PHYSICAL DIAGNOSIS

(Signs and Symptoms)

A. S. M. T. HOSSAIN

PHYSICAL DIAGNOSIS
(Signs and Symptoms)

A. S. M. T. HOSSAIN

M.D., D.Sc.(Med), M.Phill., D.T.M.& H., D.V., D.I.H., D.P.H.

Author of : *Principles and Practice of Medicine, Skin and Venereal Diseases, Quick Medical Diagnosis and Treatment, Essentials of Dermatology & Venerelogy, Practice of Clinical Medicine, Medical Emergencies in Poisoning, Prescriber's Guide, Multiple Choice Questions in Medicine, Handbook of Medical Syndromes, Laboratory Diagnosis in Medicine, Lecture Notes on Occupational Medicine, Medical Signs and Syndromes.*

AITBS PUBLISHERS, INDIA

MEDICAL PUBLISHERS

J-5/6, Krishan Nagar, Delhi-110051 (INDIA)

Phone: 011-40167052, 49067602; Fax: 011-22009074

E-mail: aitbsindia@gmail.com & aitbsindia@hotmail.com

AITBS Edition 2024

I S B N: 978-81-7473-093-0

Published by:
Virender Kumar Arya for
AITBS Publishers, India
MEDICAL PUBLISHERS
J-5/6, Krishan Nagar, Delhi - 110051 (India)
Phone: 011-40167052, 49067602; Fax: 011-22009074
E-mail: aitbsindia@gmail.com & aitbsindia@hotmail.com

Printed by AITBS, Delhi.

In admiration and appreciation
to
Professor YI-Shiong Hang
Orthopaedic Surgeon
Taipei, Taiwan

PREFACE

Local prevalence and endemicity of certain diseases can, no doubt, make the diagnosis of a particular condition comparatively easy, with reasonable reliance. This easiness, however, is not tenable in other circumstances and perhaps there is nc medical disorder which can be diagnosed clinically confidently and accurately by its manifestations alone, however characteristic they may be. On the contrary, a great similarity between the presenting featrures are usually evident among most medical disorders. A clinical diagnosis of a condition may therefore cause confusion, thus requiring a detailed knowledge of differentiation between the akin conditions. In fact, differential diagnosis plays a significant role in the field of proper diagnosis of medical disorders. PHYSICAL DIAGNOSIS (Signs and Symptoms) is therefore presented with a humble endeavour of supplying information for the purpose of accurate differential diagnosis.

We wish to express our deep appreciation to our publisher, Mr. Virender Kumar Arya of AITBS Publishers and Distributors for his enthusiasm and cooperation at every stage and for his excellent effort in bringing out this book in its present format.

We are sure that short book will be useful for students.

Healthy suggestions are welcome.

A S M T Hossain

CONTENTS

ABDOMINAL PAIN

Abdominal pain or distress is not only a frequent manifestation of gastrointestinal disturbances but also of several other ailments. The pain may be localised or generalised, or may develop as being referred from other site, while in some cases, the pain or tenderness may only be elicited on deep palpation. The pain may be acute and may accompany shock or be chronic, and the nature of it may show great variation ranging between colicky or cramping pain and dull or vague ache. Similar variations are also evident in its occurence, and the pain may be continuous, intermittent, transient, or may occur at an irregular intervals. The pain may remain almost static and one can often pin-point the site of maximum pain, or the pain may radiate at other sites or may be distributed evenly all over a large area. In other instances, there may not be any abdominal pain as such but a distressing discomfort or distension. Along with the pain there may or may not be any muscle guarding and rigidity.

Although overeating, particularly of rich foods, can at times cause abdominal pain or distress, while in some cases the pain may be psychological in origin, and there is no laboratory test or other aid available to establish the fact.

However, sometimes the pattern of abdominal pain may by itself appear suggestive for a certain ailment, to the extent even diagnostic when the pattern of the pain is taken into consideration along with other accompanying manifestations. In other instances, the pain is not specific and hence cannot aid to any diagnosis.

Conditions which present with upper adbominal pain or distress are listed below, and Table 1 illustrates a few such conditions :

- **Gastric ulcer** gives rise to epigastric distress as burning, aching, hunger pain, developing soon after food, and the pain may radiate generally to the left subcostal area. Diagnosis of the condition is made by barium meal x-ray. Endoscopy is also a helpful aid.
- **Duodenal ulcer** presents with epigastric distress as burning, aching, hunger pain, that occurs about two hours after food, and the pain generally radiate below the costal margin into the back and right shoulder. Diagnosis of the condition is made by barium meal x-ray. Endoscopy is also helpful.
- **Gastritis**, however, presents wih epigastric pain, discomfort, tenderness, nausea and vomiting. Diagnosis can be made by endoscopy and confirmed by histopathology.
- **Dyspepsia** gives rise to epigastric or substernal pain, and eating may worsen or relieve the pain. In addition, there are belching, abdominal distension, and broborygmus. There may also be nausea, anorexia, and a change in bowel habit.
- **Zollinger-Ellison syndrome** presents as an exaggerated form of peptic ulcer, and may accompany diarrhoea or steatorrhoea. The lesion may be seen at atypical locations, or may develop following successful surgical treatment of peptic ulcer.

- **Chronic pancreatitis** leads to persistent or recurrent attack of pain in the upper abdomen, which may radiate to the back and continue for hours or days. There is discomfort and distension in the upper and middle abdomen, with mild muscle guarding and perhaps paralytic ileus. Mild attack of jaundice may accompany the pain. Steatorrhoea is a common feature.
- **Acute cholecystitis** gives rise to epigastric discomfort and severe abdominal pain, along with slight fever and rigors. There is tenderness and rigidity in the right hypochondrium or epigastrium. Gall bladder is palpable.
- In **chronic cholecystitis** the patient complains of bouts of pain in epigastrium and right hypochondrium, epigastirc distress, belching, flatulence and borborygmus. The pain is usually worse alter fatty and fried foods, and may radiate to the intrascapular area. There may also be jaundice. Deep pressure causes tenderness in the right hypochondrium.
- **Cholangitis** is characterised by intermittent colicky pain in the right upper abdomen, frequently accompanied by flatulent dyspepsia, and fullness or oppression in the epigastrium, coming soon after food but worse after fruits and fatty or fried foods, and is relieved by belching or vomiting. There may also be chilliness, especially in the evening, with slight rise of body temperature.
- **Biliary cirrhosis** presents with upper abdominal discomfort, diarrhoea, and pain and tingling sensation in the feet and hands. In addition, there is symptoms and signs of obstructive jaundice.
- **Carcinoma of gall bladder** gives rise to constant pain in the right upper quadrant. A firm, tander mass, or the gall bladder, may be palpable. There may also be jaundice. History of recurrent biliary colic and chronic cholecystitis is available.
- **Cholestatic jaundice** may give rise to discomfort or pain in the right upper quadrant. There is also pruritus and jaundice.
- **Carcinoma of pancreas** presents with epigastric pain, usually dull and boring, which radiates to the neck. The pain become exaggerated following foods and from lying supine but relieved by crouching forward. In some cases, however, there may not be any epigastric pain. Painless obstructive jaundice develops and deepens progressively in the late stage of the condition. Liver becomes firm and enlarged, and the distended gall bladder may be palpable, or there may be ascites.
- **Carcinoma of stomach** may be manifested by abdominal discomfort and other symptoms mimicking peptic ulcer. There is also dysphagia, and palpable abdominal mass.
- **In cholangiocarcinoma,** there may be pain in the upper abdomen and intense generalised itching. Development of obstructive jaundice is a common accompaniment.
- **Chronic myeloid leukaemia** leads to abdominal distension with diarrhoea or constipation, and a feeling of weight and pain in the left hypochondrium. The patient complains of easy bruises and persistent bleeding from the mucous membrance. Spleen is greatly enlarged, firm, smooth and painless.
- If not asymptomatic, **gallstones** may present with abdominal distress, nausea, belching, bloating and pain, usually precipittated by fatty food. Otherwise, there may be recurrent biliary colic, or

TABLE 1

Upper Abdominal Pain

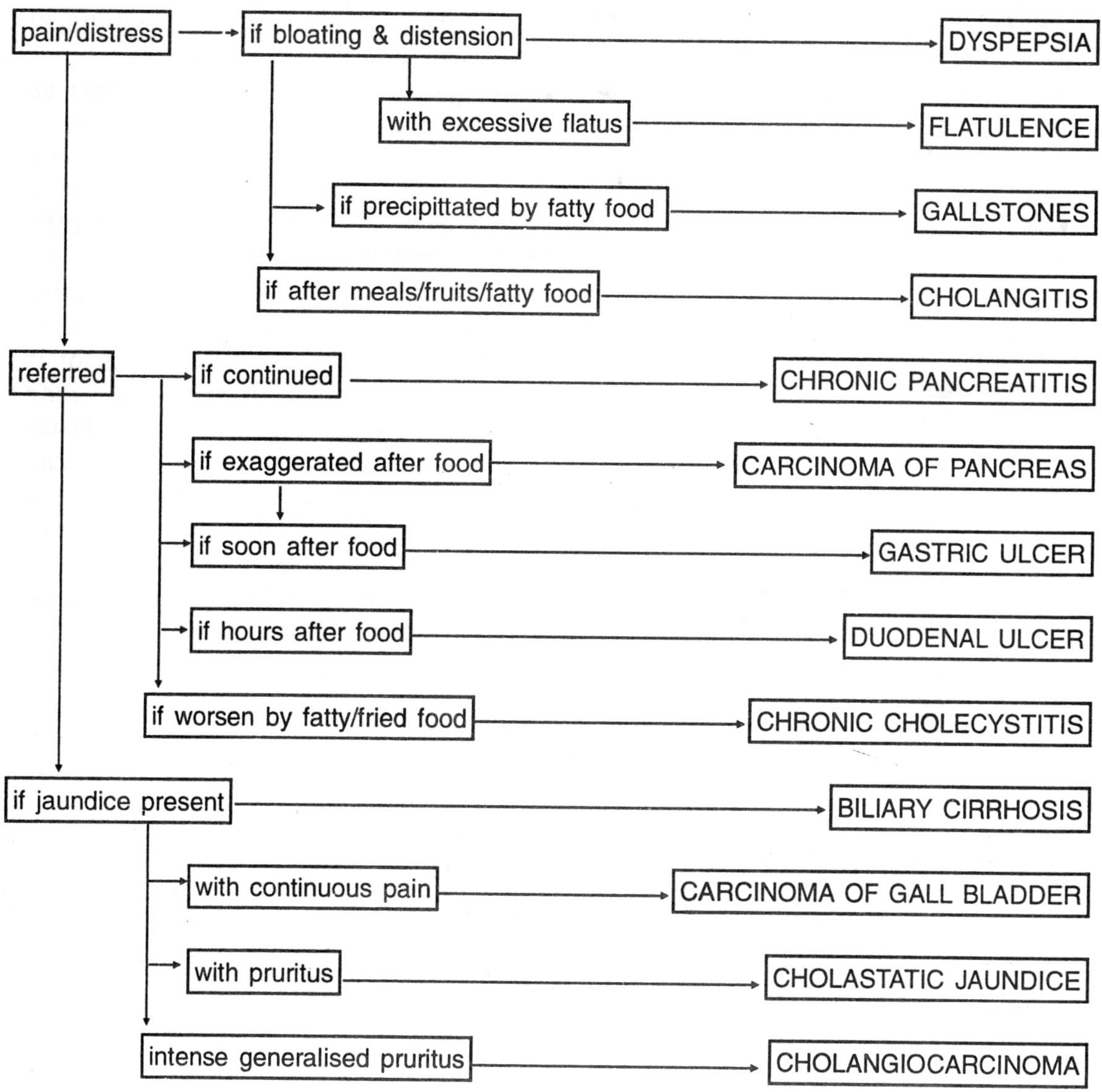

severe pain in the epigastrium and right hypochondrium. Diagnosis of the condition is made by x-ray and ultrasonogram.

- **Choledocholithiasis** may be asymptomatic. In cases when it is symptomatic, it gives rise to sudden or severe pain in the right hypochondrium or epigastrium. The pain may sometimes radiate to the right scapula or shoulder. Right hypochondrium or epigastrium may appear tender. There may also be a history of jaundice.
- **Hereditary spherocytosis** gives rise to a feeling of fullness and discomfort in the left upper quadrant, and abdominal pain due to splenic infarction. There may also be headache, fever, and mild jaundice. Spleen is often palpable and firm. History of familial incidence is available. Diagnosis is made by blood examination and red cell survival study.
- **Fatty liver** is often asymptomatic. Otherwise, the patient may complain of pain in the right upper quadrant, jaundice and, perhaps, diarrhoea.
- **Cor pulmonale** may give rise to pain at the upper quadrant, and prominent pulsations at the lower end of the sternum or at the epigastrium, along with cardiorespiratory symptoms.
- **Fasciolopsiasis** perhaps produces cramping epigastric pain, anorexia and loose motions in cases of moderate and heavy infection. In mild involvement, however, there may be only gastrointestinal irritation. The diagnosis is made from identification of the eggs or adult fluke.
- **Hiatus hernia** is usually asymptomatic unless there is strangulation or the hernia assumes large size. Occasionally, there may however be epigastric or mid-thoracic pain and occasional hiccough.
- **Lassa fever** initially begins with increasing sore throat, fever, anorexia, vomiting and epigastric pain. The abdominal pain and vomiting however increasingly become severe from the second week of the condition.
- **Q fever** may sometimes give rise to pain in right upper quadrant. There may be jaundice, and the liver is enlarged.

Sometimes the pain may predominently develop in the lower abdomen (Table 2) and therefore included several disorders, such as

- **Appendicitis** begins with vague abdominal discomfort, followed by slight nausea and anorexia, and the pain becomes persistent and continuous with occasional mild epigastric cramps. There may be episodes of vomiting. The pain shifts to the right lower quadrant and generally becomes localised, and causes tenderness with slight muscle rigidity.
- In acute form, **Crohn's disease** may present with symptoms mimicking acute abdomen, or may present with steady abdominal or colicky pain but in chronic form, recurrent episodes of pain, usually in the right lower quadrant, with local tenderness or muscle guarding, abdominal distension, and palpable tender mass on abdominal or rectal examination. Diagnosis of the condition is made from barium meal and barium enema x-rays.
- **Diverticulitis** gives rise to severe pain in the left lower quadrant but may occasionally in the suprapubic region or even in the right lower quadrant, accompanied by muscle guarding and rigidity. The severity of pain is however associated with the signs of spreading peritionitis but if there is any bowel obstruction, the pain may be cramping,

accomapnied by abdominal distension. A mass may be felt in the left lower quadrant on palpation.

- **Irritable bowel syndrome** gives rise to mild to severe abdominal pain, referred to either iliac fossa or hypogastrium, and is relieved by passing flatus or defaecation. The patient may feel urgency of defaecation frequently during or immediately after food, and passes pellet of ribbon-like stools with or without mucus. There is a sensation of incomplete emptying of bowel. The descending colon may be palpable and tender.
- In **constipation,** sometimes there may be cramping pain in the lower abdomen with bloating and passage of flatus.
- In **ulcerative colitis,** the symptoms may vary from mild to acute fulminating, with a tendency towards remissions and exacerbations. It gives rise to frequent diarrhoea with loose bloody stools, and pain in lower abdomen, usually in the left iliac fossa.
- **Amoebiasis** presents with abdominal pain or discomfort, tenesmus, urgent desire of defaecation and recurrent bouts of diarrhoea, sometimes alternating with constipation. At times however, when dehydration develops, there may be colicky pain prior to defaecation, generalised abdominal discomfort and intense rectal tenesmus. Diagnosis of the condition is made by the identification of the causative protozoa in the fresh stools and tissues obtained from the edges of the ulcers. Endoscopy may reveal the ulcerative lesions.
- In **bacillary dysentery,** though the symptoms vary depending upon the causative organism involved, in general, the condition gives rise to diarrhoea with frequent small stools which rapidly lose faecal character and become mass of mucus. Tenesmus is common. There is colicky pain in the hypogastrium, and the abdomen feels tender. In addition, there may be fever, chills, anorexia, malaise, lethargy and dehydration.
- **Dysmenorrhoea** causes cramping, colicky or constant dull pain in the lower abdomen, which is intermittent and sharp, and radiates to the back and thighs, and reaches its peak within 24 hours. In addition, the patient complains of headache, nusea, vomiting and abdominal distension.
- **Salpingo-oophoritis** presents with severe lower abdominal and pelvic pain, usually bilateral. The pain radiates down the legs. Often there is copious purulent vaginal discharge and fever, accompanied by tachycardia. Chills or chilly sensation may occur occasionally. Nausea is often present but may or may not be associated with vomiting.
- In **premenstrual tension,** there may be abdominal bloating, colicky pain in the abdomen, lethargy, fatigue, irritability, nervousness and unreasonable temper.
- **Intermenstrual pain** begins in the lower abdomen which may be very mild and brief, or be acute, severe and continuous, mimicking acute appendicitis. There is however no cramping. Only occasionally the pain may radiate slightly to the inner things. There is also no nausea, vomiting and muscle guarding.
- In **tubo-ovarian abscess** most patients usually complain of severe lower abdominal and pelvic pain. The abdomen is tender and shows muscle guarding. There is also nausea and vomiting. Tachycardia is usual, and the body temperature may swing high.

TABLE 2

Lower Abdominal Pain

Disease	Pain	Site	Muscle guarding	Abdominal distension	Palpable mass	Fever	Other features
Appendicitis	Vague/persistent	right lower quadrant	slight	no	no	yes/no	vomiting
Crohn's Disease	steady/colicky	right lower quadrant	yes	yes	yes	no	-----
Diverticulitis	severe	left lower quadrant	yes	yes, if strangulated	yes/no	no	-------
Ulcerative colitis	severe/cramping	lower abdomen	no	no	no	yes/no	bloody diarrhoea
Irritable bowel syndrome	severe	iliac fossa hypogastrium	no	no	yes	no	------
Dysmenorrhoea	cramping/colic or dull	lower abdomen	no	yes	no	no	headache/vomiting
Salpingo-oophoritis	severe	lower abdomen & pelvic	yes	no	no	yes	purulent vaginal discharge
Endometritis	severe	lower abdomen	yes	no	no	yes	lochia
Tubo-ovarian abcess	severe	lower abdomen & pelvic	yes	no	no	yes	tachyacardia
Intermenstrual pain	mild/acute	lower abdomen	no	no	no	no	-------

- **Endometritis** presents with lower abdominal pain, accompanied by malaise and anorexia. Body temperature rises to 102°–103°F (38·8°–39·4°C) and remains elevated throughout. Lochia is a common feature.
- **Endometriosis** usually presents with varying degree of pain in the lower abdomen or back. The pain may accompany the menses or may start a few days to a week before the onset of the period and becomes more severe until the flow is maximal, when the pain subsides.
- **Carcinoma of Fallopian tube** shows variable symptoms dpending on the size of the tumour and the pressure it exerts on the surrounding structures. In general, most patients however complain of lower abdomdinal pain or vague discomfort in the abdomen.
- **Carcinoma of ovary** is often asymptomatic in the early stage but otherwise may give rise to nonspecific gastrointestinal symptoms and lower abdominal discomfort. Later, there is pelvic pain. Ascites may also develop.
- **Ovarian sarcoma** is also generaly asymptomatic during the early stage. When the condition however occurs due to mixed variety, the initial symptom develops as pain in the lower abdomen due to extension of the tumour.
- **Enteric fever** may present with abdominal flatulence, perhaps with vague pain in the right iliac fossa and upper abdomen. There is however other manifestations of the condition, notably the characteristic pattern of body temperature.
- **Nonspecific urethritis** is usually asymptomatic, especially in the females. Sometimes, however, it gives rise to pain in the penis, perineum and lower abdomen in the males, and pelvic pain in the females.

In other instances, pain may not be particularly located at the upper or lower abdomen. In this situation the pain may involve the entire abdomen, back or flanks and thus, includes several conditions, such as :

- Development of the initial symptoms in **peritonitis** depend on the cause. In general, however, it presents with abdominal pain, nausea, vomiting and fever. The severity of pain is directly related to the extent of contamination. Abdomen shows diffuse, exquisite tenderness and board-like rigidity. There is also hypotension and shock.
- **Acute pancreatitis** presents with persistent, intense abdominal pain which may be generalised or be present in the epigastrium and across the back. In addition, there are nausea, vomiting, prostration and fever. There may be little or no muscle guarding and rigidity. The abdomen is distended, and the peristaltic sounds may be audible.
- In **intestinal obstruction** symptoms vary. When the lesion is high in the intestine, there is severe, crampy, intermittent, colicky pain, usually at or around the site of obstruction, with loud borborygmi. There may also be projectile and intermittent vomiting of foul-smelling fluid. Abdominal distension may however be less apparent.

  When the obstruction is low in the lower small intestine or colon, abdominal pain is less severe but abdominal distension occurs with fullness in the flanks. Vomiting is however absent or occurs lately.

  In cases of development of strangulation, there is constant severe colicky pain, with tenderness and muscle rigidity. Later, bowel sounds disappear, and shock follows.

In cases of ***paralytic ileus*** there is, however, constant dull pain with diffuse abdominal distension. The patient may pass small amount of faeces and flatus but there is no bowel sound. Malodorous fluid may be seen tickling from the corner of the mouth.

- There may be abdominal distension, vague abdominal discomfort or colicky pain in late stage of **carcinoma of rectum and colon.** An abdominal mass may also be palpable.
- **Carcinoma of liver** may show rapidly recurring abdominal pain, jaundice, ascites and oedema. The liver is enlarged and tender, and a mass may be palpable at right upper quadrant of the abdomen.
- **Portal hypertension** gives rise to abdominal pain, ascites and, perhaps, jaundice. Liver is enlarged, soft and tender. Spleen is also enlarged.
- **Intestinal lymphangiectasia** presents with abdominal pain, intermittent diarrhoea, nausea and vomiting. The condition is, however, characterised by protein-losing enteropathy.
- In some cases of **extrapulmonary tuberculosis,** abdominal pain and distension may be a feature. Evidence of tuberculosis is available elsewhere in the body.
- **Campylobacter infection** gives rise to abdominal pain, with watery and often bloody stools. There is also relapsing or intermittent fever. Both liver and spleen may be enlarged.
- **Salmonella gasteroenteritis** is featured by colicky pain in the abdomen and abrupt onset of persistent diarrhoea preceded by nausea, vomiting, low-grade fever and, often, chills. Diagnosis of the condition is made on clinical ground. Isolatation of the causative organism from stool culture can however confirm the diagnosis.
- **Renal carcinoma** causes pain in the abdomen or flanks. The condition is characterised by recurrent painless haematuria.
- **Nephrotic syndrome** presents with pain in the abdomen, weakness, anorexia, malaise, protuberant abdomen, puffy eyes, and wasting of muscles. Oliguria is a common feature.
- **Polycystic kidney disease** gives rise to discomfort, pain or colic in the lumbar region, and slowly progressive hypertension. The condition is diagnosed by ultrasonogram or retrograde pyelogram.
- **In acute nephritic syndrome** there may be discomfort or pain in the flank or upper abdomen. Other features of the condition are headache, malaise, mild fever, nausea, vomiting, and respiratory distress with shortness of breath. Puffiness around the eyes and face is a common manifestation. The patient is usually a child, and a history of streptococcal infection is often available.
- **Rapidly progressive nephritic syndrome** presents with acute nephritic syndrome-like manifestations. Abdominal pain and arthralgia are common. Haematuria is common but proteinuria is variable.
- **Membranoproliferative glomerulo-nephritis** presents with the manifestations of acute nephritic syndrome or nephrotic syndrome, and abdominal pain may be a feature of the condition. There are also oedema, proteinuria and haematuria.
- Manifestations of **IgA nephropathy** may often accompany pain in the flanks, or dysuria. There is recurrent gross or microscopic haematuria which comes and goes.

- **Acute tubulointerstitial nephritis** may present with urinary tract infection, such as chills, fever, dysuria, and pain in the flanks.
- **Acute pyelonephritis** presents with chills, fever, and pain in one or both loins, radiating to the iliac fossa and suprapubic area. Costovertebral region and hypochondrium are tender on pressure, and show muscle guarding.
- In **chronic pyelonephritis**, the patient may present with manifestations of recurrent pyelonephritis, or may give rise to vague and slight manifestations with frequency of micturition, dysuria, and lumbar pain.
- In **hydronephrosis**, there may be no pain or there may be intermittent attack of dull ache and discomfort in the flank, or excruciating or colicky pain. A mass may be palpable in the flank.
- **Hypercalcaemia** is manifested by anorexia, nausea, vomiting, constipation, abdominal pain and ileus. There may be polyuria, nocturia, and polydipsia.
- **Infective endocarditis** sometimes gives rise to pain in the abdomen or flanks, along with fever, chills and night sweat. A history of fulminating infection, or of rheumatic, congenital or atherosclerotic heart disease is often suggestive. The causative organism can be isolated from culture of blood or of bone marrow.
- **Rheumatic fever** gives rise to fever and abdominal pain, often preceded by a history of group A streptococcal infection. In many cases the causative organism may be isolated and identified from culture of throat swabs.
- **Bacterial meningitis** sometimes causes pain in the abdomen, back and extremity in addition to its other features, such as fever. Irritability, drowsiness, delirium and stupor or coma. Characteristically the condition gives rise to stiffness of the neck and back.
- In **epilepsy** there may be abdominal pain, headache and euphoria.
- **Addison's disease** may present with abdominal pain and constipation alternating with diarrhoea, along with other manifestations of adrenocortical insufficiency.
- **Hyperparathyroidism** may lead to weakness, lethargy, abdominal pain and constipation.
- **Brucellosis** presents with abdominal pain, headache and arthralgia, along with chills and fever. Agglutination titre of above 1:80 for IgG immunoglobulin is highly indicative. Isolation of the causative organism though not always possible but diagnostic. Occupational history of the patient is a useful guide.
- **Infectious mononucleosis** often presents with abdominal pain and tenderness. The condition is however characterised by the involvement of the lymph nodes of any area but more frequently of those of the posterior cervical chain. Demonstration of rising titre by immunofluorescence and other techniques are helpful for the diagnosis of the condition. Sheep cell agglutination test for heterophil antibodies is another diagnostic aid. Detectable serum IgM antibodies is diagnostic.
- In **pneumonia** there may be tenderness and rigidity in the right side of the abdomen. The condition however presents with shaking chills and fever.
- ***Diaphragmatic*** **pleurisy** occurs occasionally and presents with acute abdominal pain, usually referred to the iliac fossa, and rigidity. There may be other symptoms and signs of peritonitis.

- **Haemorrhagic fever** gives rise to abrupt worsening of the cases with abdominal pain, nausea, headache and fever. This is followed for two or more days after shock and haemorrhagic manifestations. Diagnosis is made on clinical grounds.
- **Relapsing fever** presents with abdominal pain and tenderness. Liver and spleen are frequently palpable and tender. Jaundice is a common feature.
- **Polyarteritis nodosa** may give rise to fever, sweating, abdominal pain, localised oedema and loss of body-weight. There may be peripheral neuropathy, oliguria, uraemia, convulsions and organic psychosis.
- **Schistosomiasis** may give rise to abdominal pain along with fever and other symptoms. Both liver and spleen are enlarged.
- In the adults, **carbohydrate intolerance** causes abdominal cramps and diarrhoea. In addition, there are abdominal bloating, borborygmus and flatus.
- **Gastroenteritis** presents with nausea, vomiting and borborygmus, along with abdominal discomfort and cramps, and diarrhoea.
- **Botulism** gives rise to abdominal cramps, vomiting, visual disturbance, and muscle weakness which increasingly becomes prominent.
- **Hypoparathyroidism** is manifested by tetany with muscle cramps, numbness and stiffness around the mouth. In addition, there are abdominal cramps, dyspnoea and frequency in micturition.
- **Kala-azar** characteristically presents with fever. In addition, there may be abdominal discomfort, headache, cough, epistaxis, and bleeding gum.
- **Giardiasis** may not give rise to any symptom or may produce mild abdominal cramps and discomfort, with foul eructation, flatus, and anorexia. There may also be melena. There is acute or chronic diarrhoea, usually recurrent and urgent, frequently alternating with constipation. Often there is a history of intolerance to milk or milk products.
- **Sickle cell anaemia** may, along with its usual manifestations, give rise to acute abdomen, jaundice, and episodes of severe pain, commonly occuring in the bones and spleen.
- **Tapeworm infection** is usually asymptomatic. However, heavy infection with *Hymenolepsis nana* (dwarf tapeworm) may cause abdominal pain, diarrhoea, and minor nervous disturbances, particularly in the children. Diagnosis of the condition is made by identification of the distinctive ova or proglottids in the stools.
- Only in heavy infection, **trichuriasis** may produce nausea, flatulence, abdominal distension and pain, tenesmus and diarrhoea. Diagnosis is made by identification of the eggs in the stools.
- Occasionally **ascariasis** may cause abdominal discomfort and colic. Identification of eggs in the stools can confirm the diagnosis.
- **Whipple's disease** presents with features of malabsorption, including diarrhoea, abdominal pain and distension. There may also be enteropathic arthritis-like migratory arthritis.
- **Meig's syndrome** may give rise to abdominal distension with little tenderness on palpation of abdomen. Development of ascites is common. Accumulation of fluid also occurs in the chest.

- **Gilbert's syndrome** is a benign condition of unconjugated hyperbilirubinaemia and is generally asymptomatic. Yet, sometimes it may give rise to abdominal pain which may even be severe occasionally. The patient appears more icterus than sick.
- **Melioidosis** gives rise to abdominal pain or severe diarrhoea, extreme muscle tenderness, shaking chills, fever and prostration. Liver is usually enlarged.
- **Anaphylactoid purpura** may give rise to abdominal pain and a self-limiting acute arthritis, involving one or more joints.
- **Scleroderma** is a condition of diffuse fibrosis and destructive changes of skin, articular surfaces and internal organs. At times it can however give rise to abdominal pain, distension, constipation, dilatation of segments of the small and large bowel, and obstruction.
- In **haemochromatosis** symptoms depend on the organ involved. Characteristically a laden-gray pigmentation develops on the exposed part of the skin and on the axillae, groins and genitalia. Occasionally there may also be abdominal pain and arthritis.
- **Actinomycosis** may involve the abdomen and thus may lead to abdominal colic. The condition is however characterised by the formation of multiple indurated abscesses and sinus tract.
- In **tropical sprue** there is however no abdominal pain as such but abdominal distension and borborygmus are common, with steatorrhoea.
- In **diabetes mellitus** symptoms vary widely, and there may be no or just a few symptoms, or the condition may present with classical symptoms. In children, it may however cause acute abdominal pain.

  Diabetic ketoacidosis, an important complication of the condition, can also give rise to abdominal pain, tenderness and rigidity.
- Patient with **paroxysmmal nocturnal haemoglobinuria** presents with severe anaemia, and abdominal and low back pain. The condition characteristically gives rise to dark morning urine due to haemoglobinuria which is accentuated during sleep. Gross haemoglobinuria with urine containing haemosiderin is common during the crises.
- **Rocky mountain spotted fever** presents with headache, muscle aches, bone, joint pain, abdominal pain and fever. Weil-Felix reaction with *Proteus* strains OX19 and OX2 shows rising titres.
- In **urinary tract calculus** often remains asymptomatic but otherwise may produce renal colic or excruciating intermittent pain, usually in the kidney area, that radiates across the abdomen, extending down to the genitalia and inner sides of the thighs. There may be abdominal distension, haematuria and frequency of micturition. On the other hand, vesicle calculus produces suprapubic pain.
- **Fulminant hepatic failure** presents with cranial manifestations. There is also weakness, nausea, vomitting, fever and other symptoms of impairment of liver function, with hepatic encephalopathy. Pain in the hypochondrium however only occurs rarely.
- Only occasionally **streptococcal sore throat** may give rise to abdominal pain.

ACHES AND PAINS

The term "aches and pains" is used here loosely to express any sorts of pain that is evident in a large number of ailments. Here the term includes all pains, including headache and backache, but excludes bone and joint pains, abdominal and chest pains. The occurence and the site of involvement of the symptoms vary widely. A particular condition may include every kind of aches and pains, while another may include one or more charactersitic features of them. Similarly, the intensity of the symptoms also vary widely. For the diversity of the symptoms, headache, for example, may be an accompanying component of generalised aches and pains in some conditions, while it may be a prominent feature in other instances. This therefore makes it extremely uneasy to organise them in a simple entity for descriptive purposes.

Besides these symptoms are also evident in other general circumstances as well. An extensive or unusual physical exertion or trauma may give rise to myalgia, while too much strains on eyes can eventually cause fatigue, leading to headache.

Occasionally however the presence of the symptoms along with other manifestations may be indicative or suggestive for a particular condition. Otherwise, in general, these symptoms are usually nonspecific and have no clinical significance in terms of diagnosis.

- Generalised aches and pains along with chills, malaise and anorexia are the usual manifestations of **influenza.** The condition however shows epidemic and endemic incidences at varying intervals in late-autum and winter.
- In **enteric fever,** the patient may complain of malaise, lethargy, severe headache, generalised aches and pains, and nausea in the prodromal stage of ***typhoid fever.*** Body temperature shows a characteristic pattern.
- In cases of **streptococcal sore throat** when ***scarlet fever*** eventually develops, the condition gives rise to headache and muscle aches on the second or third day of the infection and the initial fever reaches its peak.
- In **acute viral hepatitis,** generally jaundice develops but prior to this the patient complains of headache and influenza-like fever, with chills or chilliness.
- **Malaria** may give rise to headache along with chills, rigor and fever.
- **Diphtheria** begins with headache and vomiting. The condition is characterised by the formation of pseudomembrane, covering the tonsils and then extending to the pillars and pharyngeal wall.
- Manifestations of **acute coryza** include dull frontal headache and malaise.
- **Bacterial meningitis** presents with chills, fever, headache, and pain in the back, abdomen and extremity. Often there is also haemorrhagic rash.
- **Viral encephalitis** presents with headache, sore throat, and high fever. The condition gives rise to other symptoms and signs of meningeal irritation, and shows stiffness of neck.
- **Epilepsy** may sometimes give rise to headache, abdominal pain and euphoria.

- In primary **dysmenorrhoea** the patient complains of headache, lower abdominal pain, abdominal distension, nausea and vomiting.
- **Chickenpox** is manifested by mild headache, backache and moderate fever, followed by development of characteristic skin rash, and itching.
- **Coarctation of aorta** may present with headache, weakness or cramps in the legs, and other usual symptoms of the condition.
- During the late stage **bronchial carcinoma** may give rise to headache, bone ache, jaundice and epileptiform seizures or personality changes with other usual symptoms of the condition.
- **Acute nephritic syndrome** may lead to headache and respiratory distress. The condition however gives rise to puffiness around the eyes and face. It is predominently a disease of young children, and a history of streptococcal infection may be available.
- Some cases of **chronic nephritic syndrome** may complain of vague muscle and bone pain, headache, and dysnoea. The condition is characterised by proteinuria, and hypertension or uraemia.
- **Migraine** characteristically presents with severe and throbbing unilateral headache.
- **Lymphogranuloma venereum** presents with headache, joint pains, and perhaps fever. The inguinal lymph nodes, frequently unilateral, are enlarged and matted into a tender, sausage-shaped fluctuating mass.
- **Polycythaemia vera** presents with headache, drowsiness, forgetfulness, and vertigo. Blood shows increased mass and viscocity, and haemoconcentration.
- **Multiple myeloma** may give rise to headache, vertigo, dizziness, somnolence and stupor. Blood shows hyperviscocity with very high level of paraprotein.
- **Aplastic anemia** is manifested by headache, and bleeding in the skin and mucous membrance. Peripheral blood shows pancytopenia and reduced number of red cells.
- **Hypertension** is usually asymptomatic but otherwise may give rise to headache, often suboccipital.
- **Idiopathic thrombocytopenic purpura** may present with headache, dizziness, and pain, anaesthesia or paralysis from the pressure on the nerve tissue.
- Headache may be severe in **phaeochromocytoma**. Otherwise, the condition is manifested by paroxysmal or sustained hypertension, with nausea, vomiting, constipation, and sweating.
- **Brain abscess** gives rise to headache, nausea, vomiting, slight paresis, apathy and drowsiness.
- **Iron deficiency anaemia** does not usually give rise to any symptom, but when it does, the patient may complain of aches and pains, headache, weakness, lassitude, anorexia and dyspepsia.
- **Hypothryroidism** gives rise to vague muscle and joint pain, decreased sense of taste and smell, and increased sensitivity to cold. There is dryness and roughness of skin, along with other usual manifestations of the condition.
- **Hyperparathyroidism** presents with headache, and pain in the bones and joints. X-ray may show demineralisation or subperiosteal erosions in the phalanges in early stage and resorption of terminal phalanges and 'pepper-pot' appearance of the skull.
- In **hypopituitarism,** the headache may be severe due to chromophobe or acidophil adenomas.

- **Respiratory acidosis** gives rise to warm extremities, headache, drowsiness and stupor. The pulse may be bounding.
- **Tonsilitis** may give rise to fever, chills, anorexia and headache.
- **Anthrax** produces mild fever, headache and severe systemic distrubances in cases of infection acquired through inhalation of the spores.
- **Gastrointestinal bleeding** may give rise to weakness, faintness, palpitation, sweating, headache and irritability.
- Some cases of **yaws**, may present with headache, fever, and painless regional lymphadenopathy.
- In **toxaemia of pregnancy** when ***pre-eclampsia*** develops, the patient complains of headache, either frontal or occipital, as soon as the symptoms of hypertension become apparent, and the intensity and frequency of headache increases with the severity of the condition.

  In ***eclampsia,*** which follows pre-eclampsia, the headache however increasignly becomes severe and constant.
- **Puerperal infection** presents with fever, more so in the late afternoon or early evening. Headache, malaise and anorexia are always present.
- **Hypoglycaemia** presents with headache, malaise, sweating, tremor, faintness and dizziness. Skin and tongue appear moist.
- **Intracranial neoplasms** may produce drowsiness, lethargy, mood changes and impaired judgement, along with papilloedema and headache.
- Sometimes there may be progressive weakness, nausea, pruritus, vertigo and headache in **chronic renal failure**.
- **Allergic rhinitis** presents with sneezing, nasal congestion, conjunctival itching and burning, and lacrimation. In addition, there may also be headache and irritability.
- **Hereditary spherocytosis** may sometimes give rise to headache and fever. Characteristically the condition shows anaemia and jaundice.
- **Sideroblastic anaemia** may include headache, fatigue, lassitude, and breathlessness on exertion. Blood shows hypochromic microcytic anaemia, and increased level or serum iron.
- **Typhus** is manifested by malaise, generalised aches and pains, chest pain and intractably severe headache. The synptoms are however more common in *epidemic typhus* than in *scrub typhus* but quite mild in *endemic typhus.*
- **Bartonellosis** when presents as *oroya fever,* it gives rise to fever, diarrhoea, muscle and joint pains, and severe headache. There is also severe anaemia due to haemolysis.
- **Acute leukaemia** causes generalised pain, and pain and tenderness in the bone and around the joints, with rapidly advancing anaemia and perhaps haemorrhagic manifestations.
- **Erythema multiforme** may sometimes give rise to itching, burning sensation, soreness due to erosions of the mucous membrane in the mouth, genitalia and eye, aches and pains, fever, and malaise.
- In **poliomyelitis** the symptoms of aches and pains, and headache may develop, particularly in *abortive poliomyelitis* but the headache may be severe in *non-paralytic poliomyelitis.*
- In **pneumonia,** the manifestations include headache, generalised body aches, fever, and other usual symptoms of the condition.
- **Dengue** gives rise to fever, accompanied abruptly by malaise, chills, headache,

postorbital pain, backache, pain in the extremities, and sore throat. The condition characteristically presents with episodes of saddle-back tempreature.

- **Yellow fever** presents with frontal headache, backache, muscle aches, chills or rigor, and fever. Characteristically the pulse appears slow from the second day of the condition as compared to the degree of body temperature.
- **Glanders** may appear as a fulminating acute febrile illness or as a chronic indolent disease, with fever, aches and pains, and prostration. Occupational history of the patient is a helpful guide in the diagnosis of the condition.
- **Menopausal syndrome** may present with vague complaints which include malaise, dizziness, headache, myalgia and arthralgia.
- In **infective endocarditis** the patient may complain of pain in the abdomen, chest or flanks, myalgia and arthralgia or swelling and redness of the joints. In the diagnosis of the condition a history of fulminating infection or of rheumatic, congenital or atherosclerotic heart disease is often suggestive.
- In **subarachnoid haemorrhage** symptoms develop abruptly with severe headache, followed by impairment or loss of consciousness.
- **Plague** begins suddenly with chills, fever, intense headache and generalised muscular aches. In addition, there is regional lymphadenopathy. Causative organism can be isolated and identified from the bubo. There may also be a history of exposure to the rodents in the endemic area.
- **Infectious mononucleosis** presents with fever, malaise, severe frontal headache and myalgia. The condition characteristically involves the lymph nodes which are enlarged, firm, elastic, normally discrete and non-tender or slightly painful.
- In **polyarteritis nodosa**, myalgia and arthralgia are common. In addition, the condition presents with fever, sweating, tachycardia, abdominal pain, peripheral neuropathy, oliguria and localised oedema.
- In **hypocalcaemia** when the serum calcium level falls below 1·75 mmol per litre (7 mg per 100 ml) of blood, tetany develops. The condition then gives rise to paraesthesia, generalised muscular aches, prolonged or painful carpopedal spasms and spasms of the facial muscles.
- **Legionnaires' disease** presents with profound weakness, dry cough and non-remittent fever. In addition, there are dyspnoea, headache, disseminated aches and pains, and photophobia.
- **Melioidosis** presents with glanders-like manifestations, and gives rise to severe diarrhoea or abdominal pain, and severe muscle tenderness.
- **Lassa fever** gives rise to increasing sore throat, headache and severe muscle aches. Diagnosis of the condition is made by isolation of the causative organism from the blood.
- **Relapsing fever** begins with fever, chills, intense headache, and muscle and joint pain. Jaundice is common. Liver and spleen are frequently palpable and tender.
- In **schistosomiasis** there may be urticaria, cough, muscle ache, headache and abdominal pain. Fever is a usual manifestation. In addition, there are hepatomegaly and splenomegaly.
- **Toxoplasmosis** may present with malaise, sore throat, fever, headache, myalgia, arthralgia, stiff neck, urticaria and

maculopapular skin rash. Diagnosis is made from the identification of the causative protozoa.

- **Erysipelas** begins with chills, high fever, headache and vomiting.
- **Brucellosis** gives rise to headache, arthralgia and abdominal pain. There is fever which may be intermittent or chronic and undulant. Occupational history of the patient is a helpful diagnostic aid.
- **Stroke** presents with headache, dizziness, and drowsiness, but otherwise the onset may be violent and the patient may fall on the ground in deep sleep.
- **Goodpasture's syndrome** presents with severe haemoptysis and dyspnoea, usually accompanied by malaise and headache. Frank or microscopic haematuria and proteinuria are common.
- **Lyme arthritis** begins with erythema chronicum migrans, followed by prostration, including chills, fever, headache and stiff neck.
- **Q fever** presents initially with retro-orbital headache, myalgia and fever, There may also be chest pain.
- **Trench fever** begins abruptly with exhaustion, headache, severe backache and leg pain, fever and sweating.
- **Tularemia** begins abruptly with nausea, vomiting, headache, pain in the limbs, chills, high fever, and extreme prostration. History of exposure to the infected mammals and birds or of bites of ticks or other arthropods is available.
- **Rocky mountain spotted fever** presents with sore throat which progresses further till headache becomes severe and accompanies muscle aches, pain in the joints and bone, abdominal pain, chills and fever. Weil-Felix reaction with *Proteus* strains OX19 and OX2 shows rising titres. Complement-fixing antibodies also show rising titres with specific rickettsial antigens.
- In **leptospirosis** the headache is usually frontal and the muscle pain appears severe, especially in the legs and back. There is also chills and rapidly rising fever, often accompanied by severe prostration.
- **Psittacosis** presents with fever, chills, headache, myalgia and prostration. Occupational history is a useful guide in the diagnosis of the condition, which generally involves persons coming close contact with the infected birds.
- **Rickettsial pox** is manifested by chills, profuse sweatig, headache, disseminated aches and pains, and photophobia. The condition initially presents with a small papule from the bite of the infected chigger or adult mite, followed about a week after by the development of intermittent fever.
- **Rat-bite fever** presents with headache, backache, painful polyarthritis, chills and septic fever.
- **Cat-scratch disease** may give rise to malaise, headache and fever.
- **Cryptococcosis** is a fungal infection characterised by granulomatous lesions, and is manifested by severe headache, fever, blurred vision, stiffness of neck, and paralysis or convulsion.
- Headache may also be an accompanying manifestation in **acute bronchitis, pulmonary emphysema, bacillary dysentery, irritable bowel syndrome, constipation, giardiasis, trichuriasis** and **filariasis.**

Sometimes the manifestation of aches and pains may be localised when it develops from trauma or from local infection. The conditions in this catagory include -

- **Suppurative parotitis** presents with localised pain with unilateral swelling of the parotid gland and fever.
- **Mumps** may give rise to localised pain and swelling of one or both parotid glands. Otherwise, the condition presents with headache, chilly sensation and fever.
- **Herpes zoster** presents with boring pain with hyperaesthesia. There is severe pain along the distribution of the affected nerve root. There may also be malaise and fever.
- **Subacute thyroiditis** is manifested by progressively increasing neck pain. In addition, there is low-grade fever. The thyroid gland appears firm, tender and enlarged symmetrically.

There are also several conditions in which the pain predominently occurs in the back, including the perineum, such as

- **Lumbago-sciatica syndrome** gives rise to low back pain on bending (*lumbago)* but the pain in the buttock can radiate down to the posterior aspect of the thigh and calf to the outer border of the feet (*sciatica*). There may be pain and tenderness over the paravertebral muscles, and the pain aggravates on coughing, sneezing or straining.
- **Osteoporosis** gives rise to backache with varying degree of severity, which aggravates by weight bearing, and generally subsides after a few days or weeks. Local tenderness is present and the vertebrae may collapse. X-ray of the bones show characteristic changes.
- **Acute pyelonephritis** presents with pain in one or both loins, radiating to the iliac fossa and suprapubic area, with dysuria, strangury, frequent micturition of small amount of cloudy urine, rigor and fever. In the infants, there are also abdominal distension, diarrhoea, apathy and convulsions. Lumbar region and hypochondrium are tender on pressure and show muscle guarding.
- **Chronic pyelonephritis** gives rise to vague and slight manifestations of frequency of micturition, dysuria and lumbar pain.
- In **hydronephrosis**, the presentations vary and there may even be no pain. Otherwise, there may be intermittent attack of dull ache and discomfort in the flanks, or excruciating or colicky pain. There may also be haematuria, pyuria, fever and localised discomfort.
- **Ploycystic kindey disease** is manifested by discomfort, pain or colic in the lumber region, haematuria and slowly progressive hypertension. Sometimes the kidneys may be palpable as smooth, nodular mass.
- **Urinary tract calculus** may cause renal colic or excruciating pain usually in the kidney area, radiating across the abdomen, extending down to the genitalia and inner sides of the thighs. In other cases there may be no pain at all. Vesicle calculus however gives rise o suprapubic pain. There may also be abdominal distension, haematuria and frequency of micturition.
- In **renal carcinoma** there may be renal colic, long continued fever and oedema of the legs. A recurrent painless haematuria is a characteristic feature. A flank mass may be palpable.
- **Perinephric abscess** presents with chills and fever. There is pain in the flank or in the abdomen. Development of dysuria is frequent. A palpable mass may be felt in the loin or abdomen but deveopment of haematuria is occasional.
- **Hypersplenism** may give rise to pain in the splenic area, abdominal fullness,

haematemesis, and gastrointestinal bleeding.

- **Paroxysmal nocturnal haemoglobinuria** causes abdominal and low back pain. It characteristically presents with dark morning urine due to haemoglobinuria which is accentuated during sleep. Gross haemoglobinuria with urine containing haemosiderin is common during the crises. Spleen is enalrged and blood shows normochromic normocytic anaemia and thrombocytopenia.
- **Prostatitis** presents with perineal pain, low back pain, myalgia, arthralgia, and fever. There is also urgency and frequency of micturition, and the prostate appears enlarged, tender and boggy.
- **Dissecting aneurysm of aorta** gives rise to pain, beginning at the back in cases when the lesion is in the aortic arch or in the descending aorta.
- **Ankylosing spondylitis,** in general, begins with recurrent episodes of low back pain. The condition is characterised by stiffness and fusion of the axial skeleton.
- In **Gullain-Barré syndrome**, some cases may present with backache, while some with tingling and paraesthesia on the distal parts of the limbs. The condition is characterised by flaccid paralysis of the muscles.

BONE PAIN

Bone pain (Table 3) by itself is an occasional manifestation. Though a few conditions may give rise to such a symptom but otherwise most malignant conditions can eventually involve the bones through metastatic spread as complication during the late stage. Of the latter maligant tumours of the prostate, kidney, lung, breast and thyroid gland are quite frequent.

Conditions which give rise to the symptom as primary feature or as a part of general manifestations are :

- **Scurvy** when involves the infants, usually of 6 to 12 months old, may give rise to painful limbs, angular enlargement of the costochondral junctions and swelling over the ends of the long bones, with intense pain, particularly on movement. The infants remain quiet and avoid body movement, and fail to gain body weight. There may also be haemorrhagic tendency, fever and anaemia.
- Involvement of the skeleton in **hyperparathyroidism** gives rise to headache, bone pain, joint pains, pseudogout, bending of the long bones and pathological fracture. X-ray may show demineralisation or subperiosteal erosions of the phalanges in the early stage and later, resorption of terminal phalanges and 'pepper-pot' appearance of the skull.
- Cases of **menopausal syndrome** characteristically gives rise to progressive loss of bone mass and thus, leads to osteoporosis which results in kyphosis and varying degree of pain.
- **Syphilis** in its tertiary (late) stage may involve the bones, causing destructive lesions. There may be deep or boring pain, usually worse at night. There is also soft, rubbery swelling of the joint, tendon, sheath and bursae. History of primary infection may not be remembered. Conventional serological tests for syphilis are however always positive.
- **Endemic syphilis** gives rise to gummatous lesions in its late stage. There may be periosteitis of long bones, causing pain. The condition is usually diagnosed on the clinical grounds, while its occurence in an endemic area makes it much easy.
- **Yaws** when involves the bones causes tenderness, pain and swelling of the bones, osteitis, periosteitis, anterior bowing of tibia and multiple dactylitis. Bone tumours may develop at the sides of the nose. The condition is diagnosed on clinical grounds.
- **Acute leukaemia** may give rise to generalised pain, pains and tenderness in the bones and around the joints. Other features of the condition include rapidly advancing anaemia and haemorrhagic manifestations. Bone marrow examination or trephine biopsy can confirm the diagnosis.
- **Multiple myeloma** presents with constant bone pain, especially in the back and thorax, and recurrent bacterial infections, especially pneumococcal pneumonia. Pathological fractures are common, occuring as spontaneous fracture of the weight bearing bones, and vertebral collapse. Blood shows hyperviscocity with high leval of paraprotein. X-ray of the

TABLE 3
Bone Pain

Condition	Nature of pain	Aggravated by	Worsening of pain at night	Swelling	Fracture	Bending of bone	Serum calcium level
Paget's disease	deep aching	weight lifting	no	no	yes	yes	elevated
Hyperparathyroidism	vague	none	no	no	yes	yes	elevated
Osteomyelitis	localised	touch or movement	no	yes	no	no	normal
Osteomalcia	persistent	walking	no	no	no	no	decreased
Multiple myeloma	constant	none	no	no	yes	no	elevated
Acute leakaemia	generalised	none	no	no	no	no	elevated
Syphilis	deep pain	none	yes	yes	no	no	normal
Yaws	deep pain	none	no	yes	no	yes	normal

bones show typical punched out lytic lesions of diffuse osteoporosis.

- **Extrapulmonary tuberculosis** when involve the bone can cause several bone and joint disorders, and gives rise to varying degree of bone pain, sometimes occuring at night. Evidence of tuberculosis in the body may be available.
- **Bronchial carcinoma** may cause metastasis in the late stage, producing varieties of symptoms, such as headache, bone pain, and epileptiform seizures or personality changes. Diagnosis of the condition is made by X-ray.
- **Prostatic carcinoma** causes bone pain from metastasis to the pelvis or lumbar spine. The prostate gland appears stony hard, with obliterated median furrow.
- **Osteomyelitis** may give rise in acute stage the localised pain and tenderness over the bone, which is worse even on tapping over the bone but otherwise, the pain may be vague and shifting. There may be muscle spasm, redness and swelling over the involved bone, and pain on movement. Radiological findings in the early stage are nonspecific but show characteristic features in the late stage. Radionuclide scanning technique is helpful in early diagnosis.
- **Osteomalacia** presents with persistent bone pain and tenderness on pressure, and muscular weakness. The patient feels difficulties in climbing stairs or standing from sitting, and perhaps shows an waddling gait. There may also be spontaneous fracture. X-ray shows reaction of bone and symmetrical translucent bands in the ribs, spines, pelvis and lower extremities.
- **Paget's disease** is often asymptomatic. Otherwise, it gives rise to deep aching pain in the bone, aggravated by weight lifting. The overlying skin of the affected bone appears warm due to increased vascularity which is a highly characteristic feature of the condition. The bones commonly involved are the pelvis, femur, tibia, vertebrae and skull. The condition produces enlargement and deformity of the bone and later bowing of femur and tibia. There may be spontaneous fracture or fracture from trivial trauma heal spontaneously.
- **Benign tumours of bone** such as *osteoid osteoma, giant-cell tumour* and *benign osteoblastoma* are manifested by bone pain and local swelling. Diagnoses of the condition is made by x-ray but may also require biopsy.
- **Primary malignant tumours of bone** such as *osteogenic sarcoma, chondrosarcoma, malignant lymphoma of bone* and *Ewing's tumour,* all present with bone pain and local swelling. Diagnoses of the conditions are made by radiological examinations and biopsy.
- **Aneurysmal bone cyst** is a cystic bone lesion of unknown origin, and gives rise to pain and local swelling. The condition may simulate primary bone tumours in all respect.
- **Sickle cell anaemia** gives rise to increased susceptibility to cold, acute abdomen, jaundice and episodes of severe pain, commonly occuring in the bones and spleen. There is chronic punched out ulceration of the leg, haematuria and large fusiform swelling of the fingers and toes in the infants. Development of gallstone is common. Patient shows scleral icterus constantly. Blood shows abnormal haemoglobin (HbS) and increased blood viscocity.

- **Coeliac disease** may be asymptomatic or may give rise to voluminous, pale, frothy, foul-smelling stools and, in the adults, diarrhoea. There are loss of body weight, bone pain, paraesthesia and peripheral neuropathy. There may also be symptoms of nutritional deficiencies. The condition is diagnosed clinically. A trial with gluten-free diet brings an immediate dramatic improvement.
- **Chronic nephritic syndrome** when appears as symptomatic may give rise to loss of appetite, fatigue, nausea, vomiting, polyuria, thirst and pruritus. There may also be haematuria, drowsiness, hiccough, muscular twitchings, vague muscle and bone pain, headache, dyspnoea, loss of vision, fits and coma. In addition there may be hypertension. Occasionally there may be osteitis fibrosa and peripheral neuropathy. A history of acute nephritic syndrome or of nephrotic syndrome may be available.
- **Rocky mountain spotted fever** presents with bone and joint pain, abdominal pain, and harassing unproductive cough. Body temperature rises gradually to reach its peak, with perhaps remissions in the morning hours. In its diagnosis complement-fixing antibodies show rising titres with specific rickettsial antigens.

CHEST PAIN

Chest pain (Table 4) is usually a frequent manifestation of several respiratory and cardiovascular disorders. It is also encountered in some infections and inflammatory conditions, while upper gastrointestinal disorders can give rise to pain, sometimes even expressed as heartburn. On the other hand, it may be expressed as distressing sensation of tightness of the chest. The intensity and the character of pain, however, vary between stabbing or agonising and dull or boring, depending upon the conditions involved. Sometimes the characteristic of the pain is so particular that it is often suggestive of a particular condition. In other instances, it appears to be a part of the presenting manifestations and aids nothing in terms of diagnosis, to the extent that a chest pain may develop from trauma or following series of exertional coughs. However, the symptom is usually encountered in :

- **Pneumonia** characteristically presents with stabbing chest pain, the severity of which varies according to the organism involved, accompanied by cough. Presence of pleural pain is also a characteristic feature. A pleural rub may be heard on auscultation. The causative organism can be isolated from the sputum and blood. Chest x-ray gives the evidence of pneumonia.
- **Fibrinous pleurisy** presents with sharp, stabbing pain, often more pronounced during inspiration. The pain, however, aggravates by deep breathing, sneezing, coughing, yawning, and by other act which causes movement of the chest wall. Pain may be referred to the shoulder and neck or upper abdomen. The condition also gives rise to fever. Respiration is shallow with restricted rib movement. Breath sounds are diminished on the affected side or give rise to pleural friction rub.
- **Dissecting aneurysm of aorta** begins with sudden onset of severe, tearing, chest pain which may radiate into the neck, abdomen, back or legs. The site of the pain may often suggest the site of the lesion. Pain usually begins anteriorly in cases of involvement of the ascending aorta, at the back in aortic arch involvement but if the pain is located low in the back, the involvement may be at the descending aorta. In this condition one or more of the peripheral pulses, carotid or brachial, may be obliterated causing unequal or disappearances of pulses. Blood pressure in the legs appears lower than that in the arms.
- **Angina pectoris** gives rise to a sensation of oppression or tightness in the middle of the chest. The discomfort is variable, ranging between vague discomfort and intense precordial crushing sensation which may radiate backwards, upwards or downwards, causing discomfort in the arm, usually the left, wrist and, sometimes, hand. The discomfort lasts for a few minutes but may also persist maximum up to 15 minutes. The pain is induced by exertion and passes away after rest or following administration of glyceryl trinitrate. Sometimes the pain occurs at night while sleeping and awakens the patient (***nocturnal angina***) or the pain occurs while lying flat quietly (***angina decubitus***). Occasionally the pain occur

while resting (***Prinzmetal's angina, variant angina***). At times the established pattern of the occurence of anginal pain may however alter and the patient may present with serious increase in the symptoms (***unstable angina***). Breathlessness during the stage of anginal pain is a common feature. In between two attacks, there is however no abnormality and the patient remains completely free of symptoms.

- In **myocardial infarction**, the cardinal symptom is pain. The pain may however be absent or the severity of it may vary from a feeling of aching or pressure to severe agonising pain in the chest. It is similar to that of angina pectoris in terms of location and referral but is more severe and lasts longer with no effect on rest. Glyceryl trinitrate brings little or no temporary relief. Later, there is pericarditis with pain which alters by the change of position, and a pericardial friction rub is heard on auscultation. Development of pulmonary oedema and oliguria is common. ECG shows elevated S-T segment, inverted T wave, diminution of R wave and abnormal Q wave but this may not be consistent in subendocardial infarction.
- **Pleural effusion** often follows the symptoms and signs of pleurisy. It begins with little or no pleural pain, sweats, cough and expectoration, and perhaps pyrexia. Diagnosis of the condition is made by radiological examination.
- **Empyema** presents with high and remittent fever with rigors, sweating, and cough with purulent sputum. There is also pleural pain. Diagnosis of the condition is made on clinical grounds, perhaps aided by chest x-ray. Aspiration of pus can confirm the causative organism involved.
- Some cases of **aspiration pneumonia** may complain of pleural pain, and coarse crepitations may be heard on auscultation. Chest x-ray may demonstrate mottled opacities in a single lobe or segment of the lung.
- **Pulmonary tuberculosis** gives rise to shortness of breath on exertion. In cases of pleural involvement, there is pleural pain. Along with this there is other manifestations of the condition.
- In **extrapulmonary tuberculosis** when ***tuberculous pleurisy*** develops as a secondary condition, there are varying degree of chest pain and audible friction rub or signs of serofibrinous pleurisy.

  Tuberculous pericarditis develops usually from pulmonary tuberculosis or mediastinal tuberculosis, and gives rise to precordial pain, dyspnoea and orthopnoea.
- **Lung abscess** presents with chills, fever, sweats, aches and pains, and productive cough. There may be frank haemoptysis, and chest pain in pleural involvement.
- In **acute bronchitis,** following symptoms of upper respiratory tract infection, there is irritating, non-productive cough with retrosternal discomfort or pain. Later, there is a sensation of tightness in the chest. Pulmonary signs are few in uncomplicated cases.
- **Atelectasis** is manifested by dyspnoea, chest pain, fever, tachycardia and cyanosis. The chest appears flattened. There is diminished or absent chest movements towards the affected side. The condition gives rise to dull percussion note and diminished or absent vocal fremitus and breath sounds.
- **Pneumothorax** may begin with vague chest discomfort, chest pain and cough. Otherwise, it presents with chest pain,

referred to the shoulder and arm of the affected side or across the chest or over the abdomen, and is aggravated by breathing. Chest movement is decreased on the affected side.

- **Pulmonary arterial hypertension** may present with dull substernal discomfort. Pulmonary second sound is much accentuated over the pulmonary valve area, accompanied by an ejection click. A soft early diastolic murmur may be heard from pulmonary regurgitation.
- **Infective endocarditis** is menifested by fever, night sweats, pallor and tachycardia. The patient complains of pain in the chest, abdomen or flank. There may also be haemorrhagic manifestations. Embolism is common. A history of fulminating infection or of rheumatic, congenital or atherosclerotic heart disease is often suggestive. The causative organism can be isloated from the blood or bone marrow.
- In severe attack of **supraventricular tachycardia,** there is a feeling of tightness in the chest, chest pain, palpitation and shortness of breath. Heart rate is increased to 140-220 beats per minute.
- **Cardiomyopathy** when develops as *hypertrophic cardiomyopathy*, it then presents with dyspnoea, anginal pain, syncope, dizziness and palpitation. Pulse is perhaps jerky but sustained. There is double apical impulse, third heart sound, mid-systolic murmur, mitral regurgitation and signs of pulmonary hypertension. This type of cardiomyopathy is often familial in origin and the ECG shows left ventricular hypertrophy and bizarre T wave.

  In *dilated (cogestive) cardiomyopathy* however there may be atypical chest pain. The condition presents with cough or dyspnoea. Progressive left-sided cardiac failure-like symptoms usually develop. There are also gallop rhythm and atrial fibrillation, and the ECG may show nonspecific changes with left ventricular hypertrophy.
- **Aortic regurgitation** may be asymptomatic or there may be uncomfortable awarness of heart beat or exertional dyspnoea. The condition presents with other symptoms of left sided-cardiac failure, chest pain or angina pectoris, giddiness and syncope. ECG shows left ventricular hypertrophy and changes in the S-T segment and T wave.
- **Aortic stenosis**, when gives rise to symptoms, may present with fatigue and dizziness. Angina may occur from poor coronary blood flow. Radiological changes of the chest show calcified aortic cusps and left ventricular enlargement.
- **Pernicious anaemia** may sometimes give rise to anginal pain. Blood shows hyperchromic macrocytic anaemia, with marked anisocytosis, poikilocytosis and fragmented red cells, raised MCV, leucopenia with relative neutropenia, hypersegmented neutrophils, and low level of serum vitamin B_{12}.
- Long standing cases of **hypertension** may sometimes present with the symptoms of left ventricular hypertrophy, angina pectoris or myocardial infarction.
- In **pulmonary infarction** there may be no symptom or the patient may present with pleuritic chest pain and dyspnoea. There are diminished chest movement, local chest wall tenderness, presence of pleural friction rub and local crepitations. Pulmonary second sound appears abnormally accentuated.

TABLE 4.

Chest Pain

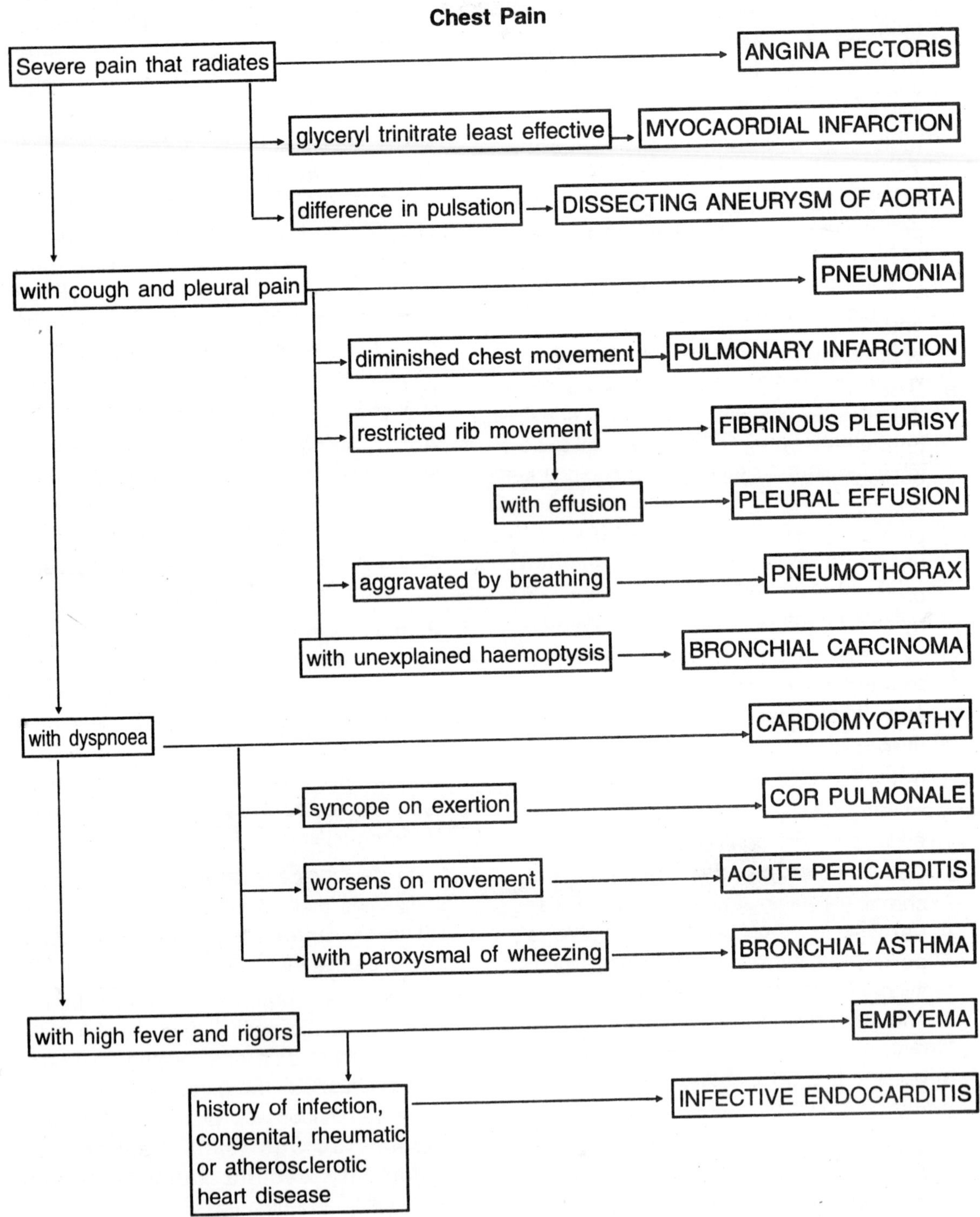

- **Acute pericarditis** may be asymptomatic or may present with mild to moderate substernal, precordial or pleuritic pain which worsens on coughing, respiration or thoracic movement, exercise or lying but relieved by sitting or standing. The pain radiates to the left arm, neck and shoulder. There is also shortness of breath. Chest x-ray may show pleural effusion, pneumonitis and cardiac dilatation.
- In **pulmonary emboilsm** there may not be any symptom or there is central chest pain and tachycardia. Diagnosis of the condition is made by radionuclide lung scanning.
- **Bronchial carcinoma** may be asymptomatic or may present with persistent cough. There may be repeated but unexplained haemoptysis. Dyspnoea appears early. In addition, there may be pleural effusion, pleural pain, pain in the chest or the upper extremity, and symtoms of secondary infection. Diagnosis is made by chest x-ray, and is confirmed by sputum cytology. Bronchoscopic examination is also helpful for the diagnosis.
- **Mitral stenosis** begins with exertional dyspnoea which progresses to paroxysmal nocturnal dyspnoea and orthopnoea. Occasionally there may also be palpitation and chest pain.
- **Cor pulmonale** usually presents with chronic productive cough and dyspnoea. Later, there are oedema, wheezing, perhaps substernal anginal pain, and syncope on exertion. There is hypoxaemia and hypercapnia, resulting fall of arterial oxygen saturation below 85% and increase of carbon dioxide combining capacity.
- **Iron deficiency anaemia** may at times give rise to tachycardia, anginal type of chest pain, systolic murmur, cardiac dilatation, and oedema of the ankles.
- **Legionnaires' disease** is a rare condition and may give rise to recurrent shaking chills and pleural pain. Development of small pleural effusion is common.
- **Actinomycosis** when involves the thorax results chills, fever, productive cough and pleural pain. Diagnosis of the condition is made by identification of the causative organism from the sputum.
- In **typhus,** prodromal symptoms include malaise, generalised aches and pains, headache and chest pain. Diagnosis is made by Weil-Felix reaction.
- The manifestations of **anxiety neuroses** may include sweating, dizziness, tremor, palpitation, precordial pain and generalised motor weakness. There is tachycardia with occasional premature beats.
- **Polyarteritis nodosa** may give rise to fever, abdominal pain, tachycardia, localised oedema, hypertension and peripheral neuropathy. There may also be precordial pain, pericarditis and myocardial infarction. Myalgia and arthralgia are common. Diagnosis of the condition is confirmed by biopsy of the artery.
- In **influenza** usually there may be substernal burning but in severe cases, there is retrosternal pain. Seasonal incidence of the condition is often suggestive for the diagnosis.
- **AIDS** may present with ill-health, weight loss, dry cough, shortness of breath, chest pain and pneumonia. Chest x-ray shows diffuse infiltration.
- Moderately severe cases of **histoplasmosis** may give rise to fever, cough and mild chest pain lasting for 5 to 15 days. Severe infection however gives rise to marked prostration, fever and occasional chest pain. The condition may

run for 1 week to 6 months. The causative organism can be identified from sputum, urine and scrapings of the ulcers.

- In **leptospirosis,** sudden cough or chest pain may develop. Otherwise, the condition usually presents with severe muscle pains, chills and rapidly rising fever. Occupational history or exposure to water or other materials contaminated with the excreta of rats, mice, wild rodents, dogs, swine and cattle is highly suggestive.
- Cases of **blastomycosis** produce pneumonia-like manifestations with dry hacking cough or productive cough, chest pain, chills, fever and dyspnoea. The causative fungus can be identified to establish the diagnosis.
- **Nocardiosis** gives rise to cough, chest pain, chills and fever. The causative organism can be identified from sputum.
- **Q fever** may give rise to chest pain along with retro-orbital headache and myalgia. Occunational history is suggestive.
- In **lassa fever**, initially chest pain and epigastric pain are common along with severe muscle pain, increasing sore throat and fever. The causative organism may be isolated from blood.
- **Coccidioidomycosis** may be asymptomatic or may present with influenza-like illness or nonspecific upper respiratory tract infection, and gives rise to chills, fever, aches, chest pain, sore throat and haemoptysis.
- In **bronchial asthma** there is no chest pain as such but muscle pain of the lower chest develops following paroxysms of wheezing, and dyspnoea.

In addition, there are several gastrointestinal disorders which may give rise to chest pain, the list of which includes :

- **Reflux oesophagitis** presents with heartburn and pain, occuring usually half-an-hour after eating, which is however dependable on the change of body posture, such as in recumbancy and in situations which increase the intra-abdominal pressure, with or without regurgitation of gastric contents into the mouth. The pain is felt retrosternally and may radiate towards the back, neck, jaw, or down the arms. Diagnosis is made by endoscopy and by biopsy.
- **Achalasia of cardia** gives rise to pre-oesophageal dysphagia for both solid and liquid foods. There may also be pain or discomfort in the retrosternal or subxiphoidal area, regurgitation, feeling of fullness behind the sternum, and nocturnal cough. The condition is diagnosed by barium meal x-ray.
- **Carrinoma of oasophagus** presents with progressively worsening dysphagia. There is also discomfort at the site of obstruction and pain in the chest. The condition is diagnosed by barium meal x-ray, and confirmed by endoscopic and cytological examinations, and by biopsy.
- **Hitatus hernia** may cause mid-thoracic or epigastric pain, and occasional hiccough. Otherwise, the condition is asymptomatic.
- In **gastritis** there may be heartburn and epigastric pain, and discomfort and tenderness in the abdomen. Endoscopic examination can diagnose the condition, and can be confirmed by biopsy.

CLUBBING OF FINGERS AND TOES

Clubbing of fingers and toes is in fact broadening and thickening of the ends of the fingers and toes, with obliteration of the angle between the nail beds and the adjacent skin. Basically clubbing is an important sign but to a conscientious patient, it is also a symptom as they may appreciate the nail changes and may thus go for proper medical advice.

It is a common feature in cyanotic heart disease and in bronchial carcinoma but can also develop in several other conditions though occasionally this may also be encountered in normal health.

- **Fallot's tetralogy,** a cognenital cyanotic heart disease, gives rise to gross clubbing of fingers. The spell of cyanosis commonly occurs after feeds or exertion, making the infant or child deeply cyanosed and flaccid for a short time. There may also be polycythaemia. There is short, harsh, systolic murmur, maximal to the left of the upper sternum. Apical impulse is absent, and the second heart sound, which is soft, may be inaudible.
- **Bronchial carcinoma** is manifested by cough, dyspnoea, and gross clubbing of fingers and toes. There may be repeated unexplained haemoptysis. The condition is diagnosed by chest x-ray and sputum cytology.
- **Asbestosis** is a condition of progressive pulmonary fibrosis, with increasing exertinonal dyspnoea. Clubbing of fingers is common. Diagnosis is made on clinical grounds, supported by the occupational history.
- **Bronchiectasis** gives rise to cough with large expectoration of purulent sputum, offensive breath after coughing, and haemoptysis. Loss of body weight, weakness, cachexia and gross clubbing of fingers and toes are common. The condition is diagnosed clinically and may be confirmed by bronchographic examination.
- **Fibrosing alveolitis** presents with symptoms and signs of pulmonary insufficiency. Development of gross clubbing of fingers and toes is common. The condition is diagnosed on clinical grounds.
- **Empyema** is characterised by fever, pleural pain and toxaemia. Chronic cases run a prolonged course with no tendency of spontaneous resorption, and present with gross clubbing of fingers. Diagnosis of the condition is made on clinical grounds and by radiological examinations.
- **Pulmonary emphysema** is characterised by dyspnoea on exertion. There may be cyanosis, especially on the lips and on the nail beds, and only occasionally that there may also be clubbing of fingers. Characteristically it presents with brief inspiration and prolonged and high-pitched expiration.
- **Infective endocarditis** may give rise to clubbing of fingers and toes, and symptoms of cardiac failure. Fever is common. Spleen is enlarged. In addition, there is haemorrhagic manifestations.
- **Cor pulmonale** is characterised by chronic cough, progressive dyspnoea and pulmonaty emphysema. In the late stage the condition however gives rise to

cyanosis, clubbing of fingers and toes, and promient pulsations at the lower end of the sternum or at the epigastrium.

- **Lung abscess** presents with septic fever and cough with large expectoration of purulent, sometimes fetid and occasionally blood-streaked, sputum. There may also be clubbing of fingers and anaemia. The condition is diagnosed by x-ray.
- In very long standing cases of **pulmonary tuberculosis,** there is chronic cough, usually troublesome in the morning, progressive shortness of breath, slowly increasing weakness and emaciation, and clubbing of fingers. Slight fever may or may not accompany the manifestations.
- **Coeliac disease** may be asymptomatic or may present with voluminous, pale, frothy, foul-smelling stools in children and, in adults, diarrhoea. In addition, there is bone pain, paraesthesia, peripheral neuropathy and clubbing of fingers. A trial with gluten-free diet brings an immediate dramatic improvement.
- **Crohn's disease** gives rise to abdominal pain, chronic diarrhoea and low-grade fever. There may also to aphthous stomatitis, clubbing of fingers and toes, erythema nodosum and peripheral arthritis. Barium meal and barium enema x-rays can often diagnose the condition. Sigmoidoscopy may however be needed to establish the diagnosis.
- **Cirrhosis of liver** may sometimes present with central cyanosis, clubbing of fingers, diffuse erythema on the palms, ascites, and peripheral neuropathy.
- **Biliary cirrhosis** is charaterised by obstructive jaundice. Pruritus is common. Clubbing of fingers however develops in its secondary or obstructive variety. Liver is enlarged and tender. Hepatocellular failure develops slowly.
- **Ulcerative colitis** presents with variable symptoms but most often with frequent diarrhoea. Blood in the stools is the cardinal feature of the condition. The condition may also occasionally give rise to minor degree of clubbing of fingers. It shows a tendency toward remissions and exacerbations.
- **Hyperthyroidism** is manifested by increased appetite, hot and sweaty hands, intolerance to warmth, nervousness, and fine tremors of fingers and tongue. Clubbing of fingers, reduced fertility, menstrual irregularity and exophthalmos are however manifested less commonly.

CONVULSIONS AND COMA

Convulsion is a state of violent spasm and is represented by involuntary contraction or series of contractions of the voluntary muscles. On the other hand, ***coma*** is a state of profound unconsciousness from which one cannot be aroused, to the extent there is no reaction even from painful stimuli. Convulsion is an important symptom, while coma may sometimes be life-threatening. Although both the symptoms may occur in a single disorder, there are also other conditions where there may be either convulsion or coma (Table 5).

- **Viral encephalitis** presents with lethargy, confusion, delirium, coma and convulsion. Tremor, stiff neck, signs of meningeal irritation and cranial nerve palsies are the common findings.
- **Subarachnoid haemorrhage** usually presents with severe headache, followed by impairment or loss of consciousness. Soon there is the development of other manifestations of the condition which include dizziness, vertigo, confusion, hemiparesis and aphasia. Stiffness of neck may develop later. In severe case, the patient may go to coma. Diagnosis of the condition is confirmed by CT scanning and cerebral angiography.
- In **malaria**, prior to the spiking fever reaches its peak, there are chills, rigor, pallor, cyanosis, headache and, in the children, even convulsions. The condition may at any time deteriorate further and may lead to impaired consciousess and coma.

  Cerebral malaria, a severe form of falciparum infection, however gives rise to high fever, confusion, delirium, seizures, and stupor, followed by coma persisting for a few hours. There may also be various paresis, and hemiplegia.

TABLE 5.

Some Cases with Convulsions or Coma or both

Disorder	Headache	Tremor	Neck stiffness	Muscle cramp or twitching	Paresis	Convulsions	Coma
Viral encephalitis	yes	yes	yes	—	present	yes	yes
Bacterial meningitis	intense	—	yes	yes	present	sometimes	yes
Subarachnoid haemorrhage	severe	—	yes (late)	—	—	occasional	yes
Brain abscess	yes	—	mild	—	slight	yes	—
Stroke	yes	—	yes	—	—	yes	yes
Intracranial neoplasms	yes	yes	—	—	present	yes	—
Respiratory acidosis	yes	yes	—	yes	—	—	yes
Tetanus	—	—	yes	yes	—	yes	—
Chronic renal failure	yes	—	—	yes	—	yes	—
Cerebral malaria	yes	—	—	—	present	—	yes
Toxaemia of pregnancy	severe	—	—	yes	—	yes	yes

- **Stroke** ***(cerebrovascular accident)*** generally represents as ischaemic condition, and presents with headache, dizziness, drowsiness and mental confusion, or there may be fever, headache, mental changes, nuchal rigidity, convulsion and coma. In other cases, the onset may be violent and the patient may fall on the ground in deep sleep, with flushed face.
- **Heat stroke** gives rise to headache, vertigo and fatigue, followed by loss of consciousness or convulsion, delirium and coma. The body temperature usually swings high.
- **Extrapulmonary tuberculosis** when presents as ***tuberculous meningitis*** gives rise to irritability, clonic contractions of muscles or generalised convulsions, cranial nerve palsies, signs of meningeal irritation, stupor and coma. There is evidence of tuberculosis elsewhere in the body.
- **Hyponatraemia** presents with lethargy, muscular weakness, mental confusion and, in severe cases, convulsions and coma. Urine output is reduced and soon oliguria supervenes and finally leads to uraemia. Muscle cramps develop when plasma sodium concentration falls to 120 mmol per litre of blood or less.
- The presenting manifestations of **hypophosphataemia** include anorexia, confusion, convulsions, coma and death. Osteomalacia is common. There may be petechial haemorrhage. Blood shows low level of phosphate but the level of serum calcium may be elevated or normal.
- In **toxaemia of pregnancy**, eclampsia develops following pre-eclampsia, when headache increasingly become constant and severe with other symptoms and signs of pre-eclampsia, along with convulsions and coma. The patient shows clonic contraction of muscles. Face becomes suffused. Opening and closing of jaw become violent. Respiratory arrest often occurs and may lead to death. Episodes of convulsion may occur for 1 to 2 times in mild cases but in severe cases, it may occur 20 times or more and may follow so closely that the convulsions appear as a single attack of prolonged duration. Coma appears for variable duration and, in severe cases, coma may continue between the convulsions.
- **Diabetes mellitus** does not give rise to any symptom in uncomplicated state but the patient appears extremely ill when *diabetic coma* develops. Then the patient presents with excessive thirst, air hunger and confusion. Finally the condition leads to coma.

  On the other hand, hypoglycaemia begins when the blood glucose level falls to 2·7 mmol per litre (50 mg/100 ml) of blood and the symptoms thereof become established when the blood level reaches to 2·2 mmol per litre of blood. At this point *hypoglycaemic coma* develops with extreme weakness, sweating, palpitation, tremor, faintness, dizziness, mental confusion and abnormal behaviour. There may be lassitude and somnolence or muscular twitching, particularly in the children. Eventually coma, sometimes with convulsions, may follow.
- **Fulminant hepatic failure** presents with cerebral disturbances, followed by restlessness, aggressive behaviour, mania, drowsiness and coma. Later, there may be confusion, slurred speech, hiccough, yawning, disorientation and finally convulsion. There may also be purpura and overt bleeding, and rapidly progressing jaundice.

- **Sheehan's syndrome** presents with decrease in breast size. Failure of lactation is a characteristic feature of the condition. Facial appearance of the patient appears flabby with thinning of eyebrows. Change in body weight is slight in mild cases but striking cachexia develops in severe cases. There is also convulsions and mental changes, and the condition finally progresses to coma and death.
- **Atrioventricular block** when develops as intermittent complete heart block, it may then cause prolonged ventricular asystole and cardiac syncope. There is rapid loss of consciousness and the patient falls on the ground. There may be convulsion and may follow death.
- In severe cases of **bacillary dysentery** there may be meningismus, delirium, convulsions and coma. Otherwise, the condition presents with abdominal pain, tenesmus, prostration, diarrhoea and pyrexia.
- In **whooping cough** convulsions may occur due to paroxysms of series of short, sharp, explosive cough. Diagnosis of the condition is made by identification of the causative organism, *Bordetella pertussis.*
- **Tetanus** is a condition of convulsions which initially begins at the site of inoculation, giving rise to stiffness of the jaw and then of the neck and other muscles. Gradually tonic spasms spread to all muscles of the trunk. There is spasm of the glottis and respiratory muscles during the convulsions, resulting in asphyxia and cyanosis.
- In **epilepsy**, Jacksonian variety gives rise to involuntary twitching or clonic movements in one part of the body which spread to another area, and the consciousness may or may not be lost. The condition may however follow a convulsive seizure.
- **Brain abscess** presents with headache, nausea, slight paresis, apathy and drowsiness. There may also be ataxia, papilloedema and convulsions. The condition is diagnosed by identification of the causative organism in the cerebrospinal fluid.
- **Hypocalcaemia** gives rise to diffuse encephalopathy, depression and psychosis. In severe cases, there may be laryngospasm and generalised convulsions. Serum calcium level is decreased but the level of serum protein is normal.
- **Hypoparathyroidism** characteristically gives rise to tetany with muscle cramp, abdominal cramp, wheezing, dyspnoea, urinary frequency, stridor and convulsions. Blood shows low level of calcium and high level of phosphate. Urinary calcium and phosphate levels are also low.
- **Pneumonia** presents with fever, chest pain, cough, dyspnoea and cyanosis. Convulsion is however frequent in the children. Diagnosis of the condition is made by x-ray of the chest.
- **Polyarteritis nodosa** is characterised by multiple nodule formation on the medium-sized arteries. The condition may give rise to fever, sweating, hypertension, asthma, peripheral neuropathy, oliguria, uraemia, convulsions and organic psychosis. Diagnosis of the condition is confirmed by biopsy of the artery.
- **Chronic renal failure** may be asymptomatic or may present with vague symptoms or with the symptoms of uraemia. The manifestations of the condition may therefore include progressive weakness, lethargy, headache and vertigo. Muscular weakness and

twitchings, peripheral nouropathy, restlessness, drowsiness, insomnia, apathy, myoclonic jerking, seizures and convulsions may develop. History of previous renal disease, symptoms of lower urinary tract obstruction or of exposure to the offending agents may be available.

- **In chronic nephritic syndrome,** symptoms vary to the extent some may remain asymptomatic. Otherwise, the condition presents with hiccough, dyspnoea, loss of vision, haematuria, drowsiness, muscular twitchings, fits and coma. The condition shows impaired renal function. Often a history of acute nephritic syndrome or of nephrotic syndrome may be available.
- **Acute pyelonephritis** presents with pain in one or both loins, dysuria, strangury, frequent micturition of small amount of cloudy urine, rigor and fever. However when the condition involves the infants and children, the condition may then also give rise to diarrhoea, apathy and convulsions.
- **Cryptococcosis** may give rise to fever, vomiting, blurred vision, stiffness of the neck, and paralysis or convulsion. Diagnosis of the condition is made by isolation and identification of the causative fungus.
- **Intracranial neoplasms** may give rise to headache, irritability, convulsions or psychomotor seizures, hemianopia, apraxia and astereognosis. Most cases are diagnosed through radiography and redionuclide encephalography.
- **Beriberi** when presents with *Wernicke's encephalopathy,* it gives rise to bilateral, symmetrical ophthalmoplegia, nystagmus, absent pupillary reflex, ataxia, and perhaps convulsions.
- **Bacterial meningitis** presents with high fever, chills, intense headache and pain in the back, abdomen and extremity. Irritability, drowsiness, delirium, stupor and coma are common accompaniment. The condition is featured by stiffness of neck and back.
- **Head injury** gives rise to loss of consciousness, lasting for seconds to minutes, with concussions of brain, and coma lasting for hours or days. Following this there may be various symptoms and signs depending on the extent of injury. In the diagnosis of the condition, a history of injury may be available. X-ray of the skull and CT scanning may demonstrate the lesion.
- In the maintenance phase of **acute renal failure** though the urinary output may be normal or there may even be polyuria, in general, there is however sustained decrease in urinary output, resulting oliguria or anuria. The condition also presents with general weakness, hiccoughs and paraesthesias. There may be mental confusion, apathy, delirium, muscular twitching, fits and coma. In addition, there may be bleeding tendency and flaccid paralysis.
- Along with the usual symptoms and signs the pharyngeal variety of **diphtheria** may also give rise to restlessness, drowsiness, stupor and coma.
- **Hypernatraemia** presents with flushed face, fever, tachycardia, confusion and seizures or coma. Blood pressure is lowered. Blood shows elevated level of urea.
- **Respiratory acidosis** is manifested by warm extremities, sweating, peripheral vasodilation, muscle twitchings, flapping tremors, drowsiness, stupor and, in severe cases, coma. Blood shows increased concentrations of hydrogen-ion, carbonic acid and $Paco_2$, but the pH is reduced.

- **Hypercalcaemia** gives rise to polyuria, polydipsia, skeletal muscle weakness and hypertension. In severe cases there may be confusion, delirium, psychosis, stupor, and coma. ECG shows shortened Q-T intervals.
- Occasionally **hypothyroidism** may lead to a life-threatening complication *myxoedema coma*, and may lead to coma with extreme hypothermia. There is shock with respiratory depressison and CO_2 retention. Further progression of the condition occurs soon to end to death.
- In **gas gangrence** toxaemia is profound and the condition gives rise to tachycardia, haemoptysis, lowered blood pressure, stupor, delirium, shock and coma.
- **Poliomyelitis** is manifested by laboured respiration, leading to respiratory failure in its bulbar variety. Lethargy or coma may also occur but convulsions rarely.
- **Aplastic anaemia** gives rise to haemorrhagic manifestations, necrotic ulcers in the mouth and throat, coma and stupor or delirium, There is normochromic normocytic anaemia. Peripheral blood shows pancytopenia and reduced number of red cells. In addition, history of exposure to radiation or to offending drugs or chemicals may be available.
- **Multiple myeloma** presents with constant bone pain. Hypercalcaemia often occurs and gives rise to nephrosclerosis, lethargy and drowsiness, leading to coma. There may be tenderness in the bone, kyphoscoliosis, muscle spasm and impaired mobility.
- In case of profound state of dehydration in **cholera** there may be severe cramps in the fingers, toes and abdominal muscles, shock, coma and death. The condition is characterised by severe diarrhoea.
- **Relapsing fever** presents with fever which subsides spontaneously and recur over a period of weeks. In its course, involvement of central nervous system may however produce paresis of cranial nerves and coma.
- In severe cases of **leptospirosis,** Cheyne-Stokes respiration, coma and finally death occur often with anuria and uraemia.
- In **candidiasis** the infection may only occasionally involve the local tissue either directly or through haematogenous spread, and may cause septicaemia, resulting shock and coma.
- **Bartonellosis,** when presents as *oroya fever*, gives rise to fever, nausea, diarrhoea, pallor, muscle and joint pain, and severe headache. It may even give rise to delirium and coma. The condition is diagnosed by identification of the causative organism, *Bartenella bacilliformis,* in the peripheral blood.
- In late stage **African trypanosomiasis** may give rise to drowsiness, tremors and coma. Diagnosis of the condition is made by isolation and identification of the caustive organism from the peripheral blood or from enlarged lymph node aspirates in the early stage but from cerebrospinal fluid in the late stage.
- **Rocky mountain spotted fever** presents with severe systemic manifestations, fever and cutaneous rash. The patient develops encephalitis with headache, irritability, restlessness, insmonia, lethargy, delirium, stupor and coma.

COUGH

Cough is one of the prominent symptoms that a patient can ever present with. It is an act of explosive forcing of air through the glottis, usually to expel mucus or other materials from the bronchus or larynx, and develops whenever there is any respiratory irritation. The cough may be painful or distressing or may just be disturbing or annoying. On the other hand, cough may be productive or unproductive. Thus, the nature of cough varies greatly with the conditions involved therewith.

The characteristic of cough, along with the productions it causes or the absence thereof, may at times be quite significant so as to be suggestive for a particular condition, while at others, it may be a part of general manifestations of no diagnostic importance.

Table 6 illustrates some causes which give rise to cough in adults, while Table 7 illustrates the same but in children.

- **Acute bronchitis** initially presents with upper respiratory tract infection followed by irritating non-productive cough, with retrosternal discomfort or pain. Later, there is wheezing and expectoration, at first scanty, mucoid, viscid, and may be streaked with blood, and then changing to mucopurulent or more copious. Pulmonary signs are few in uncomplicated cases, and the radiological findings are normal.
- **Chronic bronchitis** presents with short and dry irritating cough in the morning, with perhaps little sputum, usually in the winter, which increases in severity with the advancement of time and finally the paroxysms of cough persist throughout the year. The sputum is usually scanty, tenacious, mucoid, occasionally streaked with blood and later, may be copious and frankly purulent. The condition shows diminished vocal fremitus, hyperresonent percussion note, scattered rhonchi and coarse crepitations, and signs of coexisting emphysema.
- **Whooping cough** begins with sneezing, anorexia, malaise and low-grade fever. Soon a short, dry cough develops and persists. In paroxysmal stage, which appears after about 7 to 10 days, cough appears more frequently. It begins as a long-drawn, almost stridulous inspiration, followed by a series of short, sharp, explosive cough which follows one another rapidly, and is then followed by a high-pitched 'whoop' upon inhalation. Paroxysms may occur as often as every half-an-hour. The coughs are productive. The strain of cough make the face puffy between the attacks and may give rise to subconjunctival haemorrhage, epistaxis and blood-stained sputum. Finally, in the convalescent stage, the frequency and severity of the condition starts to decrease gradually. The 'whoop' disappears eventually though the paroxysms of cough persist for even another 3 months or more.
- **Pneumonia** begins with chills and fever but its manifestation vary on the types of organism involved.

  In *pneumococcal pneumonia*, there is stabbing chest pain and the condition usually presents with short, sharp, dry and hacking cough which is painful and explosive in efforts, and occurs in paroxysms. Later, the cough may be painless and becomes more productive with tenacious sputum, often rust coloured or, occasionally, frankly streaked with blood. The patient may also develop dyspnoea and cyanosis. Convulsion is a frequent manifestation in children. Pulse becomes rapid. Respiration is rapid, shallow and painful. Diminution of chest movement and breath sounds occur in the early stage and later, when complications occur, breath sounds become markedly diminished or absent.

Staphylococcal pneumonia abruptly changes to a very serious illness. It begins with dry cough which aggravates further and produces purulent or blood-stained sputum. There may be early signs of pleural effusion or of empyema.

In *klebsiella pneumonia* there is cough and the sputum is rusty, brick-red or bloody, and gelatinous, copious, mucoid, sticky, and difficult to expectorate.

Cough is initially non-productive but later becomes productive with blood-streaked sputum in both *mycoplasmal pneumonia* and *non-baccterial pneumonia.*

In all cases of pneumonia the causative organism can be identified except in non-bacterial pneumonia.

- In the children type, **pulmonary tuberculosis** gives rise to brassy non-productive cough, and atelectasis of the small bronchi. In adult type, however, there may not be any history of cough initially but soon there may be short and sharp cough, followed by persistent dry cough. Sputum is usually scanty at the early stage and later becomes green and purulent in caseous liquefying lesion but yellowish and mucoid in chronic cases. There may be haemoptysis which occasionaly may also be the first presenting symptom.
- In **extrapulmonary tuberculosis** when *miliary tuberculosis* develops, there may occasionally be non-productive cough, and dyspnoea. The condition usually affects the children and young adults. Diagnosis of the condition is made by chest x-ray.

  Tuberculous pleurisy however gives rise to symptoms and signs of pleurisy, with rigor, fever, dyspnoea and cough with purulent sputum. The condition always occurs as a secondary manifestation.
- **Bronchiectasis** gives rise to chronic cough, usually worse in the morning and often induced by postural changes, with large amount of purulent and sometimes foul or putrid sputum, offensive breath after coughing and haemoptysis, which vary between blood-streaked sputum and massive fatal haemorrhage. There may be wheezing, dyspnoea, fever and night sweats. Examination will reveal slight dullness at the base, weak breath sounds, rhonchi and crepitations and later, there may be diminished chest movement and vocal fremitus, and coarse crepitations over the affected area.
- **Fibrinous pleurisy** presents with pleural pain, characterised by sharp, stabbing pain, often more pronounced during inspiration. The pain aggravates by breathing, yawning, coughing and by other movements of the chest wall. There may be hacking cough of explosive effort. Slight rise of body temperature is common. Respiration appears shallow with restricted rib movements. Breath sounds are diminished on the affected side. Pleural friction rub is also present.
- **Pleural effusion** develops following symptoms and signs of pleurisy, and often presents with little or no pleural pain,

pyrexia, especially in cases of infection, sweats and cough with expectoration. Diagnosis of the condition is made by chest x-ray.

- **Pulmonary emphysema** gives rise to exertional dyspnoea and chronic cough with scanty, mucoid expectorations. Wheezing and tightness in the chest are common. Hyper-reaction of all respiratory muscles are evident during inspiraion. The lungs show diffuse hyperresonance, especially at the base, diminished vocal fremitus, scattered wheezes and rhonchi, diminished cardiac dullness on percussion, and downward depression of the liver.
- **Lung abscess** presents with chills, fever, sweats, and aches and pains. There is irritating, dry and exhaustive cough, followed by large amount of expectoration of purulent, sometimes fetid and occasionally blood-streaked, sputum, and prostration. There may also be frank haemoptysis. The condition may give rise to clubbing of fingers. Physical examination reveals small area of dullness.
- **Empyema** is manifested by high and remittent fever, with rigor, sweating and malaise. There is also cough with purulent sputum, and pleural pain. Diagnosis of the condition is made on clinical grounds, supported by the x-ray of chest. Aspirates of the pus can establish the causative micro-organism involved.
- **Cardiac failure** may present with fatigue, weakness, sweating, and cough which is usually non-productive initially but later becomes productive with frothy white or rusty or brownish sputum in left-sided cardac failure. Diagnosis of the condition is made on clinical ground, supported by the chest x-ray.
- **Cor pulmonale** usually presents with chronic productive cough, and dyspnoea which is exertional and progressive but there is no orthopnoea.
- **Pneumothroax** gives rise to dry cough along with chest pain and dyspnoea. Chest movement shows decreased activity on the affected side. Auscultation of the chest reveals absent or diminished vocal fremitus and breath sounds, and the chest appears hyperresonent.
- **Adult respiratory distress syndrome** presents with dry cough, followed by dyspnoea and progressive respiratory distress. Chest x-ray shows diffuse bilateral alveolar infiltration initially but later, snow-storm appearance in the lung field.
- **Influenza** is manifested by sore throat, nasal catarrh, substernal burning sensation, and dry cough. The condition shows a seasonal incidence, and is usually accompanied by fever.
- In **diphtheria**, laryngeal variety begins with cough and hoarse cry of the infants, and inspiratory stridor. Soon laryngeal oedema causes laryngeal obstruction, giving rise to more severe dyspnoea and high-ptiched cough.
- In **bronchiolitis** there is upper respiratory tract infection, followed by respiratory distress, wheezing and hacking cough, which may also be paroxysmal. In addition, there may be fever. X- ray of the chest shows hyperinflated lungs, prominent hilar markings and depressed diaphragm.
- Initially **acute laryngotracheobronchitis** (*croup*) presents with common cold-like symptoms, followed by noisy, violent, spasmodic cough, perhaps husky, and hoarseness of voice and stridor, commonly seen at night.
- **Acute epiglottitis** gives rise to sore throat, stridulous cough, high fever, dyspnoea,

TABLE 6

Cough in Adults

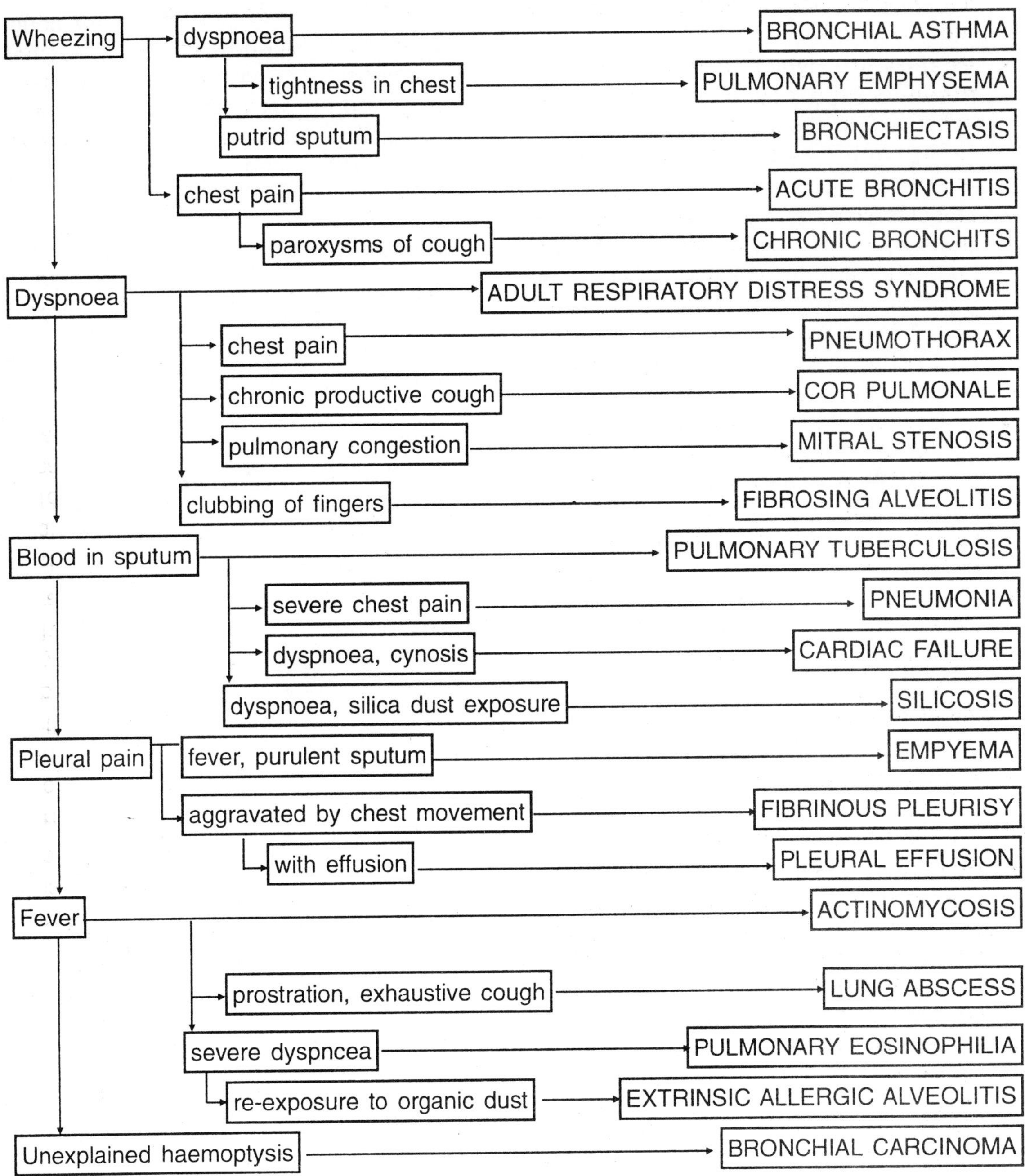

tachypnoea and inspiratory stridor. Pharynx appears highly inflammed, and the epiglottis looks oedematous and beefy red.

- **Respiratory syncytial virus infection** presents with cough, wheezing, and dyspnoea in the infants. There is also fever, and symptoms and signs of bronchiolitis.
- **Measles** presents with fever and malaise. Soon however sneezing, coryza, redness and oedema of the conjuctivae, and short dry cough develop. Koplik's spots appear after 1 to 4 days. Fever and cough persist until skin rash appears and then subsides within 1 or 2 days.
- In **laryngitis**, the patient complains of a sensation of tickling and rawness in the throat. There is also irritating, noisy and perhaps husky non-productive cough. Laryngeal oedema may cause dyspnoea, cyanosis and stridor in children.
- Chronic cases of **pharyngitis** give rise to dryness of throat and troublesome, purulent cough or recurrent episodes of throat pain. Mucous membrane of the throat may be covered with membranous or purulent exudate.
- **Acute coryza** presents with sneezing, rhinorrhoea and headache. There may be mild cough and chilly sensation.
- **Pulmonary eosinophilia** may present with high fever, cough, and severe dyspnoea, with symptoms of bronchial asthma. Blood shows increased number of eosinophils. X-ray may show localised or diffuse opacities in the lungs.
- **Bronchial asthma** is characterised by recurrent attacks of wheezing and dyspnoea. There is also cough with tenacious mucoid sputum though occasionally it may be absent in some cases.
- **Aspiration pneumonia** presents with cough and respiratory distress. Auscultation of the chest reveals coarse crepitations. X-ray shows mottled opacties in a single lobe or segment of the lung.
- **Fibrosing alveolitis** presents with progressive exertional dyspnoea. There may also be persistent dry cough. Gross clubbing of fingers and toes is common. Chest expansion during inspiration is poor. Prominent breath sounds and numerous crackling crepitations are heard on both sides of the chest.
- **Sarcoidosis** is a systemic granulomatous disorder. However, when it involves the lungs, the condition may produce cough and dyspnoea at late stage. Chest x-ray shows bilateral and often symmetrical enlargement of the hilar lymph nodes. Occasionally, there is fine miliary infiltration of the lungs with peribronchial thickening. Later, there is diffuse and confluent parenchymatous infiltrations appear throughout the lung field.
- **Bronchial carcinoma** may remain asymptomatic or may present with persistent cough. There may be repeated but unexplained haemoptysis. In addition, there may be clubbing of fingers and toes. Diagnosis of the condition is made by chest x-ray.
- **Silicosis** may or may not give rise to any respiratory symptom. Later, however, there is dyspnoea and cough which is dry at the early stage but finally bęcomes productive, frequently with blood-stained sputum, and haemoptysis. History of exposure to silica dust is available. Radiological investigation of the chest shows multiple, small, rounded, regular opacities in simple cases but nodules, interstitial fibrosis, hilar adenopathy and peripheral calcification of hilar nodes resembling egg-shell appearance in advanced cases.
- **Asbestosis** presents with increasing exertional dyspnoea. Soon cough,

wheezing and other respiratory symptoms appear. On auscultation, crackling crepitations are heard in the lung. A history of exposure to, or long-term inhalation of, asbestos fibres and dust is available.

- **Anthracosis** may not give rise to any symptom or may present with progressive shortness of breath. Soon there is cough and chronic form of bronchospasm and subsequently emphysema. In complicated cases, there is exertional dyspnoea, cough and perhaps expectoration of black sputum. There is an occupational history or of regular exposure to bituminous anthracite coal dust available.
- **Mitral stenosis** starts with exertional dyspnoea which later progresses to paroxysmal nocturnal dyspnoea and orthopnoea. There is also tachycardia. Development of pulmonary congestion gives rise to cough while development of pulmonary hypertension may cause haemoptysis.
- **AIDS** may present with ill-health, loss of body weight, dry cough, shortness of breath and pneumonia.
- **Extrinsic allergic alveolitis** is manifested by malaise, fever, dry cough and dyspnoea, occuring several hours after re-exposure to the organic dust. In cases of chronic exposure to dust, there is productive cough and progressive exertional dyspnoea.
- **Aspergillosis** may present with productive cough and dyspnoea. In addition, there are chills, fever and prostration. Radiological investigation of the chest shows a tumour-like dense opacity of round fungus ball with crescent of thin layers of air in a cavity or cyst.
- In **actinomycosis** when the infection involves the thorax, the condition presents with chills, fever, and cough with sputum formation. Identification of the causative organism from the sputum is possible, which can confirm the diagnosis.
- **Typhus** may give rise to troublesome unproductive cough, conjunctivitis, flushed face and renal insufficiency in *epidemic typhus* variety.
- **Enteric fever** presents with characteristic pattern of fever. In addition, there may be sore throat and unproductive cough.
- In **pulmonary infarction** there may be no symptom or the condition may give rise to chest pain, dyspnoea, dry and unproductive cough, and haemoptysis. There is alsc pleural effusion.
- In **hydatid disease** when a single cyst develops and ruptures, the condition gives rise to frequent cough and haemoptysis. Hydatid elements are seen in the sputum.
- In pneumonic type of **plague,** the patient develops fulminating symptoms with pneumonitis, featured by cough with copious bloody, frothy and liquid sputum.
- Moderately severe infection may develop in **histoplasmosis**, giving rise to fever, cough and mild chest pain lasting for 5 to 15 days. It however causes ulcerations fo the nasopharynx and oropharynx. The causative organism, *Histoplasma capsulatum,* can be isloated and indetified from the sputum, urine and scrapings of the ulcers.
- **Cardiomyopathy** may present with cough or dyspnoea and fatigue in its dilated (congestive) variety.
- **Schistosomiasis** presents with fever and eosinophilia. There may also be cough, urticaria, muscle aches, headache and abdominal pain.
- **Blastomycosis** gives rise to pneumonia-like manifestations with dry hacking or productive cough, chest pain, chills, fever, and profuse sweating. Chest x-ray shows patches of broncho-pneumonia.

TABLE 7

Cough in Children

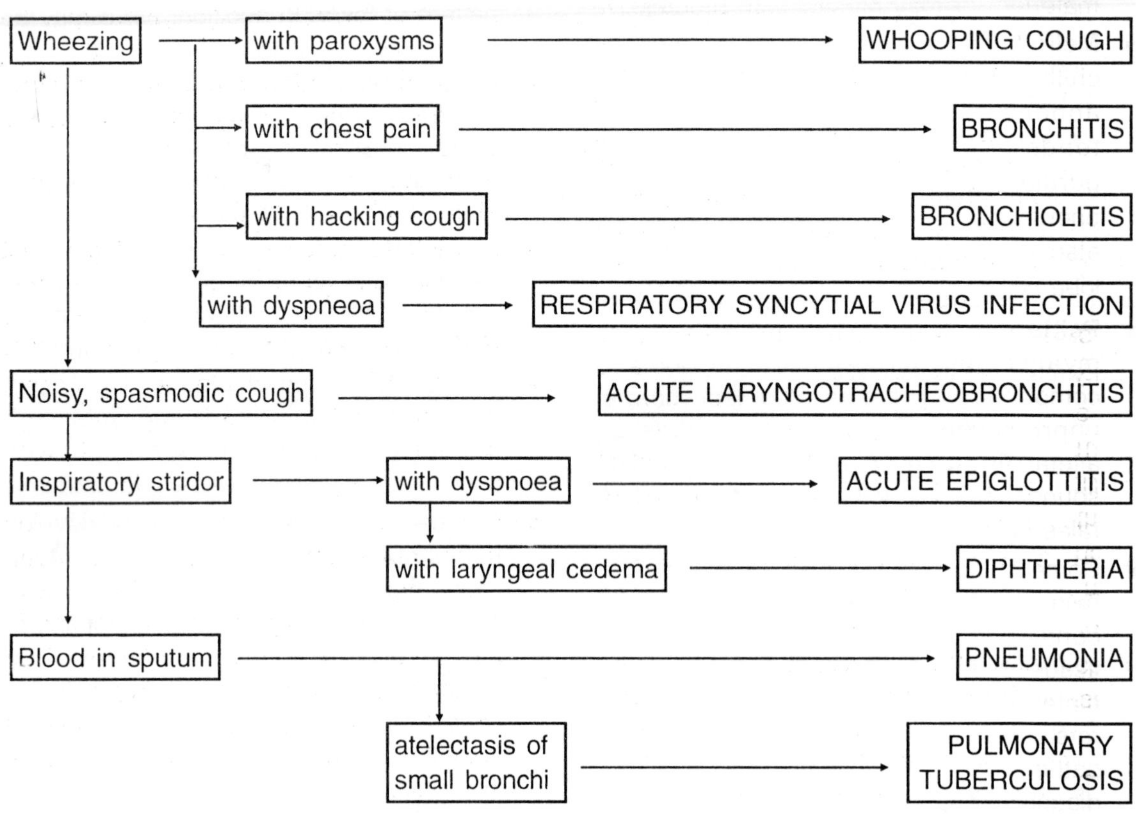

- **Nocardiosis** usually begins as pulmonary infection or may give rise to cough, chest pain, chills, fever and night sweats. Diagnosis is made by isolation and identification of *Nocardia asteroides* in the sputum, pus, spinal fluid and biopsy material.
- **Melioidosis** gives rise to fever, shaking chills, prostration, severe diarrhoea or abdominal pain, and severe muscle tenderness. Cough with bloody and purulent sputum is common. Signs of pneumonia, empyema and lung abscess also develop. Chest x-ray shows upper lobe consolidation and thick walled cysts.
- **Psittacosis** presents with chills, malaise, myalgia and prostration. The patient complains of troublesome cough, usually unproductive. The condition gives an alteration in percussion note, and breath sounds. Auscultation reveals fine, crepitant rales in localised areas over the lungs.
- Sometimes there may be cough or chest pain in **leptospirosis.** A history of direct contact with infected animal's urine or tissue or of exposure to water or other materials contaminated with the excreta of rats, mice, wild rodents, dogs, swine or cattle may be available which aids the diagnosis.
- **Infectious mononucleosis** can at times produce painful cough when there is enlargement of mediastinal glands. Otherwise, the condition is characterised by the enlargement of lymph nodes, most frequently involving the posterior cervical chain.
- **Haemorrhagic fever** is manifested by fever, headache, abdominal pain, pharyngitis, and cough.
- In **Q fever** there may be symptoms of interstitial pneumonitis with dry, non-productive cough and drenching sweating. X-ray of the chest may show marked pulmonary infiltration.
- **Lassa fever** presents with fever and severe symsemic disturbances. There may also be cough and haemorrhagic manifestations. X-ray of the chest shows basilar pneumonitis and pleural effusion.
- **Rocky mountain spotted fever** gives rise to malaise, sore throat and headache. This progresses further till headache becomes more severe and accompanies chills, muscle pain, bone and joint pain, abdominal pain, harassing unproductive cough and fever. Weil-Felix reaction with *Proteus* strain OX19 and OX2 shows rising titres.
- **Legionnaires' disease** presents with nausea, profound weakness, dry cough and non-remittent fever. As the condition progresses there may be purulent, watery, frequently blood-streaked sputum. Initially there is rales in the lungs but later consolidation develops. Chest x-ray shows patchy, often multilocular, consolidation and patchy infiltration.
- Only a small number of cases of **Goodpasture's syndrome** may give rise to fatigue, chills, fever, and cough. Otherwise, the condition presents with severe haemoptysis and dyspnoea.
- During the migration of larvae, **ascariasis** may give rise to slight fever, cough and haemoiptysis for a transient period.
- In **ancylostomiasis,** there may be cough with bloody sputum, sore throat and bronchitis during the larval migration into the lungs but for a very transient period.
- Similarly **strongyloidiasis** may also sometimes cause cough, fever and urticaria during the larval migration.

CYANOSIS

Cyanosis is, in fact, an important sign. It is also a visible symptom when develops as a generalised manifestation. It is the bluish coloration of skin and also of mucous membrane. It develops due to unsaturation of arterial blood with oxygen and thus form an increase in the amount of reduced haemoglobin in the blood. It frequently appears in conjunction with dyspnoea. It is usually evident in several cardiovascular (Table 8) and respiratory disorders.

The symptom may sometimes appear as *central cyanosis* due to imperfect oxygenation or from admixture of arterial and venous blood, or may develop as *peripheral cyanosis* due to excessive reduction of oxyhaemoglobin in the blood from the vasoconstriction, less cardiac output or stasis which makes the blood flow slow.

- In **persistent ductus arteriosus** there is central cyanosis which is more marked on the feet and toes than that is in other parts of the body. It is a congenital condition, often remains asymptomatic. Chest x-ray shows enlargement of pulmonary artery. There may also be left ventricular hypertrophy.
- **Fallot's tetralogy** is a congenital cyanotic heart disease, and presents with cyanosis which is though absent at birth but develops over the next few weeks or months. The spells of cyanosis commonly occur after feeds or exertion, making the infant or child deeply cyanosed and flaccid for a short time. Central cyanosis is common. Auscultation reveals short, harsh, systolic murmur maximal to the left of the upper sternum. Apical impulse is absent. There is a second heart sound which is soft and may be inaudible.
- Acute episodes of **cardiac failure** may present with marked dyspnoea, cyanosis and pulmonary oedema. Otherwise, there may be peripheral cyanosis due to capillary stasis in right-sided cardiac failure. Diagnosis of the condition is made on clinical grounds, supported by chest x-ray.
- In **mitral stenosis**, the patient gives an appearance of marked malar flush but otherwise there is a combination of cyanosis and pallor. The condition characteristically presents with exertional dyspnoea which later progresses to paroxysmal nocturnal dyspnoea and orthopnoea. Cough is a common feature, and may be associated with marked cyanosis or with haemoptysis. The patient may frequently give a history of rheumatic fever. X-ray of the chest shows straightening of the left cardiac border, double contour of the right border and dilatation of the upper pulmonary veins.
- **Pulmonary stenosis**, when develops as a part of Fallot's tetralogy, gives rise to cyanosis which though absent at birth, gradually develops within a few weeks or months, or the cyanotic spells develop after food or exertion. Chest x-ray shows right ventricular and atrial hypertrophy and dilatation of pulmonary artery, giving rise to absence of pulmonary artery curve.
- **Tricuspid regurgitation** may sometimes give rise to cyanosis. There is pansystolic blowing murmur, accentuated by

inspiration. The condition causes distension of jugular veins, pleural effusion, ascites and oedema.

- **Tricuspid stenosis** is a rare condition, frequently occurs in young women, and is often associated with mitral stenosis. Otherwise, there may be severe fatigue, abdominal distension and slight dyspnoea. Cyanosis may develop sometimes, and is always mild. The condition shows presystolic blowing murmur.
- **Pulmonary embolism** may give rise to pallor, cyanosis, syncope, shock and low blood pressure. Radionuclide lung scanning is often sufficient to make the diagnosis.
- **Pulmonary infarction**, when gives rise to symptoms, may present with dyspnoea, cyanosis tachycardia, and fever. Pulse and respiration appear to be rapid, and jugular venous pulsation is increased.
- **Myocardial infarction** presents with angina pectoris-like pain. Development of pulmonary oedema is common. There may be central or peripheral cyanosis. The condition gives rise to soft systolic blowing murmur.
- **Atrial septal defect** is usually asymptomatic but otherwise may give rise to exertional dyspnoea, fatigue and palpitation. Central cyanosis may develop in cases with severe pulmonary hypertension and reversed shunt.
- **Venous thrombosis** may be asymptomatic or may present with tenderness, pain, oedema, cyanosis of skin, and slight fever. Superficial arterial pulse may be lost. A hard cord may be palpable over the involved vein. Pain is maximum on dorsiflexion of the ankle with the knee extended or during straight leg raising.
- **Raynaud's disease** presents with intermittent attacks of pallor followed by cyanosis, usually in the fingers, following esposure to cold, though the condition may occasionally be precipittated by emotional stresses. The patient also complains of numbness, stiffness, diminished sensation and aching pain over the affected area. Attacks usually terminate spontaneously or on warming.
- **Acrocyanosis** results from expoure to cold and produces cold, clammy and cyanotic skin of the hands and feet, neck and ears. The cyanosis is persistent, painless and segmental, and symmetrical in distruibution. Exposure to cold intensifies the cyanosis but is relieved on warming. There may be oedema but no pain.
- **Chilblain** develops from exposure to cold and gives rise to painful, burning and itchy erythematous lesions with oedema or blistering on the fingers, toes, ears and face. The affected part appears cold, clammy and cyanotic but the colour disappears on pressure. A quick warming up of the affected part worsens the condition.
- **Cor pulmonale** presents with chronic productive cough and dyspnoea, which is exertional and progressive but there is no orthopnoea. Later, the condition may perhaps give rise to substernal anginal pain, syncope on exertion and wheezing. There is also cyanosis, prominent pulsations at the lower end of the sternum or at epigastrium, gallop rhythm and distended jugular veins.
- In **asphyxia neonatorum** the newborn fails to breathe spontaneously, and leads to the development of varying degree of cyanosis. Cardiac output falls with drops of pulse rate and blood pressure.

TABLE 8

Cardiovascular conditions with Cyanosis

Condition	Oedema	Blood Pressure	Visible Pulsation	Pulse	Apical impulse	Murmur	Other
Persistent ductus arteriosus	----	low diastolic	suprad sternal notch	Collapsing	-----	machinary like	----
Fallot's tetralogy	-----	-----	-----	----	absent	harsh systolic	soft second heart sound
Pulmonary stenosis	------	------	epigastric	-----	----	loud systolic	splitting second sound
Mitral stenosis	yes	low	left of lower sternum	low collapsing or irregular	tapping	diastolic crescendo	opening snap after second sound
Cardiac Failure	yes	normal of high	external jugular	rapid and feeble	----	systolic	diminished pulmonary sound
Myocardial infarction	-----	low or high	-----	thready	diffuse	soft systolic blowing	diastolic gallop rhythm and third and fourth heart sound
Atrial septal defect	—	—	right ventricular	—	—	mid-diastolic	splitting second heart sound
Ventricular septal defect	-----	------		----	----	pan-systolic	third heart sound at apex

- **Respiratory failure** gives rise to cyanosis and dyspnoea. Pupils begin to dilate, and respiration ceases.
- **Adult respiratory distress syndrome** presents, with dry cough followed by dyspnoea, tachypnoea, grunting respiration and progressive respiratory distress. There is cyanosis which is variable and may not show any improvement even with oxygen inhalation.
- In severe form of **acute bronchitis** there may be cyanosis. Otherwise, the condition presents with irritating unproductive cough which later becomes productive with scanty, mucoid, viscid, expectorations that later further changes to mucopurulent and more copious. There is also retrosternal discomfort or pain but later, there is a feeling of tightness in the chest.
- **Chronic bronchitis** is characterised by cough. There is tightness in the chest, wheeze and dyspnoea. There may be cyanosis due to hypoxaemia. Blood shows reduced Pao_2 due to diminished distribution of ventilation and perfusion, and sustained rise of $Paco_2$.
- **Pneumothorax** presents with cough, chest pain and dyspnoea. Shock and cyanosis may follow. History is often suggestive for the diagnosis. Chest x-ray aids the diagnosis.
- **Pneumenia** presents with chills, headache, fever and chest pain. Cyanosis is often a common feature. Respiration is rapid, shallow and painful.
- **Acute laryngotracheobronchitis** usually presents with violent spasmodic cough, and gives rise to respiratory disress. In severe cases, cyanosis occurs with shallow respiration and leads to asphyxia.
- **Atelectasis** is manifested by chest pain, tachycardia, fever, dyspnoea and cyanosis. Chest x-ray shows homogenous ground glass density, decreased volume of atelectic part of the lung, consolidation, evidence of compensatory emphysema and elevated diaphragm.
- In **whooping cough,** the paroxysms of series of short, sharp, explosive cough may produce cyanosis and convulsions. Diagnosis of the condition is made by the isolation of the causative organism.
- **Laryngitis** usually causes laryngeal oedema and may thus produce dyspnoea, cyanosis, and stridor in the children.
- **Diphtheria** causes laryngeal obstruction in *laryngeal diphtheria* and thus, produces expiratory and inspiratory stridor, cyanosis, and suffocation.

  Nasal diphtheria also gives rise to enlargement of the cervical lymph nodes, characteristic diphtheritic odour, pallor, cyanosis and oher constitutional symptoms.

  Diagnosis of the condition is usually made on clinical grounds and supported by the isolation of the causative organism.
- **Pulmonary emphysema** is characterised by exertional dyspnoea and chronic cough with scanty, mucoid expectoration. There may be cyanosis, especially on the lips and nail beds. Usually there may be clubbing of fingers. The condition causes brief inspiration and prolonged and high-pitched expiration. First sound is diminished and pulmonary second sound is abnormally accentuated.
- Cyanosis may develop in severe cases of **bronchial asthma** when the attacks worsen. The condition is characterised by recurrent attacks of wheezing and dyspnoea.

- In **extrapulmonary tuberculosis** *miliary tuberculosis* may sometimes develop, affecting predominently the children and young adults. The condition then presents with high remittent or intermittent fever, night sweats and prostration. Unproductive cough and dyspnoea occur occasionally. Sometimes cyanosis may develop disproportionately, which when occurs reckoned to be a characteristic feature of the condition. Chest x-ray shows miliary lesions, distributed symmetrically throughout the both lung fields.
- **Pleural effusion** presents with pleural pain, pyrexia, sweats, cough with expectoration and dyspnoea. Cyanosis may however appear in the advanced cases. Diagnosis of the condition is made by chest x- ray.
- **Extrinsic allergic alveolitis** results from prolonged and continuous exposure to varieties of organic dust. In chronic exposure the condition gives rise to productive cough, progressive exertional dyspnoea and, later, dyspnoea may occur at rest and gives rise to cyanosis. Chest x-ray shows diffuse interstitial fibrosis, micronodular shadows and coarse bronchovascular markings.
- **Psittacosis** presents with chills, fever and troublesome cough. In severe cases, symptoms and signs of pnoumonia with frank consolidation may appear after the first week of illness. Dyspnoea and cyanosis may however develop later. History of occupaion is a useful guide for diagnosis. The causative organism can be isolated from blood and sputum.
- **Tetanus** gives rise to spasms of the glottis and respiratory muscles during convulsions, resulting in asphyxia and cyanosis. In *neonatorum tetanus,* however, cyanosis and apnoea occur in more severe cases.
- In **malaria,** sometimes there may be pallor, headache and cyanosis before the spiking fever reaches its peak.
- In **beriberi**, the infantile variety occurs in breast-fed infants, usually of 2 to 5 months old, and gives rise to sudden cyanosis with dyspnoea, whining cry and aphonia. There are puffiness of the face, signs of cardiac failure, diminished urinary excretion, convulsions and coma.
- **Cirrhosis of liver** may be asymptomatic or may present with variable symptoms, while some may present with uneasiness and heaviness in the liver region. Sometimes the condition may also present with central cyanosis, clubbing of fingers, ascites and peripheral neuropathy.
- In severe and fulminating cases of **influenza** there may be retrosternal pain, dyspnoea, cyanosis, haemorrhagic bronchitis and pneumonia. Otherwise, the condition presents with chills, fever, malaise, aches and pains, and prostration. The condition shows a seasonal incidence.
- **Acute renal failure** presents with oliguria or anuria, general weakness, hiccoghs and paraesthaesias, In its *maintence phase,* however, respiratory embarrassement and cyanosis may develop.
- Following prodromal phase and a brief aura in the grand mal of **epilepsy**, there is a tonic stage in which the condition gives rise to loss of consciousness. The patient suddenly falls down on the ground, and then there is tonic spasm of all muscles, and the patient develops cyanosis.
- **Polycythaemia vera** may be asymptomatic or may present with fatigue, drowsiness, dizziness and vertigo. Skin

shows high colour, more so in the cold weather. Cyanosis, both central and peripheral, may be present. Spleen is usually moderately enlarged. Blood shows increased mass and viscocity, resulting to haemoconcentration.

- **Anthrax** is characterised by necrotic ulcer of the skin or of mucous membrance. Some cases may however present with mild fever, headache, cough, dyspnoea, cyanosis and severe systemic distrubances. Sometimes septicaemia develops from haematogenous spread of the infection and may cause high fever, prostration, cyanosis, shock and collapse.
- **Haemorrhagic fever** is manifested by fever, headache, nausea, vomiting and dyspepsia. Shock develops 2 to 6 days after with sudden collapse and prostration, cold and clammy extremities, weak thready pulse, and circumoral cyanosis along with haemorrhagic manifestations.

DIARRHOEA AND STEATORRHOEA

Diarrhoea indicates frequent passing of stools which may be more or less soft or loose. **Steatorrhoea,** though may not necessarily be diarrhoea as such, is the passage of abnormally increased amount of fat in faeces, resulting passing of large, bulky, offensive smell, stools which float on water surface and is difficult to flush away. Diarrhoea may develop from varieties of infection and inflammation, including gastric irritation, while steatorrhoea almost always occurs as a manifestation of malabsorption. Table 9 shows some characteristic features of a few cases of diarrhoea arising from infection, and Table 10 some cases of diarrhoea of non-infectious origin.

- **Gastroenteritis** presents with anorexia, nausea, vomiting and borborygmi. There is abdominal discomfort and cramps and persistent diarrhoea which may be watery or formed, and may or may not contain blood and mucus. Repeated attacks of diarrhoea give rise to malaise, muscular aches and prostration. Very frequent and persistent diarrhoea, perhaps along with vomiting, may lead to severe dehydration and shock. Diagnosis of the condition is made on clinical grounds.
- In **cholera** many cases may remain symptomfree or may present with mild illness and slight diarrhoea. In others, there may be explosive onset of profuse watery diarrhoea. Usually there is no abdominal pain or colic. Soon the stools loose all faecal appearances and odour, and resemble 'rice-water', containing clear fluid and flecks of mucus. The condition causes rapid loss of body fluids and electrolytes. In the endemic areas during the epidemics diagnosis of the condition is often clinical. Otherwise, diagnosis is made by identification of cholera vibrio in the excreta.
- **Salmonella gastroenteritis** may give rise to no symptom or may be manifested by diarrhoea that lasts for a few days. Otherwise, the condition presents with nausea, vomiting and usually low-grade fever, followed by colicky pain in the abdomen and abrupt onset of persistent diarrhoea, occasionally with mucus or blood. Diagnosis of the condition is made on clinical grounds, and is confirmed by the isolation of the causative organism from stool.
- **Campylobacter infection** is the commonest form of food poisoning, affectig mostly children aged between 1 and 5 years. The condition presents with fever, abdominal pain and hepatosplenomegaly. The stool is usually watery and often bloody. Diagnosis of the condition is made by the identification of the causative origanism from the blood and other body fluids.
- In **bacillary dysentery** symptoms depend on the virulence of the organism involved. In general, it gives rise to diarrhoea with frequent small stools which rapidly loose faecal character and become mucus mass composed of blood and pus, perhaps with or without faecal material. Tenesmus is common. There is colicky pain in the hypogastrium. *Shigella* species can be identified in the stools.

TABLE 9

Diarrhoea resulting from causative organisms

Condition	Fever	Steel	Pain	Tenesmus	Causative organism	Other features
Amoebic dysentery	perhaps	blood and mucus	pain/discomfort	yes	*Entamoeba histolytica*	thickened, tender celon
Bacillary dysentery	yes	mucus, pus and blood	colicky pain	yes	*Shigella* species	thickend, spasmodic colon
Cholera	hypothermia	watery	no	no	*Vibrio Cholerae*	dehydration
Salmeonella gastroenteritis	low grade	mucus or blood	colicky pain	no	*Salmonella* species	-----
Campylobacter infection	yes	watery with blood	yes	no	*Campylobacter* species	hepatoesphenomegaly
Giardiasis	no	offensive	mild	no	*Giardia lamblia*	mild catarrhal cholangitis and cholecystifis
Balantidiasis	no	blood and mucus	intermittent colic	yes	*Balantidium coli*	alternating constipation in late stage

- **Amoeblasis** or ***amoebic dysentery*** may present with lower abdominal pain or discomfort, tenesmus, nausea, vomiting, urgent desire of defaecation and recurrent bouts of diarrhoea, sometimes alternating with constipation. The stools are brown, semi-fluid with flecks of blood stained mucus or with blood, and copious mucus.

  When ***amoeboma*** develops, it gives rise to dysentery or bloody diarrhoea of moderate severity, abdominal pain and a palpable mass in the colonic area.

  Later, on development of ***hepatic amoebiasis*** it gives rise to constipation or irregularity in bowel movement.

  The causative organism can be indentified in fresh stools and in tissues obtained from the edge of the ulcers.

- **Infantile diarrhoea** predominently affects children, usually under six months old, and presents with green, slimy stools, containing mucus and streaks of blood. When however *Escherichia coli* is involved, the condition is then known as *nursery diarrhoea* and *traveller's diarrhoea*, and presents with increased frequency of passing watery stools that contain blood, pus, mucus or excess fatty material. Diagnosis of the condition is made on clinical grounds. Stool examination can reveal the causative organisms involved.

- **Giardiasis** may be asymptomatic but otherwise present with acute or chronic diarrhoea and steatorrhoea usually recurrent and urgent, often alternating with constipation. The stools are explosive, watery, pale, semi-solid, greasy, bulky and of offensive smelling. There may be mild abdominal cramps and discomfort, foul eructation, flatulence and anorexia. Often there may be a history of intolerance to milk and food containing milk. Diagnosis of the condition is made by identifcation of the cysts in the formed stools or both cysts and vegetative trophozoites in the liquid stools.

- **Balantidiasis** gives rise to amoebic dysentery-like symptoms with recurrent diarrhoea, alternating with constipation. In severe attack, there may be severe dysentery with bloody mucoid stools. There may also be tenesmus and internittent colic. Diagnosis of the condition is made by the identification of the trophozoites in liquid stools and rarely cysts and also from material obtained from the ulcers through sigmoidoscopy.

- **Strongyloidiasis** may sometimes present with gastrointestinal symptoms, accompanied by diarrhoea which may alternate with constipation or periods of normal bowel activity, and epigastric pain. In heavy infection, diarrhoea may be persistent, accompanied by malabsorption or protein-losing enteropathy, debility, and loss of body weight.

- **Ancylostomiasis** may sometimes give rise to flatulence, abdominal discomfort, diarrhoea and other symptoms of intestinal irritation. Diagnosis of the condition is made by the identification of the eggs of the worm in the stools.

- In **tapeworm infection,** heavy infestation with *Hymenolepsis nana* may produce adbominal pain and diarrhoea. Diagnosis of the condition is mde by the presence of one or more segments (proglottids) in the faeces.

- **Crohn's disease** presents with varying degree of abdominal pain, with local tenderness and muscle guarding. There is intermittent bouts of diarrhoea, flatulence, anorexia, nausea and vomiting. Development of hypochromic microcytic anaemia is common. Barium meal and barium enema x-rays demonstrate the typical lesions with alteration of intestinal mucosal pattern, showing irregularity, stiffness, ulceration, thickening of the wall and narrowing of the lumen, usually discontinuous along the length of the bowel.

- In **ulcerative colitis** the symptoms vary, and the condition show a tendency towards remission and exacerbation. The manifestations if present will include frequent diarrhoea with loose bloody stools, containing mucus and pus, and pain in the lower abdomen, usually in the left iliac fossa. Otherwise, the condition may present with bloody diarrhoea or constipation, or the patient may pass normal stools. In chronic cases, there may be persistent diarrhoea with ill-health, while rectal involvement may give rise to tenesmus, frequent stools and bleeding from the rectum. Both barium meal and barium enema x-rays show intestinal mucosal irregularity.
- **Coeliac disease** may be asymptomatic or may present with voluminous, pale, frothy, foul-smelling stools and in adults diarrhoea. The child fails to thrive, becomes irritating, shows wasting of body and a pot belly and later, retarded growth. Blood shows elevated level of alkaline phosphatase but decreased levels of calcium, proteins, sodium and potassium. A trial with gluten-free diet brings an immediate dramatic improvement.
- **Tropical sprue** is manifested by urgency of defaecation, often after meals, and the frequency is increased in severe cases. Its features include steatorrhoea with loose, bulky, frothy, pale, fatty, greasy and foul-smelling stools which float on water surface. There is no abdominal pain but abdominal discomfort and borborygmi are common. There may be hypoproteinaemic oedema and follicular dermatitis. Gluten-free diet has no influence on the condition. The condition is diagnosed on clinical grounds and is confirmed by jejunal biopsy.
- **Intestinal lymphangiectasia** presents with oedema and ascites. The patient complains of mild intermittent diarrhoea, nausea, vomiting, and abdominal pain. The diagnosis is confirmed by jejunal biopsy.
- **Carbohydrate intolerance** gives rise to episodes of diarrhoea in the children. The affected child fails to gain weight. In adults, it however presents with bloating, flatus, borborygmi, abdominal cramps and diarrhoea. Histroy of intolerance to milk is available.
- Heavy infestation in cases of **trichuriasis** may give rise to abdominal distension and pain, flatulence, nausea, vomiting, tenesmus, diarrhoea and slight fever. Diagnosis of the condition is made by identification of the eggs of *Trichuris trichuria* in stools.
- Occasionally **dracunculiasis** can cause nausea, diarrhoea, dyspnoea and giddiness. The condition is characterised by ulcers on the legs and feet.
- **Carcinoma of stomach** is generally asymptomatic during the early stage or may give rise to vague symptoms mimicking peptic ulcer. Later, however, there may be change in bowel habit and the patient complains of alternating constipation and diarrhoea. Barium meal x-ray may show the filling defect but double

contour x-ray is more helpful during the early stage.

- **Exrapulmonary tuberculosis** when presents as *intestinal tuberculosis* gives rise to watery stools, lacking practically any abdominal pain. Intestinal mucosa, especially of the lower ileum and less frequently of the rectum, shows multiple ulcerations with undermined edges but without induration.
- In **pellagra** diarrhoea is common, though sometimes this may well be absent. The diarrhoea is watery or the stools are mixed with mucus and blood. Dietary habit of the persons often appear as a helpful guide for diagnosis.
- **Starvation** and **undernutrition** give rise to weakness and loss of body weight and, in children, retardation of growth. There may also be diarrhoea, polyuria, and normochromic normocytic anaemia. Plasma levels of total amino-acids and fatty acids are elevated but the level of albumin is either normal or reduced.
- **Kwashiorkor** characteristically causes retardation of growth in the infants. The child fails to gain weight. There is oedema on the feet which may also be seen on the hands and face, and perhaps little ascites and pleural effusion. Diarrhoea with stools containing undigested food particles occur due to impaired synthesis of digestive system, atrophy of intestinal mucosa, and intestinal infection. Blood shows low levels of cholesterol, amylase, lipase, alkaline phosphatase and urea. Plasma protein is reduced but the level of gammaglobulin is well maintained or may be relatively elevated.
- **Nutritional marasmus** leads to retardation of growth, reduction of body weight and wasting of subcutanous fat and muscle. There may be watery diarrhoea or the stools may be semi-solid and bulky. Adbomen is distended with gas. Diagnostic features are same as those of kwashiorkor.
- **Chronic pancreatitis** presents with persistent or recurring pain in the upper abdomen. Mild attack of jaundice may accompany the pain. Development of steatorrhoea is a common feature. Vitamin B_{12} deficiency may be a feature of the condition. Blood shows elevated levels of amylase, bilirubin and cholesterol, and increased content of total and neutral fats in the stools, and glycosuria.
- **Cholestatic jaundice** gives rise to yellow coloration of the sclerae, skin and mucous membrane of the mouth, and clay-coloured or pale stools and steatorrhoea. Stools show increased contents of fat and blie salts.
- **Cholangitis** presents with intermittent colicky pain in the right upper abdomen. The patient often complains of flatulence, dyspepsia, fullness or oppression in the epigastrium, coming soon after foods but get worse after fruits and fatty or fried foods, and is relived after belching or vomiting. There is also chilliness, slight rise of body temperature and diarrhoea. In addition, there is obstructive jaundice. Liver is enlarged and there is tenderness in the right hypochondrium.
- **Acute viral hepatitis** presents with jaundice, headache, malaise and influenza-like fever. There may also be diarrhoea. In addition, there may be constant pain in the upper right quadrant or upper abdomen, and the intensity of the pain may vary, to the extent that may be even very severe. Diagnosis of the condition is made on clinical grounds, supported by liver function test.

TABLE 10

Diarrhoea / Steatorrhoea caused without any organism

Condition	Fever	Diarrhoea/Steatorrhoea	Pain	Association with pain	Other findings
Crohn's disease	Perhaps low-grade	intermittent bouts	intermittent abdominal	worse after foods	tenderness in right lower quadrant
Ulcerative colitis	low-grade	loose, bloody	left iliac fessa	before bowel action	tenderness over the colon
Coeliac disease	no	steatorrhoea	no	----	----
Tropical spure	no	steatorrhoea often after foods	no	----	-----
Chronic pancreatitis	no	steatorrhoea	persistent or recurring upper abdominal	mild jaundice	perhaps tenderness in costo-vertebral angle
Cholangitis	slight	diarrhoea	epigastric	soon after meals but worse after fruits, fatty or fried foods	tenderness in right hypochondrium
Biliary cirrhosis	yes	pale or clay coloured stools	upper abdominal	----	tenderness in right hypochondrium

- **Fatty liver** may give rise to no symptom or may present with non-tender hepatomegaly, or there may be pain in the right upper quadrant, jaundice, and perhaps diarrhoea. Diagnosis of the condition is made by percutaneous biopsy.
- The manifestations of **cirrhosis of liver** may include weakness, nausea, anorexia, flatulence, diarrhoea or constipation, muscle wasting and spider telangiectasia. Enlargement of spleen is common, sometimes even to a considerable size. Liver is usually enlarged in the early stage with blunt edges but later, becomes smooth and hard, often with nodular surface.
- **Indian childhood cirrhosis** presents with anorexia or voracious appetite. There is abdominal distension with flatulence, low-grade fever, constipation or diarrhoea with clay-coloured stools. Diagnosis of the condition is made on clinical grounds, and is confirmed by liver biopsy.
- **Biliary cirrhosis** presents with pururitus and later, perhaps jaundice. Liver is enlarged, hard and, sometimes, rough. Spleen is also enlarged. There may be upper abdominal discomfort, diarrhoea and pain and tingling sensation in the feet and hands. In late stage, there may be bone pain or fracture, ascites, steatorrhoea, osteomalacia or osteoporosis and occasionally, xanthomatous deposits. Diagnosis of the condition is made on clinical grounds, and is confirmed by liver biopsy.
- **Carcinoma of pancreas** gives rise to varieties of symptoms. There may or may not be abdominal pain. Obstructive jaundice develops later and deepens progressively. There may also be heamorrhagic manifestations. Sometimes steatorrhoea with pale stools and diarrhoea may develop. Liver becomes firm and enlarged, and the distended gall bladder may be palpable or there may be ascites.
- **Gastritis** may cause nausea, vomiting, heartburn and epigastric pain, discomfort and tenderness. There may also be diarrhoea. Diagnosis of the condition is made by endoscopic examination and is confirmed by histopathological studies.
- **Zollinger-Ellison syndrome** is an exaggerated form of peptic ulcer, and the patient may sometimes complain of diarrhoea or steatorrhoea. The condition is suspected when a ulcer fails to respond to the available conventional medical therapy or occurs after a successful surgical treatment, or shows its development at an unusual site. A very high level of gastrin is seen in the circulating blood.
- **Diverticulitis** presents with pain in the left lower quadrant. The condition may give rise to constipation alternating with diarrhoea or to increasing constipation. Physical examination may reveal a palpable mass in the left lower quadrant. Barium emema x-ray and sigmoidoscopy can establish the diagnosis.
- **Irritable bowel syndrome** may present with abdominal pain which is relieved by passing flatus or defaecation. There may be constipation or diarrhoea, sometimes without pain, and the stool may contain mucus. The descending colon may be palpable and tender.
- In **intestinal obstruction** when the obstruction is in the colon, there may be spurious diarrhoea. In addition, there is colicky pain and other symptoms and signs of intestinal obstruction.

- **Fasciolopsiasis** may be asymptomatic or may lead to mild gastrointestinal irritation. In heavy infection however, there may be cramping epigastric pain, nausea and loose motions, Diagnosis of the condition is made by the identification of the unembryonated operculated ovum in the stools. Adult worm may occasionally be also seen in the stools.
- **Amyloidosis** is a disorder arising due to accumulation of insoluble fibril protein (amyloid), and involves multisystem. When it involves the gastrointestinal tract, the condition presents with most intractable form of chronic diarrhoea and steatorrhoea. There may also gastric atony, defects in intestinal motility, indigestion, malabsorption, or intestinal obstruction-like symptoms.
- **AIDS** may present with unexplained and persistent lymphadenopathy, perhaps associated with fatigue, night sweats, recurrent fever, and persistent diarrhoea.
- During the prodromal phase of **enteric fever,** *typhoid fever* may give rise to abdominal flatulence and perhaps vague pain in the right iliac fessa. Bowel movement disturbance is usually present with constipation or diarrhoea. After 7 to 10 days of illness the patients are often seriously ill with marked weakness, abdominal discomfort or distension, and 'pea-soup' diarrhoea or constipation. Abdominal distension and tenderness, pronounced on the right side and upper abdomen, may be evident during the febrile period.

  In *paratyphoid fever* the gastrointestinal disturbances are, however, less pronounced.

  The condition gives rise to positive widal test after the second week of illness. The causative organism can be identified from blood and bone marrow in the first week of illness, and from stools and urine from the second week.
- **Malaria** when develops due to falciparum infection, gives rise to irreguar fever which may lack the periodicity. There may also be cough, vomiting, diarrhoea, jaundice and postural hypotension. Diagnosis of the condition is made by identification of malarial parasites in the erythrocytes.
- **Kala-azar** is characterised by irregular fever. There may be malaise, anorexia, headache, chills, dizziness, cough, sweating, diarrhoea or constipation, abdominal discomfort, epistaxis, bleeding gum and, in children, irritation and mental clouding. Diagnosis of the condition is made by identification of LD bodies in the blood, sternal bone marrow, liver or spleen.
- **Pneumonia** presents with shaking chills, headache, cough and fever. Sometimes there may also be diarrhoea and abdominal distension. In addition, there may be signs of pleural effusion or empyema. Diagnosis of the condition is made by identification of the causative organism.
- In **poliomyelitis,** *abortive poliomyelitis* appears as a mild illness, characterised by fever, headache, vomiting, sore throat, and diarrhoea or constipation.

  Non-paralytic poliomyelitis also gives rise to influnenza-like symptoms with severe headache, pain in the back and neck, myalgia, sore throat, and diarrhoea.
- **Botulism** is characterised by progressive muscle weakness. Neurological symptoms are frequently preceded by nausea, abdominal cramps, and diarrhoea. History

of conoumption of contaminated food stuff is a helpful diagnostic aid. Confirmation of diagnosis is however made by demonstration of toxin in the serum and faeces of the patient.

- **Smallpox** presents with severe headache, malaise, prostration, nausea, and diarrhoea. The condition is characterised by severe constitutional distrubances and development of a single crop of skin rash with centrifugal distribution. Disease is not found now a days.
- The manifestations of **acute renal failure** include uraemia, lethargy, and diarrhoea. Urine shows red and white cells, protein, epithelial cells, and granular and dirty brown casts. A progressive daily increase in serum creatinine is diagnostic.
- **Chronic nephritic syndrome** may be asymptomatic till late stage or may give rise to fatigue, nausea, vomiting, polyuria, thirst, pruritus and diarrhoea. A history of acute nephritic syndrome or of nephrotic syndrome may be available. Urine analysis reveals small amount of protein, red cells, granular and hyaline casts, and an increased level of creatinine. X-ray and ultrasonography demonstrate small, irregular kidneys.
- **Chronic renal failure** may give rise to the symptoms of uraemia, paraesthesias and vertigo. There may be stomatitis, bad metalic taste, thirst, diarrhoea, gastrointestinal irritation, burning sensation, and dryness of mouth. The patient may give a history of previous renal disease, symptoms of lower urinary tract obstruction or of exposure to the offending agents.
- **Acute pyelonehritis** presents with pain in one or both loins, which radiates to the iliac fossa and suprapubic area. Dysuria, frequent micturition of small amount of cloudy urine and fever are common. In the infants and children, however, the condition may give rise to abdominal distension, diarrhoea, apathy and convulsions.
- **Pernicious anaemia** gives rise to hyperchromic macrocytic anaemia with megaloblastic bone marrow changes. The condition may give rise to anorexia, nausea, vomiting, dyspepsia, indigestion, and diarrhoea.
- **Iron deficiency anaemia** causes hypochromic microcytic anaemia. It may present with weakness, lassitude, anorexia, nausea, dyspepsia, and constipation or diarrhoea.
- **Chronic myeloid leukaemia** may present with fatigue, weakness, malaise, loss of body weight, dyspepsia, nausea and vomiting. Abdominal distension with diarrhoea or constipation is present. The patient complains of a feeling of weight and pain in the left hypochondrium. Blood shows normochromic normocytic anaemia, full range of graunulocytes from myeloblasts to mature neutrophils, and a few nucleated erythrocytes.
- **Hyperthyroidism** may present with increased appetite, loss of body weight, pruritus, increased frequency of bowel movement or diarrhoea, nervousness and anxiety. There may be diffuse or nodular goitre or there may be no goitre even detectable clinically. The condition also gives rise to tachycardia or arrhythmias, palpitation, increased pulse pressure, perhaps detectable capillary pulsation and, in the hypertensives, collapsing or water-hammer pulse.
- **Addison's disease** may present with weakness, malaise, nausea, abdominal

pain, and constipation alternating with diarrhoea. There may be absence of sweating. The condition is characterised by increased excretion of sodium and decrease excretion of potassium, mainly through urine.

- **Medullary carcinoma of thyroid gland** gives rise to recent or rapid enlargement of thyroid gland, and presents with flushing, borborygmi and diarrhoea. Blood shows high levels of calcitonin, prostaglandins and 5-hydroxytryptamine.
- **Scleroderma** (*progressive systemic sclerosis*) may present with heartburn, pre-oesophageal dysphagia, reflux oesophagitis and loss of oesophageal peristalsis. Diarrhoea and malabsorption however occur late in the course.
- **Polyarteritis nodosa** is manifested by fever, sweating, abdominal pain, localised oedema, weakness, loss of body weight, peripheral neuropathy, oliguria, uraemia, convulsions and organic psychosis. The manifestations may also include bloody diarrhoea, gastrointestinal haemorrhage, proteinuria and haematuria. Development of myalgia and arthralgia is common.
- In **anthrax**, when the spores of the organism are ingested it causes *gastrointestinal anthrax* and presents with anorexia, nausea, vomiting, and abdominal pain with bloody diarrhoea. In diagnosing the condtiion, history of occupation appears to be a helpful guide.
- **Psittacosis** may give rise to wide range of symptoms from a mild inapparent infection to a severe pneumonia and sepsis. There may be diarrhoea or constipation, and abdominal distension. Occupational history of the patient usually aids the diagnosis. Causative organism can be recovered from the blood and sputum.
- **Typhus** presents with malaise, headache, mild anorexia and chest pain, followed by intractably severe headache, generalised aches and pains, prostration, high fever, delirium and stupor. In addition, there may be troublesome unproductive cough, flushed face, diarrhoea or constipation and renal insufficiency. In its diagnosis a rising titre with *Proteus* strain OX19 is most significant.
- **Relapsing fever** is characterised by sudden onset of fever which subsides spontaneously and then recur over a period of weeks. There may also be diarrhoea, hypotension and circulatory or cardiac failure. Diagnosis is made by identification of *Borrelia recurrentis* in the peripheral blood during the febrile period.
- **Legionnaires' desease** gives rise to fever, respiratory symptoms and prostration or delirium. Diarrhoea begins early in the course, and is watery in character. The condition is diagnosed by identification of *Legionella pneumophilia* in the lung tissue.
- **Bartonellosis** when presents as *oroya fever,* the condition then gives rise to fever, weakness, nausea, diarrhoea, severe headache, muscle and joint pain, and may even cause delirium and coma. Diagnosis of the condition is made by identification of the causative organism in the peripheral blood.
- **Histoplasmosis** may sometimes give rise to fever, cough, dyspnoea, diarrhoea and prostration. There are hepatomegaly, splenomegaly and lymphadenopathy. The causative fungus may be identified from the sputum, urine and scrapings of the ulcer.
- **Melioidosis** is characterised by acute or chronic lung condition or by a chronic

indolent infection. The condition is associated with high fever, shaking chills, prostration, vomiting, severe diarrhoea or abdominal pain, and severe muscle tenderness. Diagnosis of the condition is made by identification of the causative organism in the blood, sputum, pus and urine.

- **Whipple's disease** presents with diarrhoea, abdominal pain and distension, and loss of body weight. The condition gives rise to enteropathic arthritis-like non-erosive migratory arthritis. It is an uncommon condition and the diagnosis is made by lymph node or intestinal biopsy with periodic acid-Schiff (PAS) reagent.

DIZZINESS AND VERTIGO

Dizziness and vertigo are actually synonymous, and are often used to express same peculiar subjective symptoms like giddiness, faintness, unsteadiness and light-headedness. These expressions are, in fact, used to represent a sensation of irregular or whirling motion of one being or of external objects, with loss of equilibrium. While all these terminologies are often used loosely so as to describe the peculiar sensation, vertigo however deserves a special emphasis as there exists a true loss of equilibrium, feeling of insecurity or lack of confidence.

- In **anxiety neurosis** there may be tremor, dizziness, palpitations and sweating. A sense of air hunger may develop and the respiration often becomes rapid. Sleep disturbances are frequently common. There may also be tachycardia, occasional premature beats, precordial pain and generalised motor weakness.
- **Head injury** may give rise to dizziness, headache and personality changes which may follow or may occur several months after recovery.
- **Subarachnoid haemorrhage** presents with severe headache, followed by impairment or loss of consciousness. Soon the condition gives rise to dizziness, vertigo, convulsion, diplopia, hemiparesis and aphonia. Diagnosis of the condition is made on clinical grounds, and is confirmed by CT scanning and cerebral angiography.
- **Meniere's disease** gives rise to progressive deafness, followed by recurrent paroxysms of vertigo. There is fullness or pressure in the ears which progressively worsen leading to hearing loss. Tinnitus is a common feature which may be constant or intermittent, or may occur along with vertigo.
- **Intracranial neoplasms** are characterised by headache, papilloedema, personality change and an increase in cerebrospinal fluid pressure. In addition, there may be visual alterations and hallucinations, speech distrubances, monoplegia, hemiplegia, hemianaesthesia, intention tremor, vertigo, tinnitus and hearing impairment. In cases of increased intracranial pressure, the symptoms may include headache, vomiting, dizziness, drowsiness, behaviour and personality changes, clouding of consciousness, focal or generalised seizures, cranial nerve palsies, bradycardia, coma and death.
- **Multiple sclerosis** has an insidious onset and a relapsing and remittent course with extremely variable symptomatology. The manifestations may therefore include weakness of one or more limbs, hemianaesthesia to pain, vertigo, mild emotional disurbances and apathy. Diagnosis of the condition is usually made clinically. A course of repeated exacerbations and remissions, and inconsistent sites in the central nervous system involvement for the nourological symptoms and signs are often diagnostic.
- In **syringomyelia** when the condition presents as *syringobulbia,* it gives rise to sensory loss in the face, atrophy and fibrillation of the tongue, dysarthria, dysphonia, respiratory stridor, nystagmus and vertigo. CT scanning and myelography may demonstrate the malformation.

- **Heat stroke** presents with headache, vertigo and fatigue, followed by loss of consciousness or convulsions, delirium and coma.
- In **aortic regurgitation** there may be no symptom initially, or there may be an uncomfortable awareness of heart beat or dyspnoea. The condition also gives rise to fatigue, weakness, chest pain or angina pectoris, giddiness and syncope. There may be collapsing or water-hammer pulse.
- In **respiratory alkalosis** there may be tetany, circumoral paraesthesia, giddiness and syncope, along with anxiety and respiratory symptoms.
- **Hypertension** is usually asymptomatic but otherwise there is headache (usually suboccipital), dizziness, flushed face and muscular weakness.
- **Ventricular tachycardia** presents with very rapid ventricular rate and thus, results to palpitation, dizziness, dyspnoea and loss of consciousness.
- **Aortic stenosis** may initially give rise to no symptom but otherwise it may present with fatigue, pallor and dyspnoea. Dizziness is common. Restriction in cardiac output decreases the cerebral blood flow and may therefore give rise to syncope, sometimes with loss of consciousness.
- **Multiple myeloma** gives rise to hyperviscocity of blood and results to headache, vertigo, dizziness, somnolence, stupor and finally, coma. The condition shows immature and atypical plasma cells in the bone marrow.
- **Stroke** presents with headache, dizziness, drowsiness, mental confusion, and derangement of speech, thought, motion or of vision. The synptoms and signs the condition produce however depend on the site of causative lesion, and may include, in addition, numbness, tingling, disturbances in micturition, dysphagia, staggering gait, ataxia, dysarthria, deafness, vertigo, double vision, nystagmus, loss of consciousness, epileptic fits, hemiparesis, monoparesis and hemiplegia.
- **Polycythaemia vera** may give rise to no symptom or there may be headache, drowsiness, dizziness, vertigo, forgetfulness, loss of concentration and poor efficiency. The condition is characterised by increase in RBC mass and haemoconcentration.
- **Addison's diease** develops from increased excretion of sodium and decreased excretion of potassium, mainly through urine, and thus eventually causes increased water excretion, dehydration and hypotension. The patient therefore presents with dizziness, syncope and perhaps vertigo.
- Occasionally there may be paraesthesia of hands and feet, vertigo, syncope and hoarseness of voice in **premenstrual tension.**
- **Menopausal syndrome** may quite frequently give rise to dizziness and headache. There may also be tinnitus and fainting.
- In **gastrointestinal bleeding** the severity of symptoms however depend upon the source and rate of bleeding. In general, there may be weakness, fatiguability, pallor, sweating and faintness.
- **Hypoglycaemia** usually develops in *diabetes mellitus* when the patient takes too much insulin or has not taken foods for quite a long time or has undergone unaccustomed exercise, and the condition then gives rise to headache, malaise, nausea, perhaps vomiting, sweating,

tremor, palnitation, tachycardia, faintness, dizziness and mental confusion. Coma may, however, develop when blood glucose level falls to 2·2 mmol per litre of blood or below.

- **Hypothyroidism** gradually begins with weakness, lethargy, absence of sweating, dryness and roughness of skin. There may also be gain in body weight, constipation, hoarseness of voice, dizziness, dyspnoea, and pruritus. Measurement of total serum T_4 and serum TSH diagnostic but of T_3 is not always of much help.
- **Chronic renal failure** may be asymptomatic or may present with vague symptoms but nocturia may be common. In other cases, symptoms develop due to uraemia, along with headache and vertigo. History of previous renal disease, or symptoms of lower urinary tract obstruction may be available. Urine shows small amount of protein, white cells, and low levels of creatine, creatinine, uric acid and potassium.
- In **poliomyelitis,** the non-paralytic variety gives rise to influenza-like symptoms with severe headache. There may also be lethargy, irritability, vertigo and stiffness of the neck.
- **Idiopathic thrombocytopenic purpura** is a heamorrhagic condition, with increased platelet destruction. Along with its usual symptom of spontaneous or traumatic haemorrhage, the condition may give rise to headache, dizziness, and confusion from intracranial haemorrhage.
- In **pernicious anaemia** there may be anginal pain, dizziness, dimness of vision, ataxia, mental distrubances, dimentia and loss of vibration sense. Blood shows hyperchromic macrocytic anaemia, with marked anisocytosis, poikilocytosis and fragmented red cells.
- **Sideroblastic anaemia** may give rise to palpitation, dizziness, dimness of vision and paraesthesia in the fingers and toes. Blood shows hypochromic microcytic anaemia, and increased level of serum iron.
- In advanced stage, **iron deficiency anaemia** may give rise to exertional dyspnoea, giddiness and palpitation. Blood shows hypochormic microcytic anaemia with anisocytosis and poikilocytosis, reduced haemoglobin, perhaps slightly reduced red cell count, low MCH and MCV, and reduced MCHC.
- **Cardiomyopathy** can at times give rise to dizziness, palpitation, dyspnoea, and syncope in its hypertrophic variety.
- **Kala-azar** may present with malaise, chills, headache, dizziness and sweating.
- **Trench fever** begins with exhaustion, headache, severe back and leg pain, fever and dizziness. Diagnosis of the condition is made by specific complement fixation test and by positive haemagglutination test.
- **Neurofibromatosis** is characterised by formation of tumours in the skin, peripheral nerve, nerve roots and cranial nerve. Thus, when neurofibroma develops in a cranial nerve, it may give rise to dizziness, ataxia, deafness and blindness.
- In cases of **male hypogonadism** developing after puberty, it may then present with fatigue, flushing, sweating, dizziness, and loss of initiation.
- **Ankylostomiasis** can occasionally give rise to oedema of feet and ankles, palpitation, tachycardia and dizziness.
- In **giardiasis** occasionally there may be malaise, headache and dizziness. Often the patient gives a history of intolerance to milk and foods containing milk.

- **Dracunculiasis** is characterised by ulcers on the legs and feet. Sometimes the condition may give rise to urticaria, nausea, vomiting, dyspnoea, diarrhoea and dizziness. Diagnosis of the condition is made from presence of the worm in the subcutaneous tissue.
- **Lassa fever** is characterised by severe systemic disturbances. The condition gives rise to chills and high fever. There may also be tinnitus, dizziness, and haemorrhagic manifestations. The causative organism can be isloated from blood. Diagnosis can be confirmed by fluorescent antibody test and by a 4-fold increase of antibody in complement fixation test.

DYSPHAGIA

Dysphagia or painful swallowing is a manifestation of several ailments. This is however a subjective symptom and is usually nonspecific in terms of diagnosis.

- **Laryngitis** presents with a feeling of tickling and rawness in the throat. Voice becomes hoarse or there may be aphonia. Some cases may also give rise to fever, throat pain and dysphagia.
- **Pharyngitis** presents with sore throat and pain in swallowing. Throat appears red and inflammed. The mucous membrane of pharynx may be covered with membranous or purulent exudate which can be wiped off easily.
- **Acute epiglottitis** gives rise to sore throat, cough, dyspnoea, tachypnoea, high fever and dysphagia. The glottis and epiglottis may be seen covered with thick, superficial secretions.
- **Stroptococcal sore throat** may remain asymptomatic or the presentation may include sore throat, nausea, pain on swallowing, and fever. Cervical lymph nodes are enlarged and tender. The pharynx, soft palate and tonsils are red and oedematous, with purulent yellowish exudate which can be wiped off very easily.
- In **diphtheria,** *pharyngeal diphtheria* begins with pallor, headache, vomiting and low-grade fever. There may be pharyngeal oedema, sore throat and dysphagia. A dirty white or grayish yellow psoudomembrane covers the tonsils and surrounding areas, which when removed forcibly leaves bleeding surfaces, and the membrane is formed again. Diagnosis of the condition is made by identification of the causative organism.
- **Achalasia of cardia** presents with pre-oesophageal dysphagia which progresses gradually. In addition, there is regurgitation of the gastric contents, particularly in the night. Barium meal x-ray can demonstrate conical or pointed barium filling area at the lower end of the oesophagus, and tapering in the distal end. There is also absence of progressive peristaltic contraction in the oesophagus during swallowing.
- **Carcinoma of oesophagus** is characterised by progressively worsening of swallowing, to the extent swallowing of even liquid may become impossible. There is also regurgitation of food and a rapid loss of body weight. Diagnosis of the condition is made by barium meal x-ray, and is confirmed by endoscopic and cytological examinations, and by biopsy.
- **Tonsilitis** gives rise to sore throat and throat pain, especially marked on swallowing. There may be fever, chills, anorexia, malaise and headache. Tonsils appear swollen, inflammed and covered with pus. Tonsilar pillar and pharynx appear congested. The cervical lymph nodes may be enlarged and tender. Tongue appears heavily furred.
- **Hodgkin's lymphoma** is characterised by painless enlargement of one group of superficial lymph nodes. The lymph node mass may therefore produce pressure symptoms giving rise to dysphagia, dyspnoea, jaundice, venous abstruction

and paraplegia. Diagnosis of the condition is made by lymph node biopsy and presence of Reed-Strenberg cells.

- In **non-hodgkin's lymphoma** there is unexplained painless enlargement of lymph nodes, usually of cervical or inguinal nodes. The mass of enlarged glands, depending upon the site of involvement, may produce various pressure symptoms such as dysphagia and dyspnoea. Diagnosis is made from biopsy of the affected lymph node.
- **Simple goitre** may sometimes cause wheezing, dysphagia, respiratory embarrassement and venous engorgement of head and neck due to compression. The thyroid gland is enlarged and appears soft, symmetrical and smooth initially but multiple nodules and cysts may develop in long standing cases.
- **Hashimoto's thyroiditis** presents with painless enlargement of thyroid gland or the patient may complain of a just fullness in the throat. Later, there may be dysphagia. The gland appears enlarged, smooth or nodular, and firm.
- **Carcinoma of thyroid gland** may give rise to dysphagia and dyspnoea due to pressure symptoms. The tumour usually presents as a single nodule with poor function than the surrounding functioning tissue of the thyroid gland in the early stage. Later, the tumour becomes stony-hard and irregular, with adhesions to the surrounding tissue.
- When **extrapulmonary tuberculosis** presents as *tuberculous pharyngitis,* it then causes sore throat, pain and dryness of the throat and pain on swallowing. There is pallor and widespread 'worm eaten' ulcers on the mucous membrance of the pharynx. The condition always develops as secondary infection, frequently from pulmonary tuberculosis.

  Tuberculous laryngitis occurs as a complication, usually of pulmonary tuberculosis, and presents with constant hoarseness of voice. Severe pain on swallowing however develops at the late stage. There is pallor of the mucous membrane of the pharynx and palate, and irregular sized ulcers, usually bilateral.
- In **candidiasis** involvement of mouth (*thrush*) gives rise to pain and dysphagia in the infants. Diagnosis is made by isolation and identification of the causative organism from the sputum or aspirated material.
- **Actinomycosis** when involves the thorax or abdomen may give rise to chills, fever, cough, anorexia, malaise, dyspnoea, dysphagia and abdominal colic. The causative organism can be isolated from the sputum and pus. Biopsy of tissue can however confirm the diagnosis.
- **Hiatus hernia** is almost always asymptomatic. It however causes dysphagia only when the hernia assumes large size. Diagnosis of the condition is made by barium meal x-ray. Endoscopy is also helpful for the purpose.
- **Reflux oesophagitis** presents with heartburn and pain, occuring usually half-an-hour after eating, and is dependable on the change of posture. There may also be water brush, dysphagia, haematemesis and melaena. Diagnosis of the condition is made by visual examination through endoscopy and, also, by biopsy.
- In **chickenpox** painful swallowing occurs due to rupture of vesicles initially appearing

on the oropharynx. The condition is however characterised by centripetal distribution of pruritic skin lesions.

- **Scleroderma** may produce heartburn, pre-oesophageal dysphagia, reflux oesophagitis, sliding hiatus hernia and loss of oesophageal peristalsis. There may be normochromic normocytic anaemia. Blood shows elevated erythrocyte sedimentation rate.
- In **pellagra** diarrhoea is quite common. There is also anorexia, nausea, vomiting, excessive salivation, dyspnoea, soreness of mouth, and dysphagia. Tongue is swollen and painful with raw 'beefy' appearance. There is also angular stomatitis and cheilosis. Diagnosis of the condition is made clinically. Dietary habit serves a helpful guide.
- **Iron deficiency anaemia** may give rise to cracking at the angles of the mouth and sore tongue but there is no dysphagia. However in ***Plummer-Vinson syndrome,*** a rare and advanced stage of the condition, there may be dysphagia associated with pre-cricoid web. The condition gives rise to hypochromic microcytic anaemia.
- **Erythema multiforme** produces symmetrically distributed erythematous lesions on the skin and mucous membrane, with recurrences. In its acute form, ***Stevens-Johnson syndrome***, it is characterised by bullae formation and constitutional disturbances. Patients may complain of difficulties in swallowing.
- In **poliomyelitis,** *spinal poliomyelitis* gives rise to asymmetricl paralysis and shows a true flaccid lower motor neurone paralysis. The condition is manifested by facial paralysis, dysphagia, difficulty in chewing, inability to swallow or expel saliva, dysphonia, regurgitation of fluid through the nose, and neck drop.

  When however *bulbar polimyelitis* develops, it presents with facial asymmetry, deviation of jaw on opening of mouth, loss of movement of the palate or pharyngeal muscle, deviation of the tongue, pre-oesophageal dysphagia, and loss of movement of the vocal cords.
- In **rabies,** the patient develops spasmodic contractions of throat muslces on drinking and later, on mere sight, sound or mention of any fluid. Even the salivary secretions of the mouth are not swallowed because of the fear of spasms (*hydrophobia*).
- **Myasthenia gravis** is manifested by marked weakness and fatiguability of certain group of muscles. The patient experiences difficulties in speech, chewing and swallowing. There may however be pre-oesophageal dysphagia when the condition is associated with phenothiazine therapy.
- **Tetanus** is characterised by paroxysms of convulsive tonic, and sometimes clonic, contraction of voluntary muscles. The condition may give rise to dysphagia and irritability. Diagnosis of the condition is made on the clinical grounds.
- **Stroke,** depending upon the site of causative lesions, can give rise to numbness, tingling, distrubances of micturition, dysphagia, staggering gait, ataxia, deafness, vertigo, double vision, contralateral homonymous hemianopia, loss of consciousness, epileptic fits, hemiparesis, monoparesis, and hemiplegia. Diagnosis of the condition is made clinically.
- **Botulism** gives rise to visual disturabances, dry throat and mouth,

dysphagia and dyspareunia. Later, there is paresis of the skeletal, ocular, pharyngeal and respiratory muscles. The muscle weakness increasingly become prominent. History of consumption of contaminated food stuff is a helpful guide. Diagnosis of the condition is however confirmed by demonstration of toxins in the patient's serum and faeces.

- **Acute pericarditis** may present with substernal, pericardial or pleuritic pain. There is also shortness of breath. In addition, there may be tachycardia, chills, fever, cough, fatigue and perhaps pain on swallowing.
- **Carcinoma of stomach** is usually asymptomatic during the early stage or the condition may present with vague symptoms mimicking peptic ulcer. Symptoms generally develop later and include a change in bowel habit. Dysphagia is common. The loss of body weight and cachexia are marked. There are also pallor, ascites, jaundice, visible peristalsis and palpable abdominal mass.
- **Tropical sprue** characteristically presents with steatorrhoea. The patient often complains of an urgency of defaecation after meals. The tongue becomes sore, fiery red, furred and painful. This frequently causes pain and difficulty in swallowing, and leads to a very poor intake of food. Diagnosis of the condition is made on clinical grounds, and is confirmed by jejunal biopsy.
- In most cases **Sjögren's syndrome** present with rheumatoid arthritis-like symptoms. In other cases however it gives rise to dryness of the mouth, lips, tongue and all other mucous membrane and thus, eventually result in difficulty in swallowing and chewing, and dyspareunia.

DYSPNOEA

Dyspnoea means breathlessness, a sensation of subjective difficulty or distress in breathing, and is represented by shortness of breath. It is usually associated with serious disorders of the lungs or of the heart, though normal subjects too may sometimes give rise to this manifestation but following violent exercise.

In pulmonary involvement when the large bronchus is obstructed, it produces inspiratory dyspnoea but expiratory dyspnoea when the obstruction is in the small bronchi. Dyspnoea may develop only after an effort (*exertional dyspnoea*), and there may be paroxysms of it, occuring suddenly at night when the person is in sleep (*paroxysmal nocturnal dyspnoea*). *Orthopnoea* is known when dyspnoea is felt at a time of lying flat or comfortably, and the person is then forced to wake up and to remain seated upright or propped up with pillow on the bed. *Tachypnoea*, on the other hand, is just an exaggerated rapid breathing, and often accompanies dyspnoea.

It is however distressing symptom, and Table 11 illustrates some of the cases of dyspnoea in children and Table 12 that in adults.

- **Respiratory syncytial virus infection** is manifested by dyspnoea along with cough, wheezing, fever and bronchiolitis in infants. Direct fluorescence antibody stain on nasopharyngeal secretion aids in quick diagnosis of the condition.
- **Bronchiolitis** suddenly follows the symptoms of upper respiratory tract infection as respiratory distress with tachypnoea and cough. Inspiratory retractions may be seen of the intercostal, subcostal and suprasternal muscles. Later, respiration becomes shallow and laboured and may lead to respiratory acidosis.
- **Acute epiglottitis** presents with sore throat, cough, high fever, dyspnoea, tachypnoea and inspiratory stridor. There is inspiratory retractions of the respiratory muscles. The glottis and epiglottis may be seen covered with thick, superficial seceration. Auscultation reveals rhonchi and diminished breath sounds in both lungs.
- In **diphtheria,** *laryngeal diphtheria* begins with cough and hoarse cry of the infants, and inspiratory stridor. Soon laryngeal oedema develops and leads to severe dyspnoea, aphonia, high-pitched cough, expiratory and inspiratory stridor, cyanosis and suffocation. Diagnosis of the condition is made by the identification of the causative micro-organism.
- **Acute laryngotracheobronchitis** presents with respiratory distress, tachypnoea, and inspiratory retraction of the supraclavicular, suprasternal, substernal and intercostal muscles. There is also stridor, commonly seen at night. In severe cases, respiration may be shallow and may lead to asphyxia.
- **Laryngitis** begins with a sensation of tickling and rawness in the throat. It may cause laryngeal oedema, giving rise to dyspnoea, cyanosis and stridor in children.
- **Respiratory failure** leads to dyspnoea and cyanosis. The pupils begin to dilate and respiration to ceases.

TABLE 11
Dyspnoea in Children

Condition	Fever	Wheezing	Stridor	Hoarseness	Cynosis	Chest Sounds
Diphtheria	low-grade	----	yes	yes	yes	diminished vocal resonance; hyperesonant percussion note
Respiratory syncytial virus infection	yes	yes	---	----	----	fine moist crackles; hyperesonant percussion note
Acute epiglottitis	high	----	Inspiratory	yes	----	ronchi; diminished breath sounds
Acute laryngotracheobronchitis	yes/no	-----	Inspiratory at night	yes	yes	expiratory rhonchi; rales; diminished brath sounds
Bronchiolitis	yes/no	yes	---	-----	circumoral	fine moist crackles; hyperesonant percussion note
Bronchial asthma	----	yes	----	-----	lips and ears	scattered rhonchi; diminished vocal resonance; hyperresonant percussion note
Tuberculosis	low-grade	----	----	yes/no	----	fine crepitations

- **Pulmonary tuberculosis** presents with undue tiredness, malaise, lassitude, anorexia, dyspepsia, persistent loss of body weight, palpitation, tachycardia, cough and low-grade fever. There may also be shortness of breath on exertion, localised wheeze, unresolved pneumonia, and pleural or chest wall pain. The condition is diagnosed by radiological examination.
- **Extrapulmonary tuberculosis** can involve almost all organs and tissues of the body. When it develops as ***miliary tuberculosis,*** it presents with high remittent or intermittent fever, chills, severe night sweats, malaise, tachycardia and prostration. Occasionally there may also be unproductive cough and dyspnoea. Chest x-ray shows miliary lesions distributed symmetrically throughout the lung fields.

  Tuberculous pericarditis, is a manifestation of pulmonary tuberculosis or of mediastinal tuberculosis, and progressively gives rise to precordial pain, dyspnoea and orthopnoea. There are precordial friction rub, cardiac dullness with shifts in posture, bronchial or bronchovascular breath sounds and rales, and decreased pulse pressure.

  Tuberculous pleurisy is a secondary infection in which symptoms and signs of fibrinous pleurisy often precede the development of effusion. Along with other usual symptoms it gives rise to dyspnoea and cough with purulent sputum. There may be varying degree of chest pain, audible friction rub or signs of serofibrinous pleurisy.
- **Pneumonia** is characterised by varying degree of pain in the chest, chills, headache, cough and fever. There may also be dyspnoea, cyanosis, diarrhoea, tenderness and rigidity in the right side of the abdomen, and delirium. The causative organism may be found in the sputum.
- **Aspiration pneumonia** gives rise to cough and respiratory distress. Infants and young children usually present with wheezing. There may be low-grade fever. Auscultation reveals coarse crepitations. Chest x-ray shows marked opacities in a single lobe or segment, while some cases may show sign of atelectasis.
- **Acute bronchitis** initially presents with upper respiratory tract infection and sore throat, followed by irritating, unproductive cough with rotrosternal pain or discomfort. There may be malaise and slight fever. Later, there is sensation of tightness in the chest, dyspnoea, wheezing and expectoration, at first scanty, mucoid, viscid and may be streaked with blood, and then changing to mucopurulent or more copious.
- **Chronic bronchitis** gives rise to dry irritating cough in the morning with little sputum, which eventually remain present althrough the year. There is tightness in the chest, wheezes and dyspnoea. Cyanosis may develop due to hypoxaemia. Analysis of blood gas shows reduced Pao_2 and sustained rise of $Paco_2$. Hypercapnia is chaotic.
- **Bronchiecatsis** is characterised by cough with large expectoration of purulent sputum. There may be sinusitis, wheezing, dyspnoea, night sweats, fever and shivering in further acute inflammation. There may be slight dullness at the base, weak breath sounds, rhonchi and crepitations and later, there may be diminished chest movement and vocal fremitus, and coarse crepitations over the affected area.

TABLE 12

Dyspnoea in adults.

Condition	Cough	Chest pain	Wheezing	Cyanosis	Haemotysis or bloody sputum	Chest sounds	Chest x-ray findings
Chronic bronchitis	yes	yes	yes	yes/no	yes	hyperresonant percussion note ; dimished vocal fremitus : rhonchi	no changes or prominent linear shadows with propgressive alterations in lung markings.
Bronchiectasis	yes	----	yes	yes	yes	weak breath sounds ; diminished vocal fremitus, rhonchi, coarse creptations.	patchy consolidations ; increased bronchovascular markings.
Pneumonia	yes	yes	-----	yes	yes	impaired permussion note ; crepitations ; absent/diminished breath sounds.	consolidation in the lobe or in patchy distribution
Pleural effusion	yes	yes	------	yes	----	stony dull persussion ; diminished/absent breath sounds & vocal fremitus ; reduced vocal resonance.	homogenous opacity ; displaced mediustinum ; obscured costophrenic angles ; fluid in pleural spaces.
Pneumothorax	yes	yes	------	yes	----	absent/diminished vocal fremitus & breath sounds ; hyperresonance.	sharp edge of collapsed lung ; translucency with no lung marking ; mediastinal displacement.
Pulmonary emphysema	yes	----	yes	yes	-----	diffuse hyperresonance ; scattered wheezes & rhonchi; diminished vocal fremitus.	hypertranslucency of lung fields ; widened intercoastal spaces ; increased antro-posterior diameter of chest
Pulmonary tuberculosis	yes	yes	yes	-----	yes	slightly iincreased percussion note at upper chest ; weakened breath sounds.	calcified & enlarged lymph nodes ; consolidation with fibrosis.
Bronchial asthma	yes	yes	yes	perhaps	-----	hyperresonant percussion note ; diminished vocal fremitus ; high-pitched rhonchi.	nothing or increased bronchovascular markings.
Adult respiratory distress syndrome	yes	-----	-----	yes	-----	diminished breath sounds ; coarse crepitations.	diffise bilateral alveolar infiltration ; later, snow-storm appearance.
Pulmonary eosinophilia	yes	yes	-----	------	yes	hyperresonance, rhonchi and crepitations.	localised or diffuse opacity.
Diffuse fibrosing alveolitis	yes	----	-----	------	-----	preminent breath sounds ; crackling crepitations.	diffuse opacities ; high diaphragm ; later, honey-comb appearance.
Silicosis	yes	-----	yes	------	yes	hyperresonant or dull percussion note ; rhonchi.	nodular opacities ; interstitial fibrosis ; egg-shell opaciites.
Cor pulmonale	yes	yes	yes	yes	yes	crepitant rales over lung base ; diminished breath sounds.	enlargement of right ventricle & pulmonary artery ; increased bronchovascular markings.
Cardiac failure	yes	-----	yes	yes	yes	accentuated pulmonary second sound ; basal crepitations ; sometimes rhonchi.	enlarged cardiac shadow; increased bronchovascular markings.
Myocardial infacation	----	yes	------	yes	-----	soft systolic blowing murmur ; presystolic or systolic gallop rhythm.	nothing or enlarged cardiac shadow ; pulmonary oedema.
Mitral stenosis	yes	-----	------	------	yes	accentuated first sound ; doubling of first sound ; Graham Steel's murmur.	straaightening of left cardiac border ; double contour of right border.
Mitral regurgitation	yes	-----	------	------	yes	high-pitched blowing decrescendo diastolic murmur ; Dureziez murmur.	enlargement of left atrium and left ventricle.
Aortic stenosis	-----	yes	------	------	-----	gallop rhythm, loud systolic murmur at aortic area ; diminished/absent second aortic sound.	calcified aortic cusps and left ventricular enlargement.
Aortic regurgitaton	----	yes	------	------	------	Austin Flint murmur ; Cole-Cecil murmur ; blowing decrescendo diastolic murmur.	aortic dilatation and left ventricular enlargement.

- **Bronchial asthma** presents with recurrent attack of wheezing and dyspnoea. There is prolonged expiration and short and gasping inspiration. The paroxysms begin with a feeling of tightness in the chest. In acute attack, there may also be paroxysmal nocturnal dyspnoea. During an attack there are hyperresonant percussion note, diminished vocal resonance and presence of high-pitched rhonchi. The wheezing is often audible without any aid. Pulmonary function test shows increased TLC, decreased FVC and FEV_1 and increased FRC and RV.
- **Pulmonary emphysema** presents with progressive exertional dyspnoea, chronic cough with scanty, mucoid expectorations, wheezing and tightness in the chest. There may be cyanosis, especially on the lips and nail beds, and occasionally there may be clubbing of fingers. The condition leads to brief inspiration and prolonged and high-pitched expiration. First sound is diminished but pulmonary second sound is abnormally accentuated. X-ray of the chest shows increased anteroposterior diameter of the chest, widened intercostal spaces, hypertranslucency of the lung fields, thin walled translucent area of bullae, prominent hilar shadow, and low and flat diaphragm, with absence of movement during the respiration.
- **Pleural effusion** is often preceded by the symptoms and signs of pleurisy. There is dyspnoea which may also be the only initial symptom in some cases. Cyanosis may also appear in the advanced cases. There is diminished or absent chest movement on the affected side, shifting of mediastinum to the other side, stony dull percussion note over the fluid, diminished or absent breath sounds, reduced vocal resonance and diminished or absent vocal fremitus,
- **Pneumothorax** gives rise to chest pain. There is dyspnoea. Dry cough is also another accompaniment. Shock and cyanosis may follow. The affected side of the chest shows decreased movements. There is absent or diminished vocal fremitus and breath sounds, and hyperresonance. A crunching, rasping sound may be heard over the heart in the mediastinum.
- In **pulmonary eosinophilia**, the manifestations may vary, and the condition may present with high temperature, cough, severe dyspnoea, and occasional haemoptysis. There may also be symptoms of bronchial asthma. Blood shows eosinophilia. X-ray chest may show localised or diffuse opacities in the lungs.
- **Fibrosing alveolitis** is manifested by exertional dyspnoea, and may also give rise to tachypnoea and laboured breathing. In addition, there may be persistent dry cough, and gross clubbing of fingers and toes. Chest expansion during respiration appears poor. Prominent breath sounds and numerous crackling crepitations are heard on both sides of the lung. Chest x-ray shows diffuse opacity with small lung volume and high diaphragm.
- **Extrinsic allergic alveolitis** presents with malaise, chills, fever, dry cough and dyspnoea, occuring several hours after re-exposure to varieties of organic dust. Later, dypsnoea may occur at rest and gives rise to cyanosis. Chronic exposure may give rise to productive cough and progressive exertional dyspnoea. Chest x-ray shows diffuse interstitial fibrosis, micronodular shadows and coarse bronchovascular markings.

- Dyspnoea, chest pain, cyanosis, fever and tachycardia are the usual manifestations of **atelectasis.** There is diminished or absent chest movement towards the affected side. Chest x-ray reveals homogenous ground glass density of the lung field, decreased volume of atelectic part of the lung and consolidation. The diaphragm is elevated.
- **Lung abscess** presents with septic fever and cough which is initially dry and exhaustive but later produces large expectoration of purulent, sometimes fetid and occasionally blood-stained, sputum. Dyspnoea occurs in massive involvement, and the chest pain in pleural involvement. Clubbing of fingers is common. Physical examination reveals small area of dullness.
- **Adult respiratory distress syndrome** presents with cough, followed by dyspnoea, tachypnoea, grunting respiration and progressive respiratory distress. Development of cyanosis is variable and may not show any improvement even with oxygen inhalation. Blood shows increased Pao_2 and normal or low $Paco_2$, and low level of serum lactate.
- In **silicosis** initially there may not be any respiratory symptom. Later, there are dyspnoea on exertion and cough, which is dry initially but later becomes productive, frequently with blood-streaked sputum and haemoptysis. Wheezing is common. Progressive shortness of breath may eventually end to disability. Available history of exposure to silica dust made the diagnosis of the condition easy. Pulmonary function test reveals all kind of abnormalities. Chest radiography shows multiple, small, rounded, regular opacities in the simple cases but nodules, interestitial fibrosis, hilar adenopathy and calcification of peripheral hilar nodes, resembling egg-shell appearance, in the advanced cases.
- **Asbestosis** presents with increasing exertional dyspnoea. Soon cough, wheezing and other symptoms of respiratory distress may appear. Clubbing of fingers is a common feature of the condition. Occupational history of exposure to asbestos fibres or dust is available. Crackling crepitations are heard in the lungs. X-ray of the chest shows diffusely scattered irregular and linear, small, ground-glass or reticular opacities in the lower two-thirds of the lungs.
- **Anthracosis** develops from prolonged inhalation of bituminous anthracite coal dust. The condition may give rise to progressive shortness of breath, leading to complete incapacity. In complicated cases, the disability increases progressively with exertional dyspnoea, cough and perhaps expectoration of black sputum. X-ray of chest shows scattered small rounded opacities in both lung fields.
- **Sarcoidosis** perhaps gives rise to loss of body weight, fever and night sweats. There may be asymmetrical non-destructive inflammatory arthritis, associated with erythema nodosum. The condition may however, in the late stage, produce cough and dyspnoea. Blood shows very high erythrocyte sedimentation rate, and perhaps leucopenia. Chest x-ray shows bilateral and often symmetrical enlargement of the hilar lymph nodes. Occasionally, fine miliary infiltration of the lungs with peribronchial thickening may be evident. Later, there is diffuse and confluent parenchymatous infiltrations, appearing throughout the lung fields.
- **Bronchial carcinoma** may present with persistent cough and repeated but

unexplained haemoptysis. Dyspnoea appears early and is often out of proportion to the presenting symptoms. Diagnosis of the condition is made by x-ray and is confirmed by sputum cytology.

- **Cor pulmonale** usually presents with chronic productive cough, and dyspnoea, which is exertional and progressive but there is no orthopnoea. There may be substernal anginal pain and syncope on exertion. The condition produces hypoxaemia and hypercapnia and thus, causes fall of arterial oxygen saturation to below 85% and increased CO_2 combining power. X-ray of the chest shows enlargement of the right ventricle and pulmonary artery.
- **Fallot's tetralogy** gives rise to cyanosis which is though absent at birth but develops over the next few weeks or months. Older children however give rise to dyspnoea and fatigue but relieved by assuming squatting position. There is short, harsh, systolic murmur, maximal to the left of the upper sternum. Apical impulse is absent. Chest x-ray shows normal contour of the heart with absence of usual pulmonary artery curve.
- In **persistent ductus arteriosus** there may be no symptom for a long time. Otherwise, the child shows retardation of growth and development. Later, there is dyspnoea and the child develops cardiac failure. There is continuous mumbling or 'machinary-like' murmur. Diastolic pressure is low and the patient gives rise to collapsing or water-hammer pulse. Chest x-ray shows enlargement of pulmonary artery. There may also be ventricular hypertrophy.
- **Pulmonary stenosis**, when develops independently, it often does not give rise to any symptom. Otherwise, there may be dyspnoea, and exertional syncope or fatigue. Auscultation reveals an ejection sound followed by ejection systolic murmur to the left of the upper sternum, radiating towards the left shoulder, and is usually accompanied by a thrill.

  When the condition develops as a part of Fallot's tetralogy, it gives rise to dyspnoea and fatigue in the older children.

  X-ray of the chest shows right ventricular and atrial hypertrophy and dilatation of pulmonary artery giving rise to absence of pulmonary artery curve.
- **Acute pericarditis** may give rise to substernal, pericardial or pleural pain. There is also shortness of breath. Auscultation reveals intermittent pericaridial friction rub, best heard to the left of lower sternum.
- In acute episode, **cardiac failure** may present with marked cyanosis and pulmonary oedema. In left-sided cardiac failure, there are tachycardia, dyspnoea and orthopnoea, including paroxysmal nocturnal dyspnoea. There is also Cheyne-Stoke respiration.

  When the condition gives rise to *cardiac asthma*, bronchospasm or wheezing occurs as that is seen in bronchial asthma. In this condition cyanosis develops and deepens, and the patient is seen gasping for respiration.

  On the other hand, in *childhood cardiac failure*, tachycardia is common. There is often cyanosis, dyspnoea and cardiomegaly.

  Diagnosis of the condition is usually made clinically.
- **Myocardial infarction** may give no symptom or may present with pain, the

severity of which vary from a feeling of aching or pressure in the chest to severe agonizing pain which though mimic angina pectoris but lasts longer with no effect on rest. Glyceryl trinitrate brings little or no temporary relief. The manifestations also include vomiting, abdominal distension, pallor, syncope and breathlessness. There may be central or peripheral cyanosis and soft systolic murmur. Pulse is thready. Oliguria is common if blood pressure is low.

- **Angina pectoris** presents with oppression or tightness in the middle of the chest. There may be accompanying breathlessness. The discomfort lasts for a few minutes but may persist maximum up to 15 minutes. The pain is induced by exercise and passes away after rest or following administration of glyceryl trinitrate.
- In **supraventricular tachycardia** the patient may feel faint or breathless. In severe attack there is a feeling of tightness in the chest, palpitation and shortness of breath. Heart rate rises up to 140 to 220 per minute.
- **Ventricular tachycardia** is manifested by palpitation, dizziness, dyspnoea and loss of consciousness. Pulse is rapid and thready, and ventricular rate varies between 120 and 220 per minute. Carotid sinus massage causes no difference. ECG shows broad and abnormal QRS complex. P waves are often unrecognisable or even when they are recognisable, they bear no regular relationship with QRS complex.
- **Mitral stenosis** begins with exertional dyspnoea which progresses to paroxysmal nocturnal dyspnoea and orthopnoea. In addition, there is tachycarida and fatigue. The patient may often give a history of rhenumatic fever. X-ray of the chest demonstrates straightening of the left cardiac border, double contour of right border, dilatation of the upper pulmonary veins, bat-wing shadow in the hilar region, calcification and in cases of cardiac failure enlargement of the heart. Barium swallow x-ray reveals posterior displacement of the oesophagus.
- Initially **mitral regurgitation** does not give rise to any symptom. Later, it presents with fatigue, exertional dyspnoea, followed by paroxysmal nocturnal dyspnoea and orthopnoea, palpitation, and symptoms and signs of cardiac failure. The condition shows strong heaving apical impulse, pansystolic murmur maximum at the apex, perhaps associated with a thrill, displacement of apex beat to the left, prominent third sound or short mid-diastolic murmur and clicking opening snaps. A high-pitched blowing decrescendo early diastolic murmur is a characteristic feature of the condition.
- **Aortic regurgitation** may present with exertional dyspnoea, recurrent paroxysmal nocturnal dyspnoea and orthopnoea. Other features of the condition are fatigue, weakness and symptoms of left-sided cardiac failure. Chest x-ray shows aortic dilatation and left ventricular enlargement. ECG shows left ventricular hypertrophy and changes in the ST segment and T wave.
- In **aortic stenosis** there may not be any symptom or there may be fatigue, pallor and dyspnoea which is exertional initially but later, paroxysmal nocturnal and orthopnoea. Restriction in cardiac output decreases cerebral blood flow and may therefore give rise to syncope, sometimes with loss of consciousness. Radiological

investigations will demonstrate calcified aortic cusps and left ventricular enlargement. ECG shows left atrial and ventricular hypertrophy, and ST segment and T wave abnormalities.

- **Tricuspid stenosis** presents with severe fatigue, abdominal distension and slight dyspnoea. Sometimes there may be cyanosis which is always mild. The condition often develops in association with mitral stenosis. X-ray of the chest shows dilatation of right atrium and superior vena cava. ECG shows tall peaked P wave in some leads.
- In **cardiomyopathy,** *dilated (congestive) cardiomyopathy* may present with cough or dyspnoea or fatigue. Progressive left-sided cardiac failure-like symptoms usually develop. ECG may show monspecific changes and left ventricular hypertrophy.

  In *hypertrophic cardiomyopathy* the condition may present with dyspnoea, anginal pain, syncope, dizziness and palpitation. Pulse is perhaps jerky but sustained. There is double apical impulse. ECG shows left ventricular hypertrophy and bizarre T wave.
- **Pulmonary embolism** may give rise to dyspnoea, pain in the middle of the chest, pallor, tachycardia, sweating, cyanosis, syncope and low blood pressure. Radionuclide lung scanning can often diagnose the condition.
- **Pulmonary infarction** may present with pleuritic chest pain, dyspnoea, cyanosis, dry and unproductive cough, and haemoptysis. Physical examinations reveal diminished chest movement, local chest wall tenderness, presence of pleural friction rub and basal crepitations. X-ray of the chest demonstrates pulmonary opacity or linear scar, presence of pleural fluid and elevation of diaphragm.
- In **atrial septal defect** there may not be any symptom for many years. Otherwise, the condition may give rise to dyspnoea, cardiac failure and arrhythmias. Wide fixed splitting of second heart sound is a feature of the condition. Chest x-ray shows enlargement of heart and of pulmonary artery. It is a congenital disorder and is more common in females.
- Manifestations of **aplastic anaemia** include weakness, lassitude and exertional dyspnoea. It produces pallor, palpitation, tachycardia, systolic murmur and cardiac dilatation. In the diagnosis of the condition a history of exposure to radiation or to offending drugs or chemicals may be available. Blood shows normochromic normocytic anaemia, and pancytopenia with reduced number of red blood cells.
- **Chronic lymphatic leukaemia** presents with lymphadenopathy. In addition, there may be weakness, loss of body weight, malaise, fever, night sweats, and exertional dyspnoea. Pressure symptoms may develop due to enlarged lymph node mass, such as respiratory difficulties from tracheal compression. There may also be purpura and other haemorrhagic manifestations. Blood shows leucocytosis with absolute lymphocytosis, usually of small variety. Bone marrow shows reduced megakaryocytes and an increase in both large and small lymphocytes.
- In **iron deficiency anaemia** there may be weakness, lassitude, anorexia, nausea and dyspepsia. The condition gradually gives rise to exertional dyspnoea, giddiness and palpitation. There may also be coldness and paraesthesias in the fingers and toes, tachycardia, anginal type of chest pain,

cardiac dilatation, systolic murmur and oedema on the ankles. Blood shows hypochromic microcytic anaemia.

- Along with the usual symptoms of anaemia, **sideroblastic anaemia** may present with dyspepsia, headache, and breeathlessness on exertion. Blood shows hypochromic microcytic anaemia and increased level of serum iron.
- **Pernicious anaemia** gives rise to weakness, debility, soreness of tongue, palpitation and tachycardia. Exertional dysonoea is present but is not so marked. Blood shows hyperchromic macrocytic anaemia, and the bone marrow shows megaloblastic changes.
- **Hodgkin's lymphoma** presents with painless enlargement of one group of superficial lymph nodes. The enlarged lymph node mass can therefore produce pressure symptoms and can thus, give rise to dyspnoea, dysphagia, jaundice, venous obstruction and paraplegia. Diagnosis of the condition is made by lymph node biopsy.
- **Non-hodgkin's lymphoma** also gives rise to unexplained painless enlargement of lymph glands, usually of cervical or of inguinal. The mass of enlarged lymph nodes can therefore sometimes proudce pressure symptoms, and depending upon the site of involvement, can give rise to dysphagia and dyspnoea. Diagnosis of the condition is made by biopsy of the affected lymph node.
- Occasionally **simple goitre** can produce dysphagia, wheezing and even respiratory embarrassement. Venous engorgement of the head and neck may occur due to compression. The thyroid gland is enlarged and appears symmetrical, soft and smooth initially but, in long standing cases, nodules and cysts may develop.
- **Carcinoma of thyroid gland** may give rise to pressure symptoms, such as dysphagia and dyspnoea. In the early stage, the tumour usually appears as a single nodule with poor function than the surrounding tissue of the thyroid gland. Later, the tumour becomes stony hard and irregular, and shows adhesions to the surrounding tissue.
- **Hypothryroidism** presents with weakness, lethargy, absence of sweating, dryness and roughness of skin. Face appears dull and swollen with puffy eyelids, thick lips and enlarged tongue. There may also be tingling of the fingers, fatigue, deafness, hoarseness of voice, dizziness, dyspnoea and pruritus. Generally serum T_4, T_3 and T_3 uptake are low. The levels of TSH are always high in secondary hypothyrodism but low in primary hypothyroidism.
- **Hypoparathyroidism** gives rise to tetany, with muscle cramps, numbness and stiffness around the mouth, wheezing, dyspnoea, stridor, convulsion and urinary frequency. Light tapping on the facial nerve even produces contraction or twitching of the facial musclas.
- **Cushing's syndrome** presents with gain of body weight, central obesity, and accumulation of fat at lower part of the back of the neck with rounding of face, protuberant abdomen and thin extremities. There may be dyspnoea, palpitation and hypertension. It also gives rise to mental symptoms ranging from depression to frank psychosis.
- **Phaeochromocytoma** is manifested by paroxysmal or sustained hypertension, and extreme pallor or flushing of the face or of

the extremities. There may also be discomfort in the chest, dyspnoea, palpitation, postural tachycardia and cardiac enlargement. The condition may show glycosuria or hyperglycaemia with normal thyroxin level in the blood.

- **Scleroderma** may lead to progressive pulmonary fibrosis accompanied by increasing dyspnoea. The lung function may be imparied and there may be aspiration pneumonia.
- When *angio-oedema,* a state of **urticaria** involving large areas of oedema in the subcutaneous structures and dermis, involve the upper respiratory tract, it then gives rise to respiratory distress and stridor.
- **AIDS** may sometimes present with ill-health, dry cough, shortness of breath, chest pain and pneumonia, with chest x-ray showing diffuse infiltration.
- **Actinomycosis** when involves the lungs, may cause chills, fever, night sweats, cough with sputum formation, dyspnoea and pleural pain. Diagnosis of the condition is established by biopsy of the tissue.
- **Histopasmosis** is characterised by respiratory symptoms, with ulcerations of nasopharynx and oropharynx. In its acute stage there may be fever, cough, dyspnoea, prostration, diarrhoea, hepatomegaly, splenomegaly and lymphadenopathy. Diagnosis of the condition is made by isolation and identification of the causative fungus from the sputum, urine and scrapings of the ulcers.
- **Aspergillosis** may not give rise to any specific symptom, or the condition may present with productive cough and dyspnoea. X-ray of chest shows tumour-like dense opacity of round fungus ball with crescent of thin layer of air in a cavity or cyst.
- **Blastomycosis** presents with pneumonia-like manifestations, as dry hacking or productive cough, chest pain, chills, fever, dyspnoea and profuse sweating. Diagnosis of the condition is made by identification of the fungus from the sputum.
- Only when **influenza** develops as a severe and fulminating condition it may then give rise to substernal pain, dyspnoea, cyanosis and haemorrhagic bronchitis.
- *Neonatal herpes* is an extremely rare condition of **herpes simples**. Yet, when it develops, it presents with generalised vesiculation of skin, fever, jaundice, dyspnoea, haemorrhage and signs of cardiac failure. There is progressive hepatosplenomegaly.
- When **anthrax** develops due to inhalation of the spores, the condition then presents with primary pneumonia, giving rise to mild fever, malaise, headache, cough, haemoptysis, dyspnoea, cyanosis and severe systemic disturbances. History of occupation appears to be a helpful guide for the diagnosis. The causative organism can be isolated from local lesions, blood and sputum.
- **Psittacosis** is an occupational disease with wide range of symptoms from a mild inapparent infection to a severe pneumonia and sepsis. Dyspnoea and cyanosis may develop in the late stage of the condition. Diagnosis is made by identification of the causative organism from the blood and sputum.
- **Goodpasture's syndrome** gives rise to severe haemoptysis and dyspnoea.

Malaise and headache are common accompaniment. Chest x-ray shows progressive, migratory, asymmetrical, bilateral densities in the lung fields.

- **Acute renal failure** presents with the symptoms of uraemia, lethargy and diarrhoea. In its maintenance phase, there is oliguria or anuria, general weakness, hiccoughs and paraesthaesia. There may also be respiratory embarrassement and cyanosis. Blood shows elevated levels of urea, creatinine, phosphorus, sulphate and organic acids but low level of calcium in recovery phase.
- **Chronic renal failure** may remain asymptomatic or may give rise to vague complaints but nocturia may be common. Otherwise, it presents with symptoms of uraemia. There may also be shortness of breath, hiccough, pruritus, haomoptysis and haemorrhages. Urine shows small amount of protein, white cells, epithelial cells, granular and waxy casts, and low levels of creatine, creatinine, uric acid and potassium.
- **Acute nephritic syndrome** develops in the children with puffiness around the eyes and face. There may be respiratory distress, with shortness of breath. There is also discomfort or pain in the flank or upper abdomen and epigastrium. The patient may give a history of previous infection, particularly of streptococcal. Urine appears scanty, brown, smoky or frankly bloody, containing deposits of erythrocytes, leucocytes, epithelial and granular casts, with high specific gravity and a decreased level of creatinine. Proteinuria is also present.
- **Chronic nephritic syndrome** may remain asymptomatic till the late stage, or may present with fatigue, nausea, vomiting, polyuria, thirst, pruritus and diarrhoea. There may also be drowsiness, headache, dyspnoea, hiccough, loss of vision, fits and coma. Face is pale with puffiness of the eyelids and cheeks. There is also oedema on the feet and ankles, ascites, anaemia and osteomalacia.
- **Legionnaires' disease** presents with malaise, profound weakness, dry cough, non-remittent fever, shaking chills and pleural pain. In addition, there are headache, nausea, vomiting, dyspnoea, myalgia and arthralgia. X-ray of the chest shows patchy, often multilocular, consolidation and patchy infiltration.
- Sometimes the manifestations of **menopausal syndrome** may include tinnitus, fainting, palpitation, tachycardia and dyspnoea.
- **Beriberi** in general does not cause any respiratory distress. In cardiovascular beriberi there is however oedema, dyspnoea, peripheral vasodilatation, high cardiac output, cardiac failure, and retention of sodium and water.

  Infantile beriberi, occurs in breast-fed infants usually of 2 to 5 months old, and gives rise to sudden cyanosis with dyspnoea, whining cry and aphonia. There are puffiness of the face, diminished urinary excretion, and signs of cardiac failure.
- When **syphilis** presents as *tertiary syphilis* it may very rarely involve the lung and may be asymptomatic but otherwise may accompany dyspnoea, haemoptysis and night sweats. Conventional serological tests for syphilis are always positive, some even with non-treponemal antigens.

  Tabes dorsalis begins with lightening or stabbing pain down in the legs, particularly in the calves and heels, and sometimes around the abdomen. There is unsteadiness of gait and ataxia. Paroxysmal painful disorder of function of various viscera, such as laryngeal crises, may develop, giving rise to paroxysmal nocturnal dyspnoea.

- **Dracunculiasis** may sometimes give rise to nausea, vomiting, diarrhoea, dyspnoea and giddiness. The condition is characterised by ulcer formations on the legs and feet. Diagnosis is made by the presence of the warm in the subcutaneous tissue.
- **Anxiety neuroses** may give rise to sweating, tremor, dizziness, palpitations, tachycardia and precordial pain. A sense of air hunger may develop and the respiration may often become rapid. Respiratory distress may secondarily produce stiffness of the muscles of the extremities, with a pricking sensation or numbness on the fingers and toes.

DYSURIA

Dysuria (Table 13) is a painful manifestation in which one complains of difficulty or pain in micturition. It usually develops due to irritation or inflammation in the bladder neck or urethra. The symptom is often associated with increased frequency of micturition.

- In **gonorrhoea,** symptoms may vary but usually it presents with burning on micturition and dysuria. The condition gives rise to urethral discharge in males, or discharge from vagina and urethra in females. Available history of sexual exposure is a helpful guide. The causative organism, gonococcus, can be identified from the exudates.
- **Cystitis** presents with frequency of micturition, dysuria and haematuria. There is pain and tenderness in the hypogastrium. Causative organisms can be identified from urine.
- **Prostatitis** presents with perineal pain, low back pain and perhaps fever. Characteristically it gives rise to urgency and frequency of micturition and dysuria. Burning on micturition, nocturia, and even gross haematuria may also develop. Prostate gland appears to be slightly tender, firm and irregularly idurated or boggy.
- **Acute pyelonephritis** is featured by pain in one or both loins. The manifestations also include dysuria, strangury, fever, rigor, nausea, and vomiting. There is leucocytosis. Urine shows numerous pus cells, red cells, epithelial cells and fragments of renal tissue.
- **Chronic pyelonenhritis** usually presents with vague and slight manifestations of frequency of micturition, dysuria and lumbar pain. There may also be symptoms of uraemia (fatigue, nausea, vomiting and dyspepsia). History of previous urinary tract infection or of recurrent acute pyelonephritis may be available. Urine shows pus cells, granular casts, many epithelial cells, small amount of protein, and increased level of sodium. Blood shows elevated levels of urea and creatinine, and decreased levels of protein, sodium and, occasionally, potassium.
- **IgA nephropathy** is characterised by recurrent haematuria. Pain in the flanks or dysuria is a frequent accompaniment of the condition. Proteinuria is however mild. Levels of serum creatinine and complements are normal but the level of IgA is elevated.
- **Acute tubulointerstitial nephritis** gives rise to variable symptoms. Some patients may however present with chills, fever, dysuria and pain in the flanks. There may be frank or microscopic haematuria. Often a history of consumption of offending drugs is available.
- **Urinary tract calculus** may be asymptomatic or may present with renal colic or excruciating intraurethral pain. There may also be nausea, vomiting, abdominal distension, haematuria, frequency and urgency of micturition, dysuria, and interruption of urinary flow. Plain x-ray may demonstrate radio-opaque calculus but excretory or retrograde pyelography can identify calculus not radio-opaque.
- **Extrapulmonary tuberculosis** may occur as *renal tuberculosis,* and may give rise to no symptom or may present with recurrent

haematuria and dysuria. The patient may also complain of malaise, lassitude and fever. The condition always develops as blood-borne infection, affecting usually the young people.

- **Carcinoma of urinary bladder** presents with dysuria, burning, frequency of micturition and haematuria. Pyuria also develops frequently. In late stage, a suprapubic mass may be palpable. Cytology of urine frequently shows tumour cells. Cystogram reveals the growth, and excretory urogram shows the filling defect of the bladder.
- **Nonspecific urethritis** is usually asymptomatic. Only occasionally can it give rise to dysuria and frequency of micturition in females, and blood-stained urethral discharge, haematuria and strangury in males. Diagnosis of the condition is made on clinical grounds.
- In **vulvovaginitis,** pruritus is the frequent symptom, often associated with varying degree of vaginal discharge. Most patients however complain of burning sensation in micturition. In the young patients, there may be pruritus, dysuria or fornication. The condition is usually diagnosed clinically, supported by physical and vaginal examinations.
- **Vaginitis** presents with vaginal discharge. There may also be discomfort, pain and dysuria. Dyspareunia is a common feature. The condition is diagnosed on clinical grounds.
- In **carcinoma of vagina** painless bleeding is the frequent presenting feature. The bleeding is often evident following coitus. Sometimes there may also be dyspareunia, pelvic pain and dysuria. Loss of body weight is a common feature. The vagina appears swollen in the late stage.
- **Cervicitis** presents with acute inflammation and purulent vaginal discharge. There may also be dysuria and meatal tenderness. Haematuria may however occur occasionally.
- In the late stage, **sarcoma of cervix uteri** may give rise to fever, weakness, loss of body weight, pelvic pain, dysuria and tenesmus. Vaginal cytology can confirm the diagnosis.
- **Trichomoniasis** is usually asymptomatic but otherwise may cause dysuria and dyspareunia in women, and slight discomfort inside the penis or slight early morning urethral discharge before first micturition in men. Diagnosis of the condition is made by the identification of the protozoa.
- Sometimes **candidiasis** can involve the urinary tract and may give rise to dysuria and frequency of micturition.
- **Menopausal syndrome** may give rise to urgency and frequency of micturition, dysuria, incontinence and meatal tenderness. Haematuria may however occur occasionally.
- **Diverticulitis** gives rise to pain in the left lower quadrant but occasionally at suprapubic region or even at right lower quadrant, accompanied by muscle guarding and rigidity. When the inflammation spreads to the bladder, the condition then presents with urinary frequency and dysuria, Diagnosis of the condition is made by barium enema x-ray and sigmoidoscopy.

TABLE 13

Cases with Dysuria

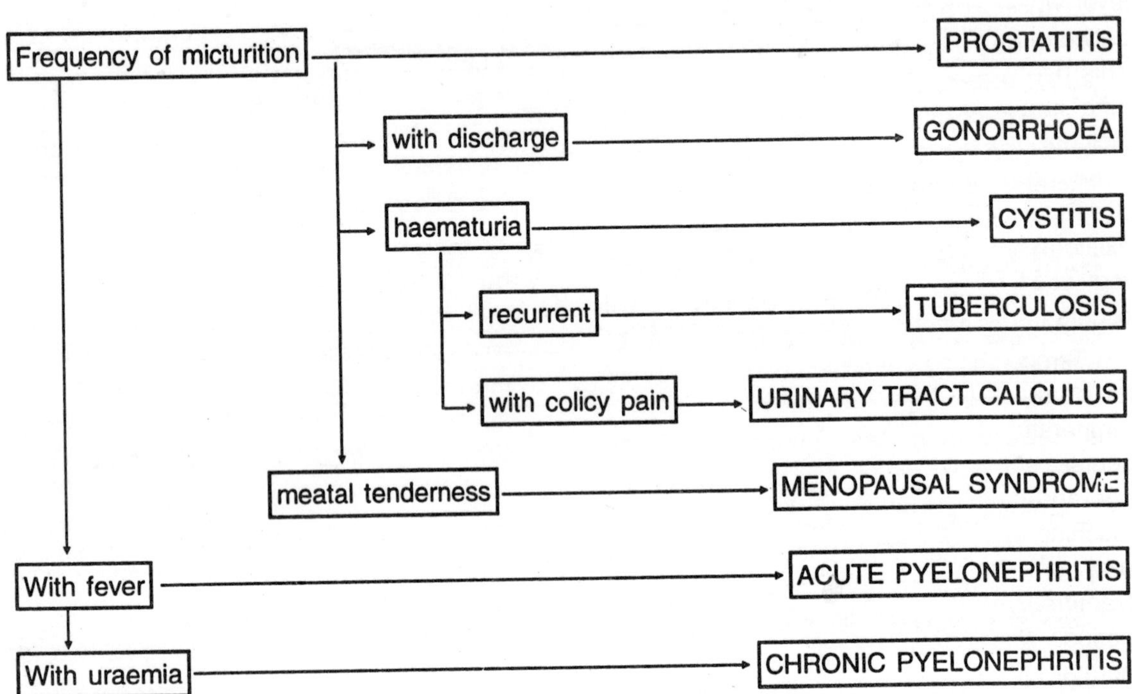

FEVER

Fever is recognised when the body temperature rises above the accepted normal level which is generally recognised as to be between 96·8°F (36·0°C) and 99·0°F (37·2°C). This rise in body temperature is encountered in a large number of condition which may include infection and inflammation, toxaemia, vascular accidents, neoplasms, collagen disease, mechanical injury, nervous excitement and disturbances in the body heat regulation. Slight rise in body temperature also occurs in the females at the time of ovulation.

Temperature may begin suddenly to reach its peak or may rise gradually. Once the temperature rises the fever runs a continuous course, showing no fluctuations of more than one-and-half degree Fahrenheit but without touching the normal level (*continued fever*), or may show fluctuation of more than 2°F (*remittent fever*) or may show alternating periods when the temperature may fall to the normal level or below even (*relapsing fever*). In other instances, fever may persist for several hours and may thus show one or more fall to normal level in 24 hours (*intermittent* or *hectic fever*).

Following the particular course the temperature may fall to normal level abruptly (*crisis*) or may gradually take several days to reach the normal level (*lysis*).

The pattern of fever, its rise, course and fall, may often lack any association with other concurrent manifestations. The fever therefore remains nonspecific in terms of diagnostic purposes. In other circumstances, however, the pattern may be so characteristic as to be suggestive of a distinct condition, and a clinical diagnosis is often made with confidence when the manifestation is taken into consideration along with other relevant facts.

Table 14 illustrates some characteristics of a few conditions and Table 15 of few exanthematous conditions.

- **Enteric fever** includes both typhoid and paratyphoid fever. In *typhoid fever* it may give rise to anorexia, malaise, lethargy, severe headache, generalised aches and pains, sore throat and unproductive cough. Body remperature rises gradually in a stepladder fashion, higher in the evening than in the morning. The pulse appears slow than that is expected from the height of the temperature. After about 7 to 10 days the temperature stablizes at 103°F-105°F (39·5°C-40·5°C) and then runs a continuous course. During the second or third week of the illness a maculopapular, slightly raised, skin rash (*rose spots*) usually appears on the upper abdomen or anterior chest, and spotaneously disappears after 2 to 4 days, which is, however, extremely difficult even to recognise in dark skinned persons. In uncomplicated cases, the patients begin to show improvement during the third and fourth week. Body temperature falls by lysis by the end of the fourth weak.

  Paratyphoid fever is however much milder in severity than typhoid fever, and the temperature returns to normal within 2 to 3 weeks. Skin rash however tends to be more abundant than that in typhoid fever.

  Blood shows leucopenia with neutropenia and relative lymphocytosis after the first week of illness. The causative organism can be identified from the blood and bone marrow in the first week of illness. Widal test becomes positive after the second week of illness.

- **Malaria** presents with chills, rigor, pallor, headache, which may continue for 15 minutes to an hour, and, even, convulsion in the children. The spiking fever reaches to 104°F (40°C) or high and may last for several hours, followed by profuse sweating, and the temperature drops. Characteristically, the fever comes and goes. The paroxysms of fever follow no definite pattern in the early stage. Later, however, the paroxysms may occur after every 48 hours in all but after 62 hours in malariae infection (quartan malaria), in general.

  In *falciparum infection* the fever is irregular and may lack the periodicity or may even occur every day, and may mimic influenza, typhoid fever or yellow fever. In severe form, it may give rise to ***cerebral malaria*** with high fever, confusion, delirium, seizures, stupor, followed by coma persisting for a few hours. Chronic type of the infection, particularly in the patients treated with quinine, may at times produce ***blackwater fever,*** which causes intravascular haemorrhage and haemoglobinuria. In addition, as the disease progresses the spleen becomes enlarged. Liver may also be enlarged and tender. Characteristic malarial parasites within the erythrocytes can be detected in the blood film, which makes the diagnosis confirmed.

- **Brucellosis** presents with fatigue, malaise, anorexia, abdominal pain, constipation and arthralgia. Body temperature rises to 102°F-104°F (39·0°C-40·0°C), and may be associated with chills. The fever may be septic, sustained, low-grade, intermittent or chronic and undulant, with emotional irritability. Temperature usually rises in the afternoon and falls in the early morning hours. Fever generally lasts for about a fortnight and falls to normal for a few days so as to recur later. Following several such undulatios, fever becomes intermittent, showing the rise in body temperature in the nights. There may be peripheral lymphadenopathy, splenomegaly and, in rare instances, hepatomegaly. It is an occupational disease involving persons coming in close contact of domestic animals, such as cattle, goats, swine and dogs. Diagnosis of the condition is possible through identification of the causative organism from the blood, cerebrospinal fluid, urine and tissue. Agglutination titre of 1:80 IgG immunoglobulin is highly indicative for the condition.

- **Relapsing fever** when develops from louse borne infection, it begins with chills, nausea, vomiting, intense headache, muscle and joint pains, and fever, rising quickly to 103°F-105°F (39·5°C- 40·5°C). There may also be varieties of skin rashes. Jaundice is common. Pulse appears rapid. Liver and spleen are frequently palpable and tender. Temperature remains high for 4 to 10 days and then falls by crisis to normal or even below, accompanied by profuse sweating. After an acute attack there may not be any relapse in some cases but in others, there may be one or more relapses after a period of remission of 4 to 10 days, along with other symptoms. The relapses are generally mild and are of short duration.

  In tick brone infection, the manifestations are similar but the condition presents with high fever of short duration, followed by a shrot period of remission. Recurrences are very common and may occur for 3 to 10 times, with declining severity and duration of illness in each attack.

Blood in relapsing fever shows leucecytosis in the acute stage but leucopenia in the afebrile period. Thrombocytopenia is common. Causative organism can be isolated from the peripheral blood during the febrile period.

- **Dengue** presents with fever, malaise, chills, headache, postorbital pain, backache, pain in the extremities and sore throat. Fever may rise to 105°F (40·5°C) with relative bradycardia, and hypotension. Spleen becomes slightly enlarged and appears soft in consistency. Cervical, epitrochlear and inguinal lymph nodes are enlarged. Fever and other symptoms usually persist for 2 to 4 days, followed by remission and profuse sweating. The remission lasts for a few hours to 2 days, followed by a second rapid rise of fever (saddle-back), though the temperature never reaches as high level as in the initial one. A maculopapular, scalatiniform or petechial rash appears on the third or fourth day of the illness. The skin rash lasts for several hours to days, and may fade leaving desquamation and itching. Blood shows leucopenia with relative lymphocytosis. Diagnosis of the condition is made from isolation of the causative organism from blood during the acute phase. Later, diagnosis is made from demonstration of neutralizing and complement-fixing antibodies and by their rising titres on paried sera.

- **Leptospirosis** may remain subclinical with mild undiagnosed fever in many cases. In others, it is ushered by headache (usually frontal), severe muscle pain, anorexia, nausea, frequent vomiting, chills and rapidly rising fever, usually ranging between 102°F and 104°F (39°C-40°C). Prostration is always severe. The pyrexial period continues for 4 to 9 days, followed by a second rise of temperature during the third week of illness, lasting for 6 to 14 days. In a large number of cases the liver as well as the spleen may be palpable. Jaundice develops in many cases on fourth to sixth day. In the early stage of mild cases, slightly raised erythematous rash, usually symmetrical in distribution, appears on the skin of the lower legs on about fifth day. Blood shows leucocytosis with abundant polymorphonuclear leucocytosis. The causative organism can be identified in blood and urine by dark-field microscopy during the first 10 days.

- **Yellow fever** presents with malaise, frontal headache, backache, muscular aches, chills or rigor, and fever which may rise up to 102°F-104°F (39°C-40°C). Pulse is initially rapid and bounding but becomes slow from the second day for the degree of temperature (Faget's sign). Albuminuria appears about the second day and increases. There may also be moderate jaundice. The presenting symptoms subside after 1 to 3 days in mild cases but in others, fever falls by lysis after 2 to 5 days, followed by a remission ranging between few hours and days, and the fever recurs with relatively slow pulse rate than that is expected from the height of the temperature. Blood shows leucopenia with lymphopenia. Mild cases can be diagnosed on Faget's sign. Diagnosis of the condition is however confirmed by isolation of the causative virus from the blood during the first few days of illness. Later, demonstration of complement-fixing and neutralizing antibodies are specific.

- **Measles** is characterised by fever which may swing as high as 105°F (40·5°C), and malaise. Soon the patient complains fo sneezing, coryza and short dry cough. There is also splenomegaly. Fever and cough persist until skin rash appears and then subsides within 1 to 2 days. The skin rash appears as pin-head sized papules or dark red macules which rapidly increases in number and coalesce to form blotchy maculopapular rash. In severe cases, the rash may coalesce further to form uniform erythema or the eruptions may become haemorrhagic. Blood usually shows leucopenia with relative lymphocytosis. Presence of Koplik's spots confirm the diagnosis.
- **Chickenpox** begins with mild headache, backache, malaise and moderate fever, rising up to 101°F to 102°F (38·3°C-38·9°C) but can also occasionally rise to 103°F (30·4°C). Soon, usually within 24 hours, pruritic cutaneous rash appears in crops over 1 to 5 days and follow a centripetal distribution. Characteristically, all stages of the eruptions are seen in any area over any period of time. The condition usually runs for about 2 weeks.
- **Smallpox** presents with severe headache, malaise, prostration, nausea and vomiting. Body temperature may rise to 105°F (40·5°C) and continues for 1 to 5 days and falls within 24 hours after the appearance of skin rash. The skin lesions it produces include macular rash with centrifugal distribution, which changes to papules, then to vesicles and finally to pustules. Characteristically the lesions are seen in the same stage of development in any area at any time.
- **Streptococcal sore throat** may be asymptomatic or may present with sore throat, pain on swallowing, nausea and fever. Cervical lymph nodes are enlarged and tender.

  Scarlet fever however presents with sudden onset of fever ranging between 100°F and 103°F (37·8°C-39·5°C), reaching its peak on the second or third day, with headache and myalgia. Vomiting may develop, and the pulse becomes rapid. Within 24 to 36 hours after the advent of fever, characteristic skin rash develops as small, firm, slightly raised, red papules, superimposed on diffusely erythematous skin surface, with no fluctuation in body temperature. The rash blanches on pressure. Sometimes the rash may also be petechial. Tongue characteristically becomes bright red initially with large papillae (strawberry tongue) but later becomes coated with enlarged papillae protruding on bright red surface. There is also exudative tonsilitis. In the early cases there is leucocytosis with an increase in polymorphonuclear leucocytes. There is also a rise in antistreptolysin O (ASO) titres.
- **Rubella** begins with malaise and low-grade fever. The temperature may rise up to 101°F (39·3°C) but may also be absent, especially in children. The suboccipital, posterior cervical and postauricular lymph nodes are characteristically enlarged, and appear tender. Within 24 hours from the onset of the first symptom, though sometimes it may be delayed till third or fourth day, fine, pink, slightly raised, maculopapular rash appears on the body. The skin rash rarely lasts for more than 3 days but, in the adults, it may be extremely itchy. In some

TABLE 14

Some cases of Fever

Condition	Pattern	Prostration	Chills & Rigor	Sweating	Liver	Spleen	Other features
Malaria	irregular & paroxysmal	present	present	profuse on remission	may be enlarged and tender	may be enlarged	usually shows periodicity
Typhoid	continuous	profound	not marked	—	—	soft, palpable	stepladder pattern of temperature
Influenza	continuous	present	chills	—	—	—	seasonal incidence
Pneumonia	continuous	present	shaking chills	—	—	—	stabbing chest pain and cough
Tuberculosis	low-grade ; irregular	none	yes	night	—	—	haemoptysis; lymphadenopathy
Kala-azar	irregular	—	not marked	at night	enlarged	soft and duffy; later enlarged and very hard	hyperpigmentation of skin; wasting and cachexia
Brucellosis	undulant	present	—	—	rarely enlarged	enlarged	chronic relapses of fever
Epidemic Typhus	sustained high	severe	—	—	—	enlarged	generalised skin rash; Weil-Felix reaction
Dengue	continuous	present	yes	profuse on remission	—	slightly enlarged and soft	saddle-back pattern of temperature; lymphadenopathy
Leptospirosis	continuous	severe	chills	—	may be payble	may be enlarged	jaundice; purpuric & other skin rash
Relapsing Fever	relapsing	present	chills	profusion remission	enlarged and tender	enlarged and tender	milder relapses; mild jaundice
Yellow Fever	continuous	severe	present	—	—	—	recurrences; Faget's sign; mild jaundice

cases however there may not be any skin rash. Blood shows leucopenia. A four-fold or greater rise in antibody in haemaggultination-inhibition test is considered diagnostic of the condition.

- **Herpes zoster** gives rise to boring pain with hyperaesthesia and later, fever, malaise and severe pain in the distribution of the affected nerve root. This is followed after a few days by the appearance of crops of vesicles over the skin supplied by the affected nerve. Scrapings and swab of the base of the vesicular lesion show multinucleated giant cells.
- **Typhus** has several varieties. Of them *epidemic typhus* presents with malaise, headache, mild anorexia and chest pain, followed usually by an abrupt onset of intractably severe headache, generalised aches and pains, high fever, delirium and stupor, Body temperature rises to 104°F (40°C) and remains unremittent for 10 to 14 days, perhaps showing slight remission in the morning, and subsides by lysis generally in 3 to 4 days. The condition also causes enlargement of spleen. Small, irregular shaped macular (sometimes popular) rash appears on fourth to seventh day of illness, on the body but spares the face, palms and soles.

  In *scrub typhus* the temperature gradually rises to 104°F-105°F (40°C-40·5°C), runs a remittent course and falls by lysis usually after twelveth to eighteenth day. About the end of the first week of fever generalised macular rash appears on the trunk and may last for a few hours or may develop to maculopapular eruptions on the trunk, face, palms and soles, and may last for a week.

  Endemic typhus shows similar manifestations as epidemic typhus. Fever develops with shaking chills and lasts for about 2 weeks and then falls by lysis. A maculopapular skin rash appears, maximum on the trunk, and fades fairly rapidly.

  Diagnosis of the condition is made by demonstration of agglutinating antibodies for *Proteus* strain OX19 (Weil-Felix reaction).
- **Brill's disease** is a recrudescence of epidemic typhus and gives rise to all the manifestations fo epidemic typhus but in a milder form. There is also fever and skin rash which follows a short course. The febrile period may last for 7 to 10 days.
- **Bacterial meningitis** presents with intense headache, pain in the back, abdomen and extremity, nausea, vomiting, malaise, chills and high fever. There may be haemorrhagic rash on any part of the skin, mucous membrane or conjunctiva, lasting for 3 to 4 days. Characteristically the condition gives rise to stiffness of the neck and back, with positive Kernig's sign and Brudziniski's sign. The causative organism can be identified from cerebrospinal fluid, blood or punctured material of the petechiae. Cerebrospinal fluid appears cloudy to frankly purulent, with elevated pressure, increased cells and protein, and decreased glucose contents.
- **Erysipelas** presents with malaise, chills, high fever, headache and vomiting. The condition gives rise to the development of small area of erythema on the face, arms or legs which spreads to form a tense, sharply demarcated with elevated margin, glistening, smooth, hot, oedematous area.
- **Respiratory syncytial virus infection** gives rise to cough, dyspnoea, wheezing and bronchiolitis in the infants but appears

TABLE 15

Few Exanthematous Conditions with Fever

Condition	Rash	Initial lesions at	Spreading to	Rash pattern
MEASLES	macule/papule changing to blotchy maculopapular	around the ears, forehead	face; sides of neck	generalised; pronounced at extensors
CHICKENPOX	crops of pruritic vesicles, later ulcerations and crust formation	oropharynx; forehead	trunk and face	centripetal
SCARLET FEVER	diffusely erythematous papule	behind ears	neck, skin fold, inner arms and things	generalised
SMALLPOX	single crop of macule -- papule -- vesicle -- pustule	face and scalp	wrists, hands, neck, back, chest, arms, legs, feet	centrifugal
HERPES ZOSTER	crops of painful vesicle or pustule	nerve root	along the course of the nerve	localised
RUBELLA	maculopapule	forehead & behind ear	trunk and extremity	generalised

as acute coryza in the adults. There is usually fever around 102°F (30°C) but in severe cases, the temperature may rise up to 105°F (40·5°C). Occasionally, there may also be erythermatous skin rash developing on the body. A quick diagnosis of the condition is possible through direct fluorescence antibody stain of nasopharyngeal smear.

- **Rickettsial pox** gives rise to eschar following inoculation of the rickettsia and then about a week after, to intermittent fever, ranging to 103°F-104°F (39·5°C-40°C), lasting for about a week. The patient also complains of chills, headache, profuse sweating and dissemninated aches and pains. During the early stage of fever it gives rise to varicella-like generalised maculopapular skin rash but spares the palms and soles. The lesion later changes to vesicles and formation of cursts that shed within 10 days. Diagnosis of the condition is made by isolation of the causative rickettsia.
- **Rat-bite fever** when develops due to *Streptobacillus* infection, it then gives rise to chills, septic fever, vomiting, headache and backache. Frequently there is polyarthralgia or arthritis. There may also to morbiliform, petechial rash on the hands and feet. The fever lasts for 2 to 3 days and does not cause any relapse.

  In *spirillium* infection, the manifestations include chills and relapsing fever. There is also splenomegaly and regional lymphadenitis. Body temperature lasts for 2 to 4 days, becomes normal by rapid fall, shows a relapse after a few days, and the relapses, in absence of treatment, may continue for weeks together or even longer. The condition also gives rise to macular or maculopapular skin rash but is less marked.

  History of bite by the wild rats or mice may cause suspicion. Diagnosis of the condition is made by isolation of the causative organism.
- **Trench fever** presents with exhaustion, headache, severe back and leg pains, sweating, fever and dizziness. Body temperature may rise to 105°F (40·5°C) and persists for 5 to 6 days. In some cases, however, fever may appear at 5 to 6 days' intervals and the recrudescence may occur for 1 to 8 times. There may be transient macular or papular skin rash. Liver is enlarged. Spleen also shows enlargement. Clinical history is often suggestive. Diagnosis of the condition is possible by specific complement fixation test and by passive haemagglutination test.
- **Rocky mountain spotted fever** presents with malaise, anorexia, nausea, headache and sore throat. This progresses further till headache becomes severe and accompanies aches and pains, chills, harassing cough and fever. Body temporature rises gradually to reach up to 103°F-104°F (39·5°C-40°C) or may even go up to 107°F (41·6°C), and remains high for some days or even weeks in severe cases, with perhaps remissions in the morning hours. In the favourable conditions, temperature finally falls by lysis. Otherwise, it may remain high, giving no hope of recovery. After 2 to 6 days of fever small macular rash appears on the skin and spreads centripetally for 2 to 4 days. The rash later becomes maculopapular, large and dark, and then petechial which coalesce to form large haemorrhagic areas and finally ulcerations. Complement-fixing antibodies show rising titres with specific rickettsial antigens.
- **Toxoplasmosis** may be asymptomatic or the condition may present as a mild, acute or chronic condition with lymphadenopathy of one or more groups of glands. The

enlarged glands are discrete and tender. There may be malaise, myalgia, sore throat, headache and fever. There may also be maculopapular skin rash and urticaria. The causative parasite can be isolated from blood, sputum, bone marrow aspirates, corebrospinal fluid, and other tissue and body fluids. Cerebrospinal fluid shows elevated level of protein and increased number of lymphocytes.

- **African trypanosomiasis** is characterised by fever and central nervous system involvement. In gambiense infection, the condition runs a chronic course with irregular fever for months or years but the rhodesiense infection runs an acute course with high fever. There is also generalised lymphadenopathy. In addition, there may be skin rash, tachycardia and enlargement of liver and spleen. The condition gives a positive Winterbotton's sign which is suggestive of the condition. Diagnosis of the condition is made in the early stage by isolation and identification of the causative organism from the pripheral blood or enlarged lymph node aspirates but from cerebrospinal fluid in the late stage.
- **Influenza** presents with chills, malaise, anorexia, aches and pains, and prostration. Body temperature rises to 102°F-104°F (39°C-40°C). Pulse rate appears to be relatively slow for the degree of body temperature. Bradycardia may develop. Occasionally there may also be erythematous or urticarial skin rash. The fever usually persists for 1 to 7 days.
- **Pulmonary tuberculosis** is manifested by low-grade fever, usually in the afternoon or evening, and night sweats. Initialy, there may not by any history of cough but soon persistent dry cough develops. Sputum is usually scanty at the early stage and later, it becomes green and purulent in caseous liquefying lesion, but yellowish and mucoid in chronic cases. There may be haemoptysis which occasionally may also be the first presenting manifestation. Diagnosis of the condition is made by identification of tubercle bacilli from the sputum and tracheal washings. Tuberculin test is a useful aid. X-ray of the chest plays an important role in the diagnosis.
- **Indian childhood cirrhosis** presents with anorexia or voracious appetite, lassitude, low-grade fever, irritability and apathy. There is also abdominal distension with flatulence, and constipation or diarrhoea with clay-coloured stools. The child shows retardation of growth. Liver is enlarged and firm with sharp, leafy border. Spleen may or may not be palpable. Diagnosis of the condition is made on clinical grounds but liver biopsy can confirm the diagnosis.
- **Diaptheria** in its pharyngeal variety begins with pallor, headache and vomiting. Usually the patient presents with low-grade fever but many cases may equally remain afebrile. Pulse becomes rapid. A dirty white or grayish yellow pseudomembrance covers the tonsils, the pillars and the pharyngeal wall. When the pseudomembrane is removed forcibly, it leaves bleeding surface and the membrane is formed again. The condition is usually diagnosed clinically, supported by the isolation of the causative organism.
- **Pernicious anaemia** is characterised by hyperchromic macrocytic anaemia with megaloblastic bone marrow changes. A low-grade fever may occur even in the absence of any infection. The condition also gives rise to pallor of skin and mucous membrane, oedema of ankles, and cardiac dilatation. Blood shows marked

anisocytosis, poikilocytosis, fragmented red cells, leucopenia with relative neutropenia, hypersegmented neutrophils and diminished platelet count.

- **Aspiration penumonia** is manifested by cough and respiratory distress. There may also be low-grade fever. Auscultation of the chest reveals coarse crepitations. X-ray of the chest shows marked opacities in a single lobe or segment. Some cases may even show signs of atelectasis.
- **Whooping cough** begins with sneezing, anorexia, malaise and low-grade fever. Soon a short, dry cough develops and persists which later follows a high-pitched "whoop" upon inhalation. Paroxysms may occur as often as every half-an-hour and involve a series of short cough of increasing intensity before a breath is taken. Blood initially shows leucopenia but later leucocytosis with absolute lymphocytosis. Clinical history is often suggestive. The diagnosis is however confirmed by the isolation of *Bordetella pertussis* from nasopharyngeal swabs or cough droplets.
- **Hyperthyroidism** may give rise to increased appetite, increased frequency of bowel movement or diarrhoea, loss of body weight, hot and sweaty hands, intolerance to warmth, nervousness, fine tremors of the fingers and tongue, wasting of muscles and bones, and low grade fever. There may be diffuse or nodular goitre or none. Blood shows relative lymphocytosis, elevated levels of calcium and glucose, low level of potassium, and marked decrease in cholesterol.
- **Subacute thyroiditis** presents with progressively increasing neck pain. In addition, there is low-grade fever. Thyroid gland appears firm, tender and symmetrically enlarged. Blood shows leucocytosis, markedly elevated erythrocyte sedimentation rate, increased level of serum T_4 and very low uptake of radioactive iodine.
- **Hodgkin's lymphoma** presents with enlargement of one group of superficial lymph nodes, which are painless, discrete, firm, rubbery, freely moveable, and is frequently associated with influenza-like symptoms. There may be progressive weakness, excessive sweating and low-grade fever persisting for several days, alternating with apyrexial periods. Diagnosis of the condition is made by lymph node boipsy and is confirmed by the presence of Reed-Strenberg cells.
- **Salmonella gastroenteritis** usually presents with low-grade fever, often accompanied by chills. Soon there is colicky pain in the abdomen, and abrupt onset of persistent diarrhoea. Diagnosis of the condition is made clinically and is confirmed by the isolation of the causative organism from the stool.
- **Kala-azar** presents with fever, generally mild, and lack any association with prostration, but may be high in some cases or may even show a daily double rise of temperature in the afternoon and evening. Temperature is usually irregular, remittent or intermittent, may well be sustained or there may be wide swings of temperature. On the other hand, there may be some cases who do not give any history of fever except that of sweating in the night. Fever, however, may continue even for months, perhaps separated by apyrexial periods. There may be malaise, chills, anorexia, headache, dizziness, cough, sweating, abdominal discomfort and, in children, irritation and mental clouding. Spleen is

soft and doughy at first but later usually becomes enlarged and very hard. Liver is also enlarged in the later stage. The patients looks wasted and cachexic, with increasing pigmentation on the skin. Blood shows marked leucopenia with relative lymphocytosis and monocytosis. Peripheral blood generally shows absence of eosinophil. Diagnosis of the condition is confirmed by identification of LD bodies in the blood, sternal bone marrow, liver or spleen.

- **Tonsillitis** presents with sore throat and pain, especially marked on swallowing. There may be malaise, headache, anorexia, chills and fever, rising to 100°F to 104°F (37·8°C-40°C). Tonsils are swollen, inflammed and covered with pus. Tonsillar pillar and pharynx appear congested. The condition is diagnosed clinically.
- **Pneumonia** is manifested by shaking chills, headache and fever which may rise to 103°F-105°F (39·5°C-40·5°C) or even higher during the period of bacteraemia. There is also stabbing chest pain and cough, which later becomes productive with tenacious sputum and, depending upon the organisms involved, may be rusty, frankly streaked with blood or bloody. There may also be pleural pain. Pulse becomes rapid. Respiration is rapid, shallow and painful. The condition gives rise to diminution of chest movement and of breath sounds in the early stage but later, when consolidation occurs, breath sounds become markedly diminished or absent. The causative organism can be identified from the suptum except in non-bacterial pneumonia.
- **Rheumatic fever** is often preceded by a history of group A streptococcal infection. The onset may be acute with high temperature, usually around 102°F to 103°F (39°C-39·5°C) or may be insidious with low-grade fever. There may be profuse sweating in the adults which may however be absent in the children. In addition, the condition gives rise to fleeting or migratory non-suppurative polyarthritis, Tongue appears coated and urine is scanty and high-coloured. History of β-haemolytic streptococcal infection may aid diagnosis. The causative organism can be isolated from throat swab. Some cases may give a raised ASO (antistreptolysin O) titre.
- **Acute epiglottitis** gives rise to cough, high fever, dysphagia, dyspnoea, tachypnoea, and inspiratory stridor. Pharynx is highly inflammed and the epiglottis appears oedematous and beefy red.
- **Laryngitis** presents with dryness and soreness of tongue. Voice becomes hoarse or there may even be aphonia. There may also be malaise, fever, throat pain and dysphagia in some cases. The condition shows marked erythema and oedema of mucous membrane of the larynx, covered with mucus.
- **Pharyngitis** gives rise to sore throat and pain in swallowing. In some cases there may be malaise and fever. Cervical lymph glands may be enlarged. The mucous membrane of the pharynx may be covered with membranous or purulent exudate which could be wiped off easily.
- **Bacillary dysentery** is characterised by abdominal pain, tenesmus, prostration and diarrhoea. In addition, there may be anorexia, malaise, lethargy, chills and fever. Haemoconcentration is a common feature and plasma CO_2 level is usually low. Blood pH is also lowered. Stool examination can identify the causative organism involved.

- **Campylobacter infection** gives rise to relapsing or intermittent fever, rising to 100°F-104°F (37·8°C-40°C), and malaise. The condition is characterised by watery stool, often bloody. Physical examination reveals enlargement of both liver and spleen. The condition is diagnosed by isolation and identification of the causative organism from the blood and other body fluids.
- **Amoebiasis** presents with recurrent bouts of diarrhoea. Although in many cases there may not be any elevation of body temperature, occasionally some may present with low-grade fever.

  When the infection however involves the liver (***hepatic amoebiasis***), it gives rise to irregular fever interspersed by apyrexial periods that may run for months.

  Later, when ***amoebic liver abscess*** develops the condition gives rise to intermittent fever, chills, sweating, nausea, vomiting and, in some cases, diarrhoea or dysentery. The liver becomes enlarged and tender.

  The causative protozoa can be identified in the fresh stools and tissues obtained from the edges of the ulcers. In other cases, indirect haemoglutination test may be helpful.
- **Extrapulmonary tuberculosis** may at times present as ***miliary tuberculosis,*** and may usually be manifested by high remittent or intermittent fever, reaching to 103°F (39·5°C) in the evening but normal in the morning. There are also chills, malaise and profuse night sweats. Liver is often enlarged. Spleen may also be palpable and tender. The condition develops from massive invasion of blood by tubercle bacilli, and predominently affect the children and young adults. Chest x-ray shows miliary lesions distributed symmetrically throughout both the lung fields.

  In the adults, ***tuberculous meningitis*** gives rise to malaise, loss of appetite, vomiting, fever, and persistent and severe headache. General manifestations of the condition include irritability, clonic contraction of muscles or generalised convulsions, cranial nerve palsies, signs of meningeal irritation, stupor and coma, Ophthalmic examination can reveal choroid tubercle. The condition develops from haematogenous spread of tubercle bacilli from a localised focus and usually involves children aged between 1 and 5 years.

  Tuberculous pleurisy develops with symptoms and signs of pleurisy, preceded by the development of effusion. The condition gives rise to malaise, rigor, fever, dyspnoea and cough with purulent sputum.

  Tuberculous pericarditis presents with vague malaise and low-grade fever, or may start as an acute febrile illness. It progressively gives rise to pericardial pain, dyspnoea and orthopnoea. There is also enlargement of liver, and development of ascites. X-ray of the chest shows enlarged cardiac shadow. ECG demonistrates changes in the T wave and ST segment.

  Renal tuberculosis may be asymptomatic or the condition may present with recurrent haematuria and dysuria. In addition, there are malaise, lassitude, fever and loss of body weight. It also causes frequency of micturition. Characteristically, the urine though shows pyuria but is sterile.

  Tuberculous peritonitis usually affects children aged over 2 years and presents with malaise, wasting, fever, abdominal pain and abdominal distension.

  Tuberculous lymphadenitis produces some degree of fever and other constitutional symptoms. It commonly involves the hilar, mediastinal and tracheobronchial lymph glands but involvement of the upper cervical glands is more common. The lymph nodes are usually non-tender, enlarged, matted together and may perforate when caseation and liquefaction develop. Massive involvement of the glands may sometimes produce pressure symptoms.

Tuberculous epididymitis presents with swelling, local rise of temperature, pain, tenderness and fever. The testes may become enlarged and tender, and the entire mass may become fluctuating.

Tuberculous salpingo-oophoritis, the commonest variety of tubereculosis of female pelvic organs, may also involve the ovaries and may thus give rise to pain, fever, tenderness and guarding of pelvic muscles.

In the diagnosis of the extrapulmonary tuberculosis, evidence of active or past tuberculous infection may be available in some cases. In other cases, isolation of the tubercle bacilli may be needed for the diagnosis. The remaining cases may need biopsy or x-ray. Tuberculin test may be a helpful aid in some cases.

- Initially **acute bronchitis** presents with upper respiratory tract infection and slight sore throat, followed by irritating, un-productive cough with retrosternal discomfort or pain. There may be malaise, chilliness, slight fever and muscle pain. If there is no complication the fever perisists for a few days, and the condition runs for 7 to 10 days, though a slight cough may persist for another week or so.
- **Bronchiectasis** is manifested by cough with large expectoration of purulent sputum. There is also recurrent pneumonia in the affected area of the lung. In addition, there may be sinusitis, wheezing, dyspnoea, fever, night sweats and shivering on further acute inflammation. Lassitude, anorexia and clubbing of fingers and toes are common. Diagnosis of the condition is made on clinical grounds.
- **Fibrinous pleurisy** begins with sharp, stabbing chest pain. Body tomperature is usually elevated and rarely exceeds 100°F-101°F (38·0°C-38·5°C). Respiration appears shallow, with restricted rib movements. The breath sounds are diminished on the affected side. The condition gives rise to pleural friction rub.
- **Pleural effusion** often presents with symptoms and signs of pleurisy and begins with little or no pleural pain, cough, expectoration, fever, especially in the infective cases, and sweating. Chest x-ray shows sign of fluid in the pleural space with homogenous opacity, obscured costophrenic angles, displaed mediastinum, and retraction and even collapse of lungs. Diaphragm shows no movement on respiration.
- **Heat stroke** presents with headache, vertigo and fatigue, followed by loss of consciousness and convulsion, delirium and coma. Skin appears hot, dry and flushed with absence of sweating. Body temperature usually swings high to 105°F-108°F (40·5°C-42·2°C) or may even go higher. Pulse rate increases to 160-180 per minute. Respiration rate may also be increased.
- In **sunburn,** symptoms and signs develop upon the intensity of exposure, and is characterised by scaling and hyperpigmentation. In severe cases there may also be nausea, chills, fever,

tachycardia, shock and oedema of the ankles, legs, face and other parts of the body.

- **Exfoliative dermatitis** presents as erythema over large areas on the body surface, covered with lamellated scales. There may also be itching, malaise, chills, rigors, fever or excessive heat loss and, in late stage, loss of hair and nails. Generalised lymphadenopathy and hypoproteinaemia are common manifestations.
- **Osteomyelitis** usually starts in the infants with severe systemic symptoms of toxicity but in the children, it is ushered by fever, chills, malaise and sweating. In the adults, the onset is however less striking. There may be localised pain and tenderness over the bone, and a tapping over the bone can make the pain worse. There is also muscle spasm, and redness and swelling over the affected bone. Culture of blood and aspirates of bone or of joint effusion are helpful for the diagnosis.
- **Acute pyelonephritis** presents with pain in one or both loins. The patient complains of dysuria, frequent micturition of small amount of cloudy urine, fever, rigor, nausea and vomiting. Urine shows numerous pus cells, red cells, epithelial cells and fragments of renal tissue. Blood shows leucocytosis.
- **Acute nephritic syndrome** presents with puffiness around the eyes and face in children. There may be headache, malaise, mild fever, anorexia, vomiting and respiratory distress with shortness of breath. The condition gives rise to oedema, particularly around the ankles. Pulse rate is increased, blood pressure becomes elevated and the jugular venous pressure is raised. In diagnosis of the condition a history of previous infection, particularly of streptococcal, may be available. Blood shows elevated levels of urea and creatinine, and a decreased level of sodium. Proteinuria is also present. Urine is scanty, brown, smoky or frankly bloody, containing deposits of erythrocytes, leucocytes, epithelial and granular casts, with high specific gravity.
- **Rapidly progressive nephritic syndrome** presents with acute nephritic syndrome-like manifestations, which include fever, anorexia, nausea, vomiting, fatigue and weakness. Abdominal pain and arthralgia are common. Haematuria is always present but proteinuria is variable.
- **Acute tubulointerstitial nephritis** gives rise to chills, fever, dysuria, and pain in the flanks. Often a history of consumption of offending drug is available.
- In **cystitis**, acute infection may cause malaise, chills and fever. The patient presents with urgency and frequent urge of voiding but passes small volume of urine, often turbid, and may also be blood stained. Micturition is always associated with burning or pain.
- The manifestations of **acute viral hepatitis** include chills or chilliness, headache, malaise, and influenza-like fever which may even rise to 101°F (38·3°C) in hepatitis A virus infection. This is followed by the development of jaundice. Diagnosis of the condition is made on clinical grounds. Blood shows leucopenia with relative lymphocytosis. Hyperbilirubinaemia is a characteristic feature of the condition. Liver function tests reflect hepatocellular damage.
- In **poliomyelitis,** *abortive poliomyelitis* is the commonest form and gives rise to

fever, headache, sore throat, vomiting and diarrhoea or constipation. In most cases, the patients however recover from the illness in a few days.

Another variety, *non-paralytic poliomyelitis* may present with influenza-like symptoms with severe headache, pain in the back and neck, deep muscle pain, sore throat and vomiting or diarrhoea.

- **Mumps** may remain clinically inapparent but otherwise the condition presents with malaise, chilly sensation, headache and anorexia though, in some cases, the prodromal symptoms may remain absent. Fever, about 102°F (39°C), is always present but often in the children. Fever is usually high when the condition accompanies any complication. Usually pain and swelling occur on one side, followed by the other in a day or two, or both the parotid glands may be affected at the same time, or the swelling may remain confined to one side and the other side may escape altogether. The glands are firm and moderately or extremely tender. Blood shows leucocytosis with relative lymphocytosis, and elevated level of amylase. Demonstration of a four-fold increase in complement-fixing antibodies in paried sera is diagnositic for the condition.
- Development of fever in **infective endocarditis** is a common manifestation. Fever is high with rigors in acute type but continuous, low-grade or irregular and occurs for months in subacute type. There is also chills, malaise, lassitude, anorexia, pallor, night sweats and tachycardia. There may be haemorrhage, petechial haemorrhage, and the spleen is just palpable and enlarged. Development of embolism is common, which may however be gross or minute. In diagnosis of the condition a history of fulminating infection or of rehumatic, congenital or atherosderotic heart disease is often suggestive. The causative organism can be recovered from blood and bone marrow. A suspicion of the condition should arise whenever a patient comes with unexplained fever, accompanied by heart murmur. The condition presents with a murmur at the apex or base of the heart, corresponding to the mitral or aortic valve.
- **Infective arthritis** usually involves a single large joint with extreme pain, swinging fever and severe malaise. Radiological examination reveals soft tissue swelling, periarticular osteoporosis, narrowing of joint space, periosteitis and articular erosion. The condition is diagnosed by identification of the causative organism in the joint aspirates and blood.
- **Suppurative parotitis** presents with malaise, chills, fever and pain. The affected gland is firm and tender, and the overlying skin appears oedematous.
- The manifestations of **lung abscess** include high and remittent or intermittent fever, chills, malaise, anorexia, sweats, and aches and pains. The condition gives rise to irritating, dry and exhaustive cough, followed by large amount of expectoration of purulent, sometimes fetid and occasionally blood-streaked, sputum, and prostration. X-ray of the chest shows dense homogenous opacities with segmental or lobular consolidation in the early stage and later, horizontal fluid level in a cavity which is not changed irrespective of the change in posture. There is also increased lung markings.
- **Atelectasis** presents with chest pain, dyspnoea, cyanosis, fever and tachycardia. Both heart and mediastinum are displaced

towards the affected area. There is dull percussion note and diminished or absent vocal fremitus and breath sounds. Chest x-ray shows homogenous ground glass density, decreased volume of atelectic part of the lung, consolidation, evidence of compensatory emphysema and elevated diaphragm.

- In **empyema** the symptoms may be obscured or slight but otherwise the condition may present with high and remittent fever with rigor, sweating, malaise and anorexia. There is also cough, pleural pain and, in cases of large deposition of pus, buldging of intercostal space of the affected side, reduced or diminished movements of the ribs, reduced or absent breath sounds over the affected area, and stony dull percussion note. Blood shows leucocytosis with an increase in number of polymorphonuclear leucocytes. Chest x-ray reveals collection of fluid.
- **Bronchiolitis** begins with the symptoms of upper respiratory tract infection followed suddenly by respiratory distress and tachypnoea, tachycardia, wheezing and hacking cough. There may also be fever. Blood shows leucocytosis with lymphocytosis. X-ray of the chest shows hyperinflated lungs, depressed diaphragm and prominent hilar markings.
- **Actue coryza** presents with slight sore throat and later, malaise, dull frontal headache and chilly sensation. There may be little or no fever, or there may be high temperature. The condition also gives rise to pain in the limbs and back.
- **Aspergillosis** is a non-invasive pulmonary disorder and may sometimes present with chills, fever, prostration, delirium and hypotension. Diagnosis of the condition is made on clinical grounds, supported by the identification of the causative organism and from characteristic radiological picture.
- The features of **pulmonary eosinophilia** vary. It may present with low-grade fever and minimum respiratory symptoms or there may be high temperature, cough and severe dyspnoea with symptoms of bronchial asthma. Blood shows increased number of eosinophils.
- **Extrinsic allergic alveolitis** presents with malaise, chills, fever, dry cough and dyspnoea, occuring several hours after re-exposure to organic dust. The symptoms subside after an hour but a repeated attack may lead to pulmonary fibrosis. The condition is diagnosed on clinical grounds, aided by a history of exposure to organic dust.
- **Herpes simplex** may give rise to *herpetic gingivostomatitis* which involves children aged 1 to 3 years, and presents with extensive vesiculoulcerative lesions in the oral cavity, sometimes extending to the posterior pharynx. The condition gives rise to fever which may rise up to 105°F (40·5°C) and may persist for about a week.
- **Acute pancreatitis** presents with persistent, intense abdominal pain. There may be nausea, vomiting, prostration and fever, rising to 100°F-102°F (37·8°C-39°C). The serum and urinary levels of amylase and lipase are elevated. Proteinuria is common.
- **Fulminant hepatic failure** produces severe impairment of liver function, and hepatic encephalopathy. The condition gives rise or weakness, nausea, vomiting sweating, fever, delirium, and hypotension.
- **Acute cholecystitis** gives rise to slight fever, rigor, epigastric discomfort and severe abdominal pain, tenderness and

rigidity in the right hypochondrium or epigastrium. The gall bladder may be palpable. Diagonis of the condition is made on clinical grounds. Plain x-ray may show radio-opaque shadow of gall stone.

- **Cholangitis** is manifested by colicky pain in the right upper abdomen. There may be chilliness, especially in the evening, with slight rise in body temperature. Development of obstructive jaundice occurs. Liver is enlarged, and there is tenderness in the right hypochondrium. Clinical features are usually suggestive for the diagnosis.
- **Chronic active hepatitis** gives rise to fatigue and anorexia. There may be mild or moderate jaundice but may even be absent as well. The condition also presents with fever, epistaxis, superficial bruising, spider telangiectasia, arthralgia, and hepatosplenomegaly. Diagnosis of the condition is confirmed by liver biopsy.
- **Choledocholithiasis** may give rise to sudden and severe pain in the right hypochondrium or epigastrium, intermittent jaundice and hepatocellular dysfunction. There may also be fever, and a history of biliary colic and jaundice. Diagnosis of the condition is made on clinical grounds. Cholangiography, ultrasonography or CT scanning may be needed in cases of doubt.
- **Cirrhosis of liver** can only occasionally give rise to fever, encephalopathy, purpura, thrombocytopenia, osteoporosis, renal failure, and gynaecomastia.
- **Carcinoma of liver** gives rise to unexplained deterioration of the cirrhotic patients. The condition leads to weakness, cachexia, abdominal pain, jaundice, and ascites and oedema. There may also be fever. Liver is enlarged and tender, and a mass may be palpable at right upper quadrant. Cytology of ascites may show malignant cells. Liver biopsy can diagnose the condition.
- The secondary (obstructive) variety of **biliary cirrhosis** gives rise to intermittent or chronic jaundice over months or years. In addition, there are abdominal pain, chills, rigor, fever and bone pain. Liver is enlarged and tender. In late stage, cirrhosis, portal hypertension and ascites develop. Diagnosis of the condition is made on clinical grounds and is confirmed by liver biopsy.
- Acute stage of **prostatitis** is manifested by perineal pain, low back pain, chills and fever. Urgency and frequency of micturition, dysuria and myalgia are common features of the condition. Prostate gland appears irregular, tender and boggy, and a mere palpation of it may result in expression of copious purulent discharge.
- **Gallstones** may occasionally present with obstructive jaundice, fever from biliary infection, or the condition may lead to septicaemia with shock. Plain abdominal x-ray may reveal radio-opaque shadow. The diagnosis can be confirmed by ultrasonogram.
- **Pulmonary infarction** may not give rise to any symptom or may present with pleuritic chest pain, dyspnoea, tachycardia, fever, cyanosis, dry and unproductive cough, and haemoptysis. Pleural effusion may develop. Both pulse and respiration become rapid. Blood shows polymorphonuclear leucocytosis. X-ray of the chest shows pulmonary opacity or linear scar, elevation of diaphragm, and presence of pleural fluid.

- **Venous thrombosis** may give ro tenderness, pain, oedema, local warmth, and cyanosis of skin over the area of the involved vein. There is also slight fever. Superficial arterial pulse may be lost. A hard cord may be palpable over the involved veins. The condition is diagnosed by venography and may be confirmed by impedence plethysmography, phlebography or ^{123}I fibrinogen scanning.
- **Acute pericarditis** may present with mild to moderate substernal, precordial or pleuritic pain which worsens on cough, respiration or thoracic movement, exercise or lying but relieved by sitting or standing. There may also be tachycardia, chills, fever, cough, fatigue, perhaps pain on swallowing, and other symptoms according to the underlying cause. Peripheral blood shows leucocytosis and a raised erythrocyte sedimentation rate. Presence of pericardial friction rub is diagnostic.
- **Myocardial infarction** may not give rise to any pain or there may be chest pain, the severity of which varies and may even resemble angina pectoris but lasts longer, shows no relation with rest, and glyceryl trinitrate gives little or no relief. There are also nausea, vomiting, pallor, sweating, excessive fatigue, breathlessness, syncope, fever and shock. Development of pulmonary oedema is a common feature. Blood shows leucocytosis and elevated levels of creatine kinase, lactate dehydrogenase (L.D., L.D.H.), asperate aminotransferase and, also, alanine aminotransferase. Prothrombin time may be increased. ECG shows elevated ST segment, inverted T wave, diminution of R wave and abnormal Q wave.
- **Agranulocytosis** presents with sore throat, fever, chills, extreme weakness and severe prostration. The condition causes progressive necrotic ulceration on oral mucosa and throat, with little pus formation. There may be available history of exposure to offending agents. Blood shows reduction of absolute number or absence of granular leucocytes. Platelet count may however be high.
- **Acute leukaemia** may present with weakness, easy fatiguability, malaise, anorexia, fever and prostration. Other manifestions of the condition include rapidly advancing anaemia, pallor, ulcers in the mouth and enlarged tonsils or stomatitis. There are also enlargement of liver, spleen and lymph nodes. Peripheral blood shows blast cells and other primitive cells, neutropenia, thrombocytopenia and normochromic normocytic anaemia.
- **Chronic lymphatic leukaemia** is manifested by enlargement of the superficial lymph nodes in the cervical, axillary and inguinal regions. The enlarged lymph nodes are firm, rubbery, discrete and painless, and are distributed symmetrically. There may also be weakness, fatigue, malaise, anorexia, fever, night sweats and exertional dyspnoea. Anaemia is mild but of progressively increasing. Blood shows leucocytosis with absolute lymphocytosis, usually of small variety, low or normal platelet count, low level of immunoglobulins and elevated level of uric acid.
- **Chronic myeloid leukaemia** gives rise to fatigue, weakness, malaise, fever, night sweats, and abdominal distension with diarrhoea or constipation. Easy bruises, persistent bleeding from mucous membrane, epistaxis, sternal tenderness and occasional bone or joint pain also

develop. Spleen appears firm, smooth, painless and greatly enlarged, and gives a friction rub. Liver is usually moderately enlarged with smooth surface. Lymph nodes are not generally enlarged. Bone marrow shows replacement by cellular elements, mostly granulocyte but few blasts and reduced erythropoietic tissue.

- **Anaphylactoid purpura** presents with effusion of blood and plasma into the subcutaneous, submucous and subserous surfaces. There may be erythematous rash or urticaria, and non-thrombocytopenic purpura, especially seen on the areas of pressure. Fever and malaise are common.
- **Infectious mononucleosis** begins with sudden onset of fever, often with vomiting, and the tempareture may range between 100°F and 103°F (37·8°C-39·5°C). Characteristically the condition involves the lymph nodes of any area, often the posterior cervical chain, which become enlarged, firm, elastic, normally discrete, non-tender or slightly painful and non-suppurative. Initially blood shows granulocytopenia followed by lymphocytosis with many atypical lympocytes which are larger than the normal and show cytoplasmic vocuolation.
- **Sarcoidosis** when involves the pulmonary system may give rise to fever and night sweats. The patient looses body weight. There may be symmetrical non-destructive inflammatory arthritis associated with erythema nodosum. Cough and dyspnoea may occur in the late stage. Blood shows very high erythrocyte sedimentation rate. There may be leucopenia. Serum uric acid level may be elevated in some cases. There is also elevated levels of calcium and phosphorus. Hypergammaglobulinaemia is common. Radiological findings are highly characteristic. Skin test (Kveim test) with reliable antigen is helpful.
- In **Crohn's disease** symptoms vary widely. In its acute variety, the condition may mimic acute abdomen, while in others there may be recurrent episodes of pain. The symptoms generally include local tenderness or muscle guarding, abdominal distension, intermittent bouts of diarrhoea, nausea, vomiting and low-grade fever. Development of hypochromic microcytic anaemia is common. Barium meal and barium enema x-ray can domonstrate the typical lesions with alternation on intestinal mucosal pattern. Long standing cases may show stricture. A tender mass may be palpable on adbominal or rectal examination.
- **Ulecrative colitis** is characterised by suppurative ulceration of the mucous membrane of the colon, and gives rise to bloody diarrhoea. In severe form, there may be dehydration, tachycardia and high swinging fever with signs of toxaemia, in addition. Barium meal and barium enema x-rays show intestinal mucosal irregularity.
- **Stroke** presents with headache, dizziness, mental confusion, derrangement of speech, thought, motion or of vision, or there may be fever, headache, vomiting, mental changes, nuchal rigidity, convulsion and coma but consciousness may or may not be lost. In other cases, the symstoms may however vary depending upon the site of the lesion.
- **Salpingo-oophoritis** presents with severe lower abdominal and pelvic pain. Often there is also copious purulent vaginal discharge. A high fever is usual and may reach to 104°F (40°C), accompanied by tachycardia. Chills or chilly senstation may occur occasionally. Pelvic examination

reveals tenderness on movement of the cervix, uterus or adnexa. An adnexal mass may be palpable.

- **Tubo-ovarian abscess** gives rise to severe lower abdominal and pelvic pain. There is also nausea and vomiting. Tachycardia is uaually present and the body temperature may swing high. Abdomen appears tender and shows muscle guarding. Pelvic examination is often extremely difficult due to tenderness. Yet, when it is done, tender adnexal mass may be palpable.
- **Septic abortion** though initially presents with hypothermia, fever appears later. The temperature is generally moderate but at times may swing as high as 105°F (40·5°C). There may be abdominal and pelvic pain. The condition shows marked tenderness in the suprapubic area.
- **Puerperal infection** presents with chills and fever. Body temperature rises to 100·5°F (38°C), and is more apparent in the later afternoon or early evening. The temperature occurs following the first 24 hours after delivery. There is disproportionately rapid pulse, and lowering of blood pressure. There may also be pallor and tachycardia. Lochia is usually profuse and malodorus. Uterus is soft, enlarged, tender and boggy.
- **Endometritis** presents with lower abdominal pain, accompanied by malaise and anorexia. Body temperature rises to 102°F-103°F (38·8°C-39·4°C), and remains elevated throughout. Tachycardia is always evident. Lochia is a common feature. The condition is diagnosed clinically.
- At the late stage **sarcoma of cervix uteri** may give rise ot weakness, fever, pelvic pain, dysuria, tenesmus and loss of body weight. Vaginal cytology can establish the diagnosis.
- When the abscess is not encapsulated, **brain abscess** gives rise to chills and fever with slowed pulse and respiration rate. Body temperature does not rise over 102°F (39°C). The condition also gives rise to alteration in mental and general condition of the patient. Cerebrospinal fluid shows increased pressure, mild elevation of protein. Mild pleocytosis is also evident. The causative organism can be recovered from the cerebrospinal fluid.
- **Plague** begins with chills, fever, malaise, intense headache and generalised muscular aches. Pulse appears rapid and thready. Both liver and spleen may be palpable. The *bubonic plague* characteristically presents with regional lymphadenopathy, while the *pneumonic plague* gives rise to fulminating symptoms with pneumonitis. The caustive organism, *Yersiana (Pasteurella) pestis* can be isolated from the aspirates of the bubo and from culture of the bubo aspirates or pus and blood.
- **Viral encephalitis** presents with high fever, malaise, sore throat, headache, nausea and vomiting. Tremor, stiff neck, signs of meningeal irritation and cranial nerve palsies are common finditngs. Deep tendon reflexes may show exaggeration but the superficial reflexes are absent. Cerebrospinal fluid is clear but the pressure and protein content are often elevated with normal level of glucose content.
- **Hypernatraemia** presents with flushed face, fever, tachycardia, confusion and seizurs or coma. Blood pressure is lowered. The condition is diagnosed on clinical grounds. Blood however shows elevated level of urea.

- **AIDS** may be asymptomatic or may present subclinically with fever, lymphadenopathy and skin rash. Some cases may present with fatigue, malaise, night sweats, loss of body weight, recurrent fever, persistent diarrhoea and candidiasis. Demonstration of cellular immune deficiency and immunofluorescence are helpful for the diagnosis.
- **Idiopathic pulmonary haemosiderosis** gives rise to hemoptysis, accompanied by recurrent episodes of fever. Chest auscultation reveals widespread coarse crepitations. Chest x-ray shows diffuse stippled shadow, particularly in the mid-zone.
- Some cases of **juvenile chronic arthritis** may begin with profound systemic disturbances, and may cause high intermittent fever. The condition is often accompanied by small macular rash but is not specific. Along with this there are congestion of eyes, myalagia and arthralgia. Anaemia is common. Blood shows polymorphonuclear leucocytosis, and an elevated erythrocyte sedimentation rate.
- **Polyarteritis nodosa** may begin with fever, sweating, abdominal pain, tachycardia, hypertension, asthma, peripheral neuropathy, oliguria, uraemia, convulsions and organic psychosis. Blood shows leucocytosis. Urine shows proteinuria and microscopic haematuria.
- **Polymyalgia rheumatica** begins with symmetrical pain and stiffness in the neck, back, or shoulder or pelvic girdle. In addition, there may be malaise, anorexia, fever, depression and loss of body weight. Blood shows mild normochormic normocytic anaemia, and moderately high erythrocyte sedimentation rate. Biopsy of the temporal artery may show giant cell arteritis.
- **Peritonitis** gives rise to malaise, nausea, vomiting and septic fever. Prostration may be severe. There is pain and tenderness in the abdomen which may be localised or generalised, with varying degree of muscle guarding and rigidity. Later, there may be adbominal distension. Diagnosis of the condition is made on clinical grounds.
- **Perinephric abscess** presents with chills, fever and pain in the abdomen or in one flank, Dysuria is a common feature. Development of nausea, vomiting and haematuria are occasional. A palpable mass may be felt in the loin or abdomen.
- **Sickle cell anaemia** gives rise to fatigue, increased susceptibility to infection, acute abdomen, malaise, jaundice and episodes of severe pain, commonly occuring in the bones and spleen. Cardiac enlargement may be a common accomaniment. Episodes of arthralgia with fever may occur. Aseptic necrosis of the head of femur is common. There is constant scleral icterus. Blood shows abnormal haemoglobin (HbS), leucocytosis, increased reticulocytes, increased viscosity, and elevated level of serum bilirubin.
- **Non-Hodgkin's lymphoma** is characterised by unexplained enlargement of lymph glands, usually of the cervical or inguinal lymph nodes. There may also be malaise, tiredness, occasional fever, night sweats, and pressure symptoms due to enlarged lymph node mass. Diagnosis of the condition is made from biopsy of the lymph gland. Bone marrow aspirate and trephine biopsy can also be done to establish the diagnosis.

- **Gastritis** presents with nausea, vomiting, heartburn, and epigastric pain, discomfort and tenderness. There may also be haematemesis and gastrointestinal haemorrhage. Occasionally, the condition may give rise to muscle cramps, prostration, chills and fever. Diagnosis of the condition is made by endoscopic examination, and is confirmed by histopathological studies.
- **Urinary tract calculus** may remain symptomfree or may present with renal colic or excruciating intermittent pain. There may also be nausea, vomiting, frequency of micturition, haematuria, chills and fever. Plain x-ray can detect radio-opaque calculus but excretory or retrograde pyelography is needed to identify non-opaque calculus.
- **Renal carcinoma** gives rise to recurrent painless haematuria. There may be pain in the abdomen or flank, and many patients may complain of renal colic due to blood clot. There may also be long continued fever, oedema of the legs and symptoms of metasteses in the lungs, liver or bones. X-ray may show enlarged kidney. Presence of tumour can be detected by excretory urography, retrograde pyelography, renal angiography and ultrasonography.
- **Wilm's tumour** is usually asymptomatic and most frequently presents with palpable abdominal mass. Only occasionally in the advanced cases that there may be pain, fever, anorexia and vomiting. The condition is suspected whenever a child presents with intrarenal mass in a functioning kidney. In older children however CT scanning may be helpful.
- Symptoms vary in **hydronephrosis**. There may be no pain or the patient may present with intermittent attack of dull ache and discomfort in flank, or there may be excruciating or colicky pain. There may also be haematuria, pyuria, fever and localised discomfort. A mass may be palpable in the flank. A history of unexplained, vague gastrointestinal symptoms, particularly in the children, may cause suspicion of the condition. Otherwise, the condition is diagnosed by excretory urography, retrograde pyelography and cystoscopy. Ultrasonography is also another helpful aid.
- In acute stage, **gout** gives rise to throbbing or excruciating pain, most commonly in the metatarsophalangeal joint of great toe, though other joints may also be involved. There may be fever, chills, rigors and tachycardia. Blood shows leucocytosis and elevated level of uric acid. Erythrocyte sedimentation rate is also high.
- **Fascioliasis** is asymptomatic when there is light infection but may produce mild fever and tender hepatomegaly due to migration of the metacercariae. Heavy infection however gives rise to fever and abdominal rigidity. There may also be acute cholangitis, obstruction of bile duct and jaundice. Liver is enlarged and tender. Blood shows eosinophilia. Diagnosis of the condition is made by identification of unembryonated operculated eggs of *Fasciola hepatica* in stools or in duodenal aspirates.
- **Clonorchiasis** does not give rise to any symptom unless in heavy infection when it presents with fever, chills and mild jaundice. Liver is enlarged and tender. Blood shows eosinophilia and elevated levels of alkaline phosphatase and bilirubin. Diagnosis of the condition is

made by identification of small operculated and embryonated ovum in the faeces or duodenal contents. Plain x-ray of the abdomen may show interhepatic calcification.

- **Lymphogranuloma venereum** presents with tenderness in the groin, fever, anorexia, headache and joint pain. The inguinal lymph nodes, frequently unilateral, are enlarged and matted into a tender, sausage-shaped fluctuating mass, with reddened overlying skin. Diagnosis of the condition is usually made on clinical grounds, often supported by a history of suspected sexual exposure.
- In **amyloidosis,** clinical features vary and are nonspecific, and depend upon the organ and system involved. In general, it gives rise to weakness, fever, and loss of body weight. Diagnosis of the condition is made by biopsy.
- **Systemic lupus erythematosus** does not give rise to any fever. However, when the condition develops as drug-induced, it gives rise to fever, skin lesions, polyarthritis and pulmonary infiltration.
- **Hypersplenism** is manifested by abdominal fullness, pain over the splenic area, fever, haematemesis, gastrointestinal bleeding and purpura, Spleen is enlarged and palpable, and gives an audible splenic friction rub and bruits. Blood shows mild normochromic normocytic anaemia, leucopenia, thrombocytopenia, elevation of reticulocytes and prolongation of bleeding time.
- **Erythema multiforme** is characterised by erythematous lesions on the skin or mucous membrane. There may be itching, burning sensation, soreness due to erosion of mucous membrane lesion in the mouth, genitalia and eyes, aches and pains, fever and malaise. The condition is diagnosed on clinical grounds.
- **Erythema nodosum** causes development of bilateral, tender nodules in the skin. It also gives rise to fever, malaise, and aches and pains. The condition develops as secondary manifestation of an underlying systemic disease due to infection or to drug reaction.
- **Miliaria** presents with acute inflammatory skin eruptions accompanied by severe itching, burning and irritation. In severe cases there may also be fever and heat prostration.
- **Rabies** presents with malaise, anorexia, nausea, vomiting, sore throat and fever. The patient may show restlessness, increasing to uncontrollable excitement. The patient develops spasmodic convulsions of throat muscles on drinking and later, on mere sight, sound or even mention of any fluid. History of bite by rabid animal or contact of infected saliva of rabid animal on fresh skin abrasion or mucous membrane can make the diagnosis easy.
- **Tetanus** is characterised by paroxysms of convulsive tonic, and sometimes clonic, contraction of voluntary muscles. Body temperature of the patients usually remain normal or slightly raised but may swing up to a very high level before death. The condition is diagnosed on clinical grounds.
- In **filariasis** episodes of fever, with or without inflammation of the lymphatics and nodes, come and go. There may be chills, headache, malaise and urticaria. Later, interference of normal lymphatic flow may produce hydrocele and scrotal lymphoedema in males, and lymphatic varices and elephantiasis in both sexes.

Diagnosis of the condition is made by identification of the microfilariae in the blood.

- In cases of **schistosomiasis,** following development of localised papular pruritic dermatitis at the site of penetration of the cercariae, there is a symptom-free period of several weeks, and then the condition gives rise to fever and show eosinophilia. There may also be urticaria, cough, muscle aches, headache, abdominal pain, hepatomegaly, splenomegaly and lymphadenopathy. Diagnosis of the condition is made by identification of eggs in the faeces and rectal snip.
- Larval migration in **ankylostomiasis** may cause sore throat, cough, bloody sputum and even fever for a very transient period of time.
- Larval migration in **strongyloidiasis** may produce malaise, anorexia, fever, cough and urticaria for a very transient period.
- Larval migration in **ascariasis** may cause fever, cough, haemoptysis and signs of lobular involvement of lung for a very transient priod.
- Heavy infestation in **trichuriasis** may cause abdominal pain, tenesmus, nausea, vomiting, slight fever and headache. It is diagnosed by identification of eggs of *Trichuris trichuria* in stools.
- **Anthrax** is manifested by localised necrotic ulcer of the skin or mucous membrane. The condition gives rise to high fever, prostration, shock, cyanosis, sweating and even death in cases of septicaemia occuring due to haematogenous spread of the infection. The fever may however be mild along with symptoms and signs of primary pneumonia when the condition develops due to inhalation of spores. History of occupation can serve a helpful diagnostic aid. The causative organism can be identified from local lesions and also from blood and sputum.
- **Gas gangrene** is characterised by local cellulitis and anaerobic myositis. The wound gives a foul-smelling brown to blood-stained serous discharge. Body temperature may be elevated and there may also be palpable gas bubbles in the tissue.
- **Actinomycosis** when involves the thorax or abdomen, the condition then presents with chills, fever, night sweats, cough with sputum, pleural pain, dyspnoea, anorexia, malaise, dysphagia and abdominal colic. Identification of the causative organism from pus and sputum is possible. The diagnosis is however confirmed by tissue biopsy.
- **Coccidioidomycosis** is a systemic mycotic infection, and gives rise to sore throat, chills, fever, aches, chest pain and haemoptysis. Otherwise, in a very small number of cases, it may give rise to continuous low-grade fever, severe anorexia, loss of body weight and strength. Blood shows leucocytosis, usually with esoinophilia. Diagnosis of the condition is confirmed by identification of the causative fungus in the sputum, pleural fluid, gastric aspirates, and cerebrospinal fluid.
- Moderately severe cases of **histoplasmosis** gives rise to fever, cough and mild chest pain, lasting for 5 to 15 days. In severe cases, it gives rise to marked prostration, fever and occasional chest pain. The illness may run for 1 week to 6 months. Causative organism, *Histoplasma capsulatum,* can be identified from sputum, urine and scraping of the ulcers.

- **Sporotrichosis** is characterised by chronic idolent ulceration on an area supplied by a particular lymphatic chain. There may also be local pain, heat, chills, fever, malaise, and anorexia. Diagnosis is made by identification of the causative fungus.
- **Blastomycosis** gives rise to pneumonia-like manifestations with dry hacking or productive cough, chest pain, dyspnoea, chills, fever and profuse sweating. Chest x-ray shows bronchopneumonia. Diagnosis is made by identification of the causative fungus.
- **Nocardiosis** begins with pulmonary infection but otherwise gives rise to cough, chest pain, chills, fever, night sweats and anorexia. It is characterised by granulomatous ulcer formation. Diagnosis is made by identification of *Nocardia asteroides* from sputum, pus, spinal fluid, and from biopsy material.
- **Cryptococcosis** commonly presents with the features of chronic meningitis with severe headache, malaise, vomiting, fever, blurred vision, stiffness of neck, paralysis or convulsions. Diagnosis of the condition is made from identification of the causative fungus from sputum, pus, body fluids and cerebrospinal fluid.
- **Yaws** is characterised by syphilitic-type of lesions, occuring amongst the people living near to Equator. There may also be accompanying headache, fever, painless regional lymphadenitis, and bone pain, worse at night. Diagnosis is made on clinical grounds. Causative treponema can be identified on darkfield microscopy from the exudate of skin lesions and from lymph node aspirates.
- **Heamorrhagic fever** presents with symptoms and signs of dengue but the patient's condition shows abrupt worsening. Shock develops 2 to 6 days after. Clinical manifestation with abrupt fever in a dengue endemic area, followed 2 or more days after by shock and haemorrhagic manifestations with thrombocytoponia is highly suggestive of the condition.
- **Hereditary spherocytosis** presents with anaemia, mild jaundice, fatigue, and feeling of fullness and discomfort in the left upper quadrant. There is also headache and fever. Spleen is often palpable and firm. There may also be enlargement of liver but lymphadenopathy is absent. Blood shows decreased number of red cells with increased osmotic fragility, and presence of spherocytes. The patient may give a familial history.
- **Warm type autoimmune haemolytic anaemia** is characterised by anaemia due to haemolysis. There may be prostration, fever and vomiting. Enlargement of spleen is a common feature. Some cases may also give rise to enlargement of liver. Blood shows polychromasia and spherocytes. Detection of antibodies by Coombs (direct antiglobulin) test is diagnostic.
- **Psittacosis** presents with chills, fever, malaise, anorexia, headache, myalgia and prostration. An occupational history of contact with birds (e.g. parrots, pigeons, ducks, chicken, geese, parakeets, badgerigars, canaries, pheasants, etc.) is suggestive. The causative organism can be isolated from blood and sputum.
- **Lyme arthritis** begins with red, non-itching, macule or papule (*erythema chronicum migran*) on the trunk and peripheral part of the extremities which may last for weeks or may show relapses. This is followed by signs of prostration, including malaise, fatigue, chills, fever,

headache and stiff neck. Joint involvement may occur at any time since appearance of skin rash, and gives rise to migratory polyarthritis but with no swelling.

- **Legionnaires' disease** presents with anorexia, malaise, profound weakness, dry cough and non-remittent fever. Body temperature rises like typhoid fever in a stepladder fashion and may exceed 103°F (39·5°C), with relative bradycardia. There may also be recurrent shaking chills and pleural pain. As the condition progresses there may be purulent, watery, frequently blood-stained sputum. Blood shows leucocytosis but development of leuconenia is considered to be of grave prognostic value. Diagnosis is made by identification of *Legionella pneumophilia* from the lung tissue.
- **Goodpasture's syndrome** gives rise to severe haemoptysis and dyspnoea. Malaise and headache are the common accompaniment of the condition. In some cases, however, there may also be cough, fatigue, chills and fever. Frank or microscopic haematuria and proteinuria are also common. Chest x-ray shows progressive, migratory, asymmetrical, bilateral densities.
- **American trypanosomiasis** presents with fever and acute regional lymphadenitis. Both liver and spleen become enlarged. The condition characterically shows unilateral swelling of the eyelid, particularly in children. Diagnosis is made by identification of the causative organism from peripheral blood and lymph node biopsy, and through xenodiagnosis.
- **Tularaemia** begins with nausea, vomiting, malaise, headache, chills, fever, profuse sweating and extreme prostration. Fever usually remains elevated for 3 to 4 weeks and then falls by lysis. Human being acquire the infection from contact with infected mammals and birds, and from bites of ticks and other arthropods, and a primary lesion often appears after 24 to 48 hours as papule at the site of inoculation. Occupational history may therefore serve a useful purpose in the diagnosis. The diagnosis is confirmed by isolation of the causative organism from the liver, lymph nodes or sputum.
- **Glanders** is characterised by ulceration and necrosis of the nasal mucosa and septum, laryngitis and sepsis. It may occur as a fulminating acute febrile illness or as a chronic indolent disease, with fever, chills, aches and pains, and prostration. Occupational history may be a useful guide. Diagnosis of the condition is confirmed by demonstration of rising agglutination titre and a positive mallein skin test.
- In **cat-scratch disease** a papule or pustule develops at the site of scratch or bite a few days after contact with a cat. Regional lymphadenopathy commonly occurs within 2 weeks time. There are also malaise, headache, anorexia and fever. Lymphaadenitis may persist 1 to 3 weeks or more.
- In adults, **listeriosis** presents with meningoencephalitis with or without bacteraemia. There may be typhoid fever-like menifestations with high fever. In infants, the condtion may give rise to nausea, vomiting, hypothermia, cardiopulmonary distress, and granulomas on the skin and fauces. When the condition involves the pregnant women, it may give rise to influenza-like nonspecific manifestations. Diagnosis of the condition is made from isolation of *Listeria*

monocytogenes from the cord blood, meconium and cerebrospinal fluid in infants, from blood in adults, and from cervical or vaginal exudate, lochia and placenta in pregnant woman or delivering mother.

- **Q fever** presents with malaise, chills, fever, retro-orbital headache and myalgia. Body temperature may rise up to 104°F (40°C) and may persist for as short as 1 day or as long as 3 weeks. There may also be symptoms of interstitial pneumonitis. Occupational history of handling domestic animals, particularly cattle, sheep and goats, are useful guide for diagnosis. Blood shows leucopenia.
- **Lassa fever** usually gives rise to increasing sore throat, headache, severe muscle aches, malaise, anorexia, chills and high fever. Body temperature usually lasts for about 7 to 17 days but may sometimes be prolonged in fatal cases. There may also be non-tender generalised lymphadenopathy and haemorrhagic manifestations. Blood shows leucopenia with relative polymorphonuclear leucocytosis. Proteinuria is common. X-ray of the chest shows basilar pneumonitis and pleural effusion.
- *Oroya fever* in **bartonellosis** gives rise to sudden onset of fever, weakness, nausea, vomiting, diarrhoea, muscle and joint pain, and severe headache. Both liver and spleen become enlarged and tender. Diagnosis of the condition is made by identification of *Bartonella bacilliformis* in the peripheral blood.
- In **melioidosis** symptoms vary from an asymptomatic condition to a fulminating course with septicaemia. In acute condition, pulmonary infection may be the commonest form of presentation. It is associated with high fever, shaking chills, vomiting and prostration. Cough with bloody or purulent sputum is a common feature. Liver is usually enlarged, and there may be jaundice. Chest x-ray shows upper lobe consolidation and thin-walled cysts.
- **Whipple's disease** is a rare condition and presents with the features of malabsorption, such as diarrhoea, abdominal pain and distension, loss of body weight, and anaemia. There may also be fever, pigmentation of skin and enteropathic arthritis-like non-erosive migratory arthritis. The condition is diagnosed by lymph node or intestinal biopsy with PAS reagent.

RETARDATION OF GROWTH

Retardation of growth is a characteristic feature in which in infant's normal body growth or development is retarded or delayed. The symptom usually develops in cases of nutritional deficiencies or of hormonal distrubances. Sometimes the symptom may also develop due to other reasons.

- **Undernutrition** is an important cause of retardation of growth in children. In this skin appears thin, dry, loose, inelastic and cold, and may show patchy pigmentation. There may also be diarrhoea, polyuria, and normochromic normocytic anaemia. Development of famine oedema in common. Diagnosis of the condition is usually made on clinical grounds.
- **Starvation** gives rise to weakness and loss of body weight and, in children, retardation of growth. The patient appears emaciated, thin and skinny. Skin is thin, dry, loose, inelastic and cold, and may show patchy pigmentation.
- **Nutritional marasmus** gives rise to retardation of growth, reduction of body weight, and wasting of subcutaneous fat and muscle. There may be watery diarrhoea or the stools may be semi-solid and bulky. Abdomen is distended with gas. Dietary habit is suggestive. Reduced body weight for age in comparison to normal standard is diagnostic for protein-energy malnutrition.
- In **kwashiorkor** the infant looks apathetic and miserable, and presents with retardation of growth. The child fails to gain weight. Wasting of muscles becomes a prominent feature. There is oedema on feet which may also develop on hands and face, and perhaps little ascites. Liver is enlarged. Although the dietary habits aid the diagnosis, a reduced body weight for age in comparison to normal standard is diagnostic for protein-energy malnutrition.
- **Rickets** presents with retardation of growth, and the infant shows delay in teething, sitting, standing, crawling and walking. The condition also gives rise to irritability, restlessness, abdominal distension, and sweating of the forehead and hands, particularly at night. Body muscles appear flabby. The condition is characterised by 'bossing of skull', 'pigeon chest' and 'bowing' of legs. A history of inadequate intake of vitamin D or of insufficient exposure to sunlight is suggestive of the diagnosis.
- **Hypovitaminosis** A usually presents with symptoms and signs of other vitamin deficiency or of nutrition as well. In some children the condition may lead to retardation of growth. The condition is otherwise characterised by night blindness or visual disturbances. Blood shows decreased lebel of retinol.
- In **coeliac disease,** the affected child fails to thrive, becomes irritable, shows wasting of muscles and presents with pot belly and, later, retardation of growth. The condition can be diagnosed by biopsy of jejunum but otherwise a trial with gluten-free diet brings an immediate dramatic improvement and confirms the diagnosis.
- **Indian childhood cirrhosis** presents with anorexia, voracious appetite, abdominal

distension with flatulence and constipation or diarrhoea with clay-coloured stools. The child shows retarded growth. Liver is enlarged and firm with sharp, leafy border. The condition is diagnosed on clinical grounds and is confirmed by liver biopsy.

- **Hypothyroidism** in the children (*juvenile hypothyroidism*) gives rise to an arrest or slowing of growth, delayed dentition, mental retardation and lack of interest in normal children's games and play.

  In *cretinism*, the infants show retardation of growth and slow teething. The condition leads to poor appetite, cold extremities, thick lips, large tongue, coarse facies with broad flat nose, hoarse cry, and dryness and brittleness of hair. Later, the patient presents with pot belly and umbilical hernia.

  Diagnosis of hypothyroidism is made from measurement of serum T_4 and TSH but that of T_3 is not always helpful. X-ray of bone epiphyses in children and of ossification centres in infants showed delayed skeletal maturation.

- **Hypopituitarism** characterically gives rise to retardation of growth in childhood. Pallor is often marked in this condition, and the child shows lack of resistance to stress and infection. Blood shows low fasting blood sugar level and a flat glucose tolerance curve. X-ray can reveal the lesion in or above the sella turcica and, in growing children, delay in bone age.

- **Fallot's tetralogy**, the commonest congenital cyanotic heart disease, gives rise to retardation of growth, which is however evident only in severe cases. Diagnosis of the condition is made on clinical grounds. Chest x- ray shows normal contour of the heart with absence of usual pulmonary artery curve.

- **Persistent ductus arteriosus** may remain asymptomatic for a long time. Otherwise, the affected child shows retardation of growth and development. Later, there is dyspnoea and development of cardiac failure. X-ray of the chest shows enlargement of pulmonary artery, and may also show left ventricular hypertrophy.

- **Thalassaemia** is characterised by progressively severe anaemia and splenomegaly. Sometimes it may also give rise to retardation of growth, brittleness of long bones and cardiac enlargement. The patient appears small in stature with bony deformities.

- **Sickle call anaemia,** in addition to its usual symptoms and signs of anaemia, may also cause growth retardation, delayed puberty and bossing of the skull in infancy. Blood shows abnormal haemoglobin (HbS), increased reticulocytes, increased blood viscosity, elevated level of bilirubin and low erythrocyte sedimentation rate.

- **Juvenile chronic arthritis** is a rheumatoid arthritis-like disorder of children, and presents with profound systemic disturbances. The child shows retardation of growth and loss of body weight. Tests for rheumatoid factor and antinuclear factor are, however, negative in the condition.

GYNAECOMASTIA

Gynaecomastia represents excessive development of male mammary glands, sometimes even secreting milk. The symptom is however not encountered so frequently, nor does it cause any suffering. Nevertheless, the symptom may appear annoying and quite distressing.

The development of hyperplasia of the mammary glands may however be quite common during adoloscence in normal health, and the condition usually involves mammary glands of both sides. Occasionally, it may also develop in the old people, involving usually unilaterally.

Sometimes the manifestation may also be encountered in persons with oestrogen therapy for the carcinoma of the prostate or having hypertensive therapy.

This manifestation is generally short-lived and of no significance, and majority of them usually subside spontaneously within a year or so. Only in a few cases the condition may persist for long period.

- **Male hypogonadism**, when develops before puberty, gives rise to poor growth and development, excessive tallness and high-pitched voice. The patient shows underdeveloped external genitalia, scanty secondary sex characteristics, hairless face and, during the adulthood, there may be obesity, particularly over the girdle, gynaecomastia, cryptorchidism or small testes, underdeveloped prostate and absence of spermatogenesis. Diagnosis of the condition may be made from measurement of plasma testosterone, FSH and LH, and may be confirmed by testicular biopsy.
- **Tumours of testes** give rise to painless enlargement of the testes. There may however be dragging pain in the inguinal region due to enlarged testes. When the tumour develops as *choriocarcinoma,* it also gives rise to gynaecomastia, and both plasma and urine may show high concentration of gonadotrophins. *Teratoma* similarly presents with progressively increasing scrotal mass with nodular changes and the condition often produces gynaecomastia.
- **Cushing's syndrome** is characterised by deposition of 'fat pads', central obesity and rounding of face with plethoric appearance. The condition may also give rise to gynaecomastia, testicular atrophy, loss of libido and impotence in males. The condition is diagnosed clinically. Blood shows elevated levels of sodium and cholride, and decreased level of potassium. Plasma level of cortisol is also high.
- In **hyperthyroidism** there may or may not be any goitre, and the patient presents with increased appetite, loss of body weight, hot and sweaty hands, intolerance to warmth, nervousness, anxiety, fine tremors of fingers and tongue, mild weakness of proximal muscles, and wasting of muscles and bones. Occasionally, the condition may give rise to gynaecomastia.
- **Cirrhosis of liver** may be asymptomatic or may present with variable symptoms, and the condition is characterised by fibrous and nodular regeneration and destruction of liver architecture. There may be mild or no jaundice, which may however be progressive in presence of liver failure. There may also be gynaecomastia, loss of libido, impotence, sterility and osteoporosis.

HAEMATEMESIS

Heamatemesis (Table 16) represents vomiting of blood from the stomach, and sometimes may need careful differentiation from epistaxis. The nature and extent of haematemesis however depend upon the site and severity of bleeding. The vomitus may therefore be small or large, and the contents may be fresh red blood or dark brown of 'coffee ground'.

Principally gastrointestinal bleeding is the main cause of haematemisis. The gastrointestinal bleeding may however develop from varieties of disorders, including consumption of ulcerogenic drugs, such as aspirin, non-steroidal anti-inflammatory drugs, corticosteroids, and hence omissions or duplication of certain disorders may be unaviodable here.

- In **gastrointestinal bleeding** the presenting manifestations depend on the source and rate of bleeding. Generally the condition gives rise to weakness, faintness, sweating, palpitation, pallor, headache, haematemesis and melena. Symptoms of shock and renal failure develop from massive haemorrhage. The condition is diagnosed on the history and clinical features. Endoscopy may reveal the source of bleeding.
- **Reflux oesophagitis** begins with heartburn and pain, occuring after meals and dependable on changes of posture. There may also be water brush, dysphagia, haematemesis, melaena and iron deficiency anaemia. Diagnosis of the condition is made through endoscopy and by biopsy.
- **Gastritis** may give rise to no symptom or may present with anorexia, heartburn and epigastric pain. There may also be diarrhoea, haematemesis, melaena, chills, fever and prostration. Diagnosis of the condition is made through endoscopic examination, and is confirmed by biopsy.
- In ***peptic ulcer***, both **gastric ulcer** and **duodenal ulcer** give rise to epigastric distress as burning, aching and hunger-pain. The condition presents with epigastric tenderness and voluntary muscle guarding, anaemia and perhaps occult blood. Development of varying degree of heamatemesis may not be infrequent. The condition is diagnosed by barium meal x-ray.
- **Carcinoma of stomach** is usually asymptomatic during the early stage or there may be vague complaints of abdominal discomfort. Later, there is change in bowel habit, and the patient complains of alternating constipation and diarrhoea. Loss of body weight and development of cachexia appear more marked. The features also include pallor, ascites, jaundice, anaemia, haematemesis, melaena, visible peristalsis and palpable abdominal mass. Diagnosis of the condition is confirmed by endoscopic examination and biopsy. Exfoliative cytology is also helpful.
- In **cirrhosis of liver** the symptoms may be variable. While the condition may sometimes give rise to certain symptoms of its own but otherwise the symptoms develop due to its complications, including

liver failure. There may be central cyanosis, clubbing of fingers, diffuse erythema on the palms, pigmentation of skin, ascites and, perhaps, jaundice. There may also be thrombocytopenia, anaemia, purpura, epistaxis, haematemesis and melaena. Blood shows increased levels of alkaline phosphatase, acid phosphatase, amylase, lactic dehydrogenase, total lipids, cholesterol concentration, bilirubin, AST (formerly SGOT) and ALT (formerly SGPT).

- In the intermediate stage of **Indian childhood cirrhosis,** enalrgement of liver continues, giving rise to more firm and nodular surface with sharp, irregular border. There may also be symptoms of portal hypertension, ascites, haematemesis and melena. Diagnosis is usually made clinically and is confirmed by liver biopsy.
- **Portal hypertension** gives rise to abdominal pain and ascites. Liver is enlarged, soft and tender. Spleen is also enlarged. Evidence of gastrointestinal bleeding, including haematemesis, may be available when collateral circulation. develops.
- **Malignant hypertension** may give rise to haematemesis, haemoptysis, haematuria and other haemorrhagic manifestations. The condition is characterised by papilloedema with or without retinal exudate or haemorrhage. The diastolic pressure is 130 mm of Hg or over.
- **Hypersplensim** may present with abdominal fullness, pain over the splenic area, haematemesis, gastrointestinal bleeding and purpura. Spleen is enlarged and palpable, and gives an audible splenic friction rub or bruit. There may be portal hypertension as well. Splenic venography, ultrasonography and CT scanning are useful diagnostic aids of the condition.
- **Hereditary haemorrhagic telangiectasia** Is characterised by multiple telangiectasiae. There may also be epistaxis, haemoptysis, haematemesis, and gastrointestinal bleeding.
- **Idiopathic thrombocytopenic purpura** presents with haemorrhage, either spontaneous or due to trauma, including epistaxis, bleeding gum, gastrointestinal bleeding, haematemesis and haematuria. Blood shows thrombocytopenia or absence of platelet in the peripheral blood, prolonged bleeding time but normal clotting time, and increased capillary fragility.
- **Acute leukaemia** gives rise to weakness, easy fatiguability, fever, prostration, generalised pain, sore throat, and pain and tenderness in the bone and about the joints. There may also be haemorrhagic manifestations, including haematemesis, genitourinary bleeding, and haemorrhage into the eyes or ears. Blood shows abnormal white cells. Bone marrow examination and trephine biopsy can confirm the diagnosis.
- **Chronic lymphatic leukaemia** begins with lymphadenopathy. There may be weakness, fatigue, weight loss, malaise, night sweats, fever and exertional dyspnoea. There may also be purpua and other haemorrhagic manifestations, including sometimes haematemesis. There is splenomegaly and mild to moderate hepatomegaly. Blood shows leucocytosis with absolute lymphocytosis, usually of small variety.
- **Yellow fever** characteristically gives rise to severe prostration, fever with slower pulse rate and haemorrhagic manifestations. Vomitus may be 'coffee ground' or even black with altered blood. Diagnosis of the condition is made by isolation of the

TABLE 16

Cases of Haematemesis

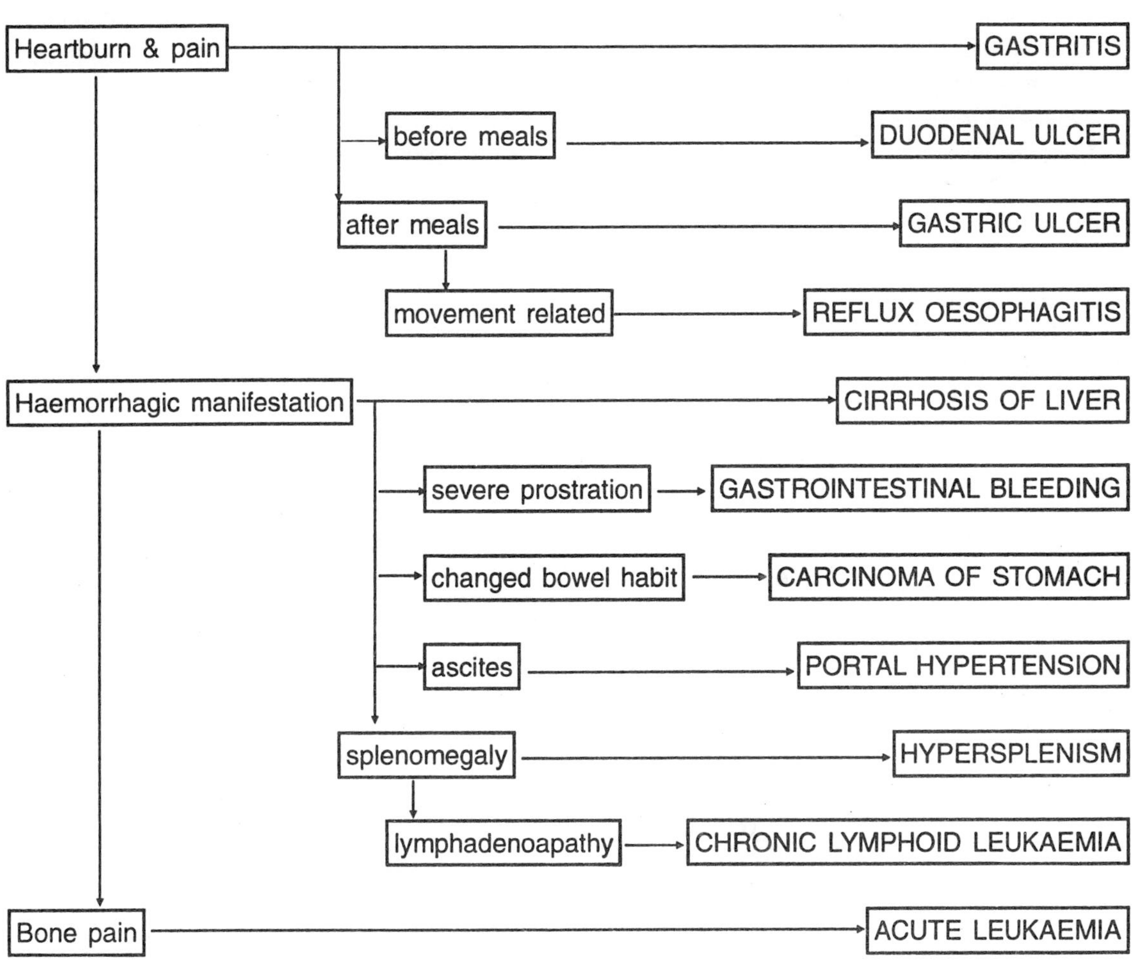

causative virus from blood during the first few days of illness but later, by demonstration of complement-fixing and neutralizing antibodies.

- **Haemorrhagic fever** presents with symptoms and signs of dengue and the patient's condition shows abrupt worsening. Shock develops 2 to 6 days after with sudden collapse or prostration. Occasionally, there may also be haematemesis, epistaxis, melaena or even subarachnoid haemorrhage. Diagnosis of the condition can be made on clinical grounds in dengue endemic area.
- **Chronic nephritic syndrome** is usually asymptomatic till the late stage. Otherwise, there may be nausea, vomiting, polyuria, thirst, pruritus, haematuria, hiccough, and drowsiness. Lately, the condition may sometimes give rise to epistaxis, gum bleeding, purpura, haematemesis and melaena. Often the patient may give a history of acute nephritic syndrome or of nephrotic syndrome.

HAEMATURIA

Haematuria (Table 17) is an important symptom, and urine may contain fresh blood or a mixture of blood, or may give a smoky appearance. On the other hand, haematuria may be frank and thus, may be apparent, while in some cases, it may not be so apparent visually and hence be microscopic. Any sort of injury, either direct or indicrect, including urethral angiomas, can cause haematuria. Certain durgs, such as salicylates and suplhonamides, can at times cause haematuria. The symptom can also be encountered in males due to excessive sexual indulgence.

Distinction, however, needs to be made between haematuria and haemoglobinuria, and the latter contains haemoglobin in urine. The symptom is, however, almost always present with haematuria, and presence of haemoglobinuria alone is rare.

- **Rapidly progressive nephritic syndrome** develops insidiously and often presents with acute nephritic syndrome-like manifestations. Abdominal pain and arthralgia are common manifestations. Haematuria is also common but proteinuria is variable. Urine shows red cells, white cells, granular and waxy casts. Blood shows elevated levels or urea and other nitrogenous products.
- **Focal segmental glomerulosclerosis** presents with nephritic syndrome-like manifestations, and proteinuria. Haematuria and hypertension are also common. Signs of renal function impairment appear as the condition progresses.
- **Membranoproliferative glomerulonephritis** is characterised by the manifestations of acute nephritic syndrome or of nephrotic syndrome. Some cases may remain asymptomatic except presenting with proteinuria and haematuria. Others may give rise to anorexia, malaise, abdominal pain and wasting of muscles. There are proteinuria, haematuria and oedema. The patient presents with puffy eyelids.
- **IgA nephropathy** usually presents as a benign condition but often runs progressive course with recurrent gross or microscopic haematuria. Haematuria lasts for a few days, subsides, and then recur every few months. Pain in the flanks or dysuria may often accompany. There may also be hypertension. Proteinuria is however mild but a proportion of cases may show nephrotic type of proteinuria.
- **Acute nephritic syndrome** characteristically causes puffiness around the eyes and face, and generally involves young children. The patient may complain of low urinary output with blood-stained urine. There may also be discomfort or pain in the flank or upper abdomen, and epistaxis.
- **Membranous glomerulonephritis** begins insidiously in previously healthy persons with nephrotic syndrome. In others, proteinuria is the earliest manifestation which may be mild or undetectable. Generalised oedema however develops with pale and puffy face when proteinuria is severe. Some cases may also present with haematuria and mild hypertension.

TABLE 17
Some disorders with Haematuria

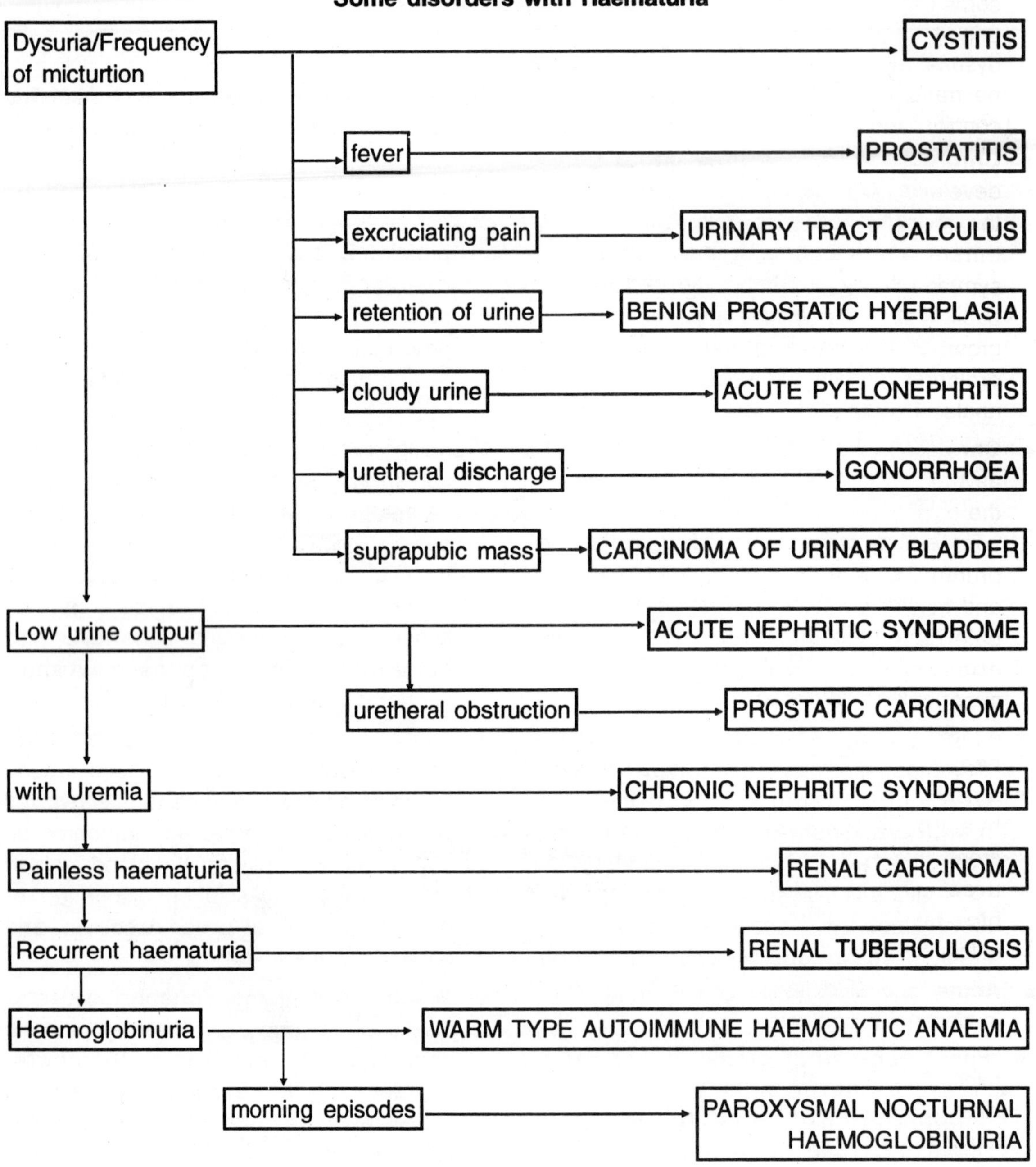

- **Acute tubulointerstitial nephritis** presents with variable symptoms, and some cases may give rise to symptoms of urinary tract infection, such as chills, fever, dysuria and pain in the flanks. There may be frank or microscopic haematuria. The condition is characterised by sterile pyuria.
- **Chronic tubulointerstitial nephritis** when develops due to analgesic nephropathy, the manifestations include polyuria and thirst. Headache and gastrointestinal symptoms are common. Tips of necrotic papillae may be passed in urine, causing gross haematuria or renal colic. History of prolonged or excessive consumption of analgesics may be available.
- **Chronic nephritic syndrome** may remain asymptomatic till its late stage. Otherwise, the condition gives rise to fatigue, nausea, vomiting, polyuria, haematuria, hiccough, pruritus, drowsiness, and vague muscle and bone pain. The patient presents with pale face, and the eyelids and checks appear puffy. There may also be hypertension. The patient may often give a history of acute nephritic syndrome or of nephrotic syndrome. Urine shows small amount of protein, red cells, granular and hyaline casts, and increased level of creatinine. Blood shows elevated levels of urea, creatinine, phosphate and bicarbonates, and decreased level of calcium.
- **Acute pyelonephritis** presents with pain in one or both loins, fever, rigor, nausea, vomiting, dysuria, strangury and frequent micturition of small amount of cloudy urine. Kidney is usually enlarged and palpable. Urine shows numerous pus cells, red cells and epithelial cells. The causative organism may be identified from urine and blood.
- Symptoms of **hydronephrosis** vary widely. There may be no pain,, or there may be intermittent attack of dull ache and discomfort in the flank, or excruciating or even colicky pain. There may also be haematuria, pyuria and fever. Diagnosis of the condition is made by excretory urography, retrograde pyelography and cystoscopy.
- Sometimes **polycystic kidney disease** develop in early or middle adult life, and gives rise to discomfort, pain or colic disc in the lumbar region, haematuria and slowly progressive hypertension. Some patients may complain of passing blood clots through urination along with renal colic. In others, there may be haematuria followed by polyuria and proteinuria. Gradually symptoms of uraemia develop. The kidneys may sometimes be palpable as smooth, nodular mass. Diagnosis of the condition is made by ultrasonography or retrograde pyelography.
- **Renal carcinoma** presents with recurrent painless haematuria. Renal colic develops but only when there is blood clot. There may also be pain in the abdomen or flank, and long continued fever. A flank mass may be palpable. X-ray may show enlarged kidney, and excretory urography and retrograde pyelography can reveal the tumour.
- **Urinary tract calculus** may be asymptomatic. Otherwise, it gives rise to renal colic or excruciating intermittent pain, usually in the kidney area and that radiates across the abdomen, and down to the genitalia and inner sides of the thigh. Vesicle calculus however produces suprapubic pain. In addition, there may be dysuria, frequency and urgency of micturition, haematuria, chills and fever. Plain x-ray can reveal radio-opaque

calculus. Non-opaque calculus can be identified by retrograde pyelography.

- **Cystitis** gives rise to haematuria. The patient complains of frequency of micturition, dysuria and strangury. There is pain and tenderness in the hypogastrium. The condition usually develops in women and girls, most commonly due to *Escherichia coli.* The causative organism can be identified from urine. Excretory urography can establish other causes.
- **Carcinoma of urinary bladder** presents with dysuria, burning, frequency of micturition and haematuria. A suprapubic mass may be palpable in the late stage of the condition. Cytotolgy of urine shows tumour cells. The diagnosis is confirmed by cystoscopy and biopsy of transurethral resection.
- **Wilm's tumour** usually remains asymptomatic. Haematuria may however develop late in the condition. It is suggestive when a child presents with intrarenal mass in a functioning kidney. Diagnosis of the condition is made by retrograde pyelography or ultrasonography. CT scanning is however helpful in cases of older children.
- **Prostatitis**, though gives variable symptoms in chronic stage, in its acute stage gives rise to perineal pain, low back pain, fever and chills. The patient complains of urinary frequency and urgency, dysuria, nocturia and haematuria. The prostate gland may appear slightly tender, firm and irregularly indurated or boggy. Prostatic secretion shows clumps of leucocytes and lipid-laden macrophages, pus cells and bacteria.
- Manifestations of **benign prostatic hyperplasia** include urgency and frequency of micturition, nocturia, sensation of incomplete urination, decreased size and force of urinary streams, terminal dribbling, and acute urinary retention. There may also be haematuria and bleeding from the urethra. Prostate may be enlarged, rubbery and uniform in consistency, and frequently shows loss of median furrow. Excretory urography can identify the prostatic enlargement and the residual urine in the bladder.
- **Prostatic carcinoma** is asymptomatic till it produces urtheral obstruction. There may be haematuria and pyuria. The prostate appears firm and stony hard, with obliterated median furrow. Transrectal or transperitoneal needle biopsy may be used to confirm the diagnosis in more extensive cases.
- **Gonorrhea** often appears asymptomatic, more so in women. Otherwise, burning on micturition, slight frequency of micturition, and a uretharal or vaginal discharge are usually common manifestations. Only occasionally can the condition gives rise to haematuria but in men only. The condition is diagnosed from history of sexual exposure and from identification of *Neisseria gonorrhoeae* from the unethral or vaginal discharge.
- Alike gonococcal urethritis **nonspecific urethritis** too is often asymtomatic but otherwise it may give rise to symptoms of urethritis. Only occasionally the condition may present with haematuria in the males. Diagnosis of the condition is made on clinical grounds.
- **Perinephric abscess** presents with fever, chills and unilateral flank or abdominal pain, often with dysuria. Haematuria occurs occasionally. Chest x-ray may show collapse of the base of the lung. There may also be slight pleural effusion.

- **Goodpasture's syndrome** presents with severe haemoptysis and dyspnoea. Development of frank or microscopic haematuria is also common. The condition leads to progressive renal failure. Diagnosis of the condition is made on clinical grounds
- **Malignant hypertension** is charactrised by papilloedema with or without retinal haemorrhage or exudate, or by other haemorrhagic manifestations, such as haemoptysis, haematuria and haematemesis, The diastolic pressure goes to 130 mm of Hg or over.
- **Extrapulmonary tuberculosis** usually affects young children when it develops as *renal tuberculosis,* and may give rise to recurrent haematuria and dysuria. The condition always occurs as blood borne infection from tuberculous focus elsewhere in the body.
- **Aplastic anaemia** presents with weakness, lassitude and exertional dyspnoea. There is also bleeding in the skin and mucous membrane, epistaxis, haematuria, other haemorrhagic tendency, and necrotic ulcers in the mouth and throat. Peripheral blood shows pancytopenia, reduced number of red cells and platelets, and perhaps decreased reticulocytes. History of exposure to radiation or to offending drugs or chemicals may be available.
- **Sickle cell anaemia** presents with fatigue, acute abdomen, malaise, jaundice and episodes of severe pain, commonly occuring in the bones and spleen. There may also be haematuria. Development of gallstone is common.

  Sickle cell trait however does not give rise to any symptom except occasional painless haematuria.

  Sickle cell anaemia is an inherited chronic haemolytic disorder, and blood shows abnormal haemoglobin (HbS).
- **Idiopathic thrombocytopenic purpura** is manifested by haemorrhage, occuring either spontaneously or from trauma, petechial haemorrhage and ecchymoses on skin, epistaxis, bleeding gum, gastrointestinal bleeding, haematuria and vaginal bleeding. Blood shows thrombocytopenia or absence of platelet in the peripheral blood, prolonged bleeding time but normal clotting time, with poor clot reaction, and increased capillary fragility.
- **Anaphylactoid purpura** commonly follows upper respiratory tract infection, and presents with effusion of blood and plasma into the subcutaneous, submucous and subserous surface. In severe cases, there may however be renal involvement, resulting haematuria and proteinuria. Diagnosis of the condition is made on clinical grounds.
- **Endometriosis** principally presents with abnormal bleeding per vagina and pain in the lower abdomen or back. Occasionally there may also be haematuria, ureteral colic, constipation and painful defaecation.
- **Menopausal syndrome** is characterised by varieties of vasomotor, emotional and systemic disturbances. In addition, haematuria may occur occasionally. Characteristically the condition presents with progressive loss of bone mass due to increased bone resorption and thus, leads to osteoporosis.
- **Polyarteritis nodosa** may give rise to fever, sweating, abdominal pain, localised oedema, hypertension, peripheral neuropathy, oliguria, uraemia, convulsions and organic psychosis, There may also be bloody diarrhoea, gastrointestinal bleeding, haematuria and proteinuria. Biopsy of medium-sized artery shows necrotic

inflammation in the modia whioh extends into the adventitia.

- During the late stage **bronchial carcinoma** may produce symptoms, such as bone pain, jaundice, epileptiform seizures or personality changes, skin pigmentation and nodule formation, and haematuria, due to metastasis. Diagnosis of the condition is made by x-ray of the chest.
- **Schistosomiasis**, when develops due to *Schistosoma haematobium*, usually begins with painless terminal haematuria. Later, there may be frequency of micturition and pain over the iliac fossa. There may be haemospermia in males or sterility in females. Diagnosis of the condition is made by identification of characteristic haematobium eggs in the urine. The egg may sometimes be also seen in stools and in rectal snip.
- Patient with **paroxysmal nocturnal haemoglobinuria** presents with symptoms of severe anaemia. Haemoglobinuria and haemoglobinaemia are common features. It characteristically presents with dark morning urine. Splenomegaly is also common. There may be mild hyperbilirubinaemia during the attack. Gross haemoglobinuria with urine containing haemosiderin is common during the crisis. Clinical features are often suggestive of the condition.
- **Warm type antoimmune haemolytic anaemia** characteristically presents with anaemia due to haemolysis. Haemoglobinuria and haemosiderinuria occur occasionally. Splenomegaly is common. Blood shows polychromasia and spherocytes. Detection of antibodies by Coombs (direct antiglobulin) test is diagnostic.
- In cases of **glucose 6-phosphate dehydrogenase deficiency,** there may be anaemia, haemoglobinuria, and other symptoms and signs of haemolysis. Blood shows irregularly contracted cells, reticulocytosis and Heinz bodies. The condition is diagnosed by specific erythrocyte enzyme assay.
- In **malaria,** chronic falciparum infection, especially in patients treated with quinine, can give rise to a serious complication, ***blackwater fever***, which presents with intravascular haemorrhage and haemoglobinuria, in addition. Diagnosis of the condition is made by detection of characteristic malarial parasites in the erythrocytes.
- **Acute leukaemia** is characterised by increased number of abnormal white cells in the blood, and may give rise to weakness, easy fatiguability, malaise, fever, generalised pain, sore throat, and pain and tenderness in the bone and about the joints. There is rapidly advancing anaemia. There may also be haemorrhagic manifestations, including gastrointestinal and genitourinary bleeding, and may thus occasionally give rise to haemoglobinuria. Diagnosis of the condition is confirmed by bone marrow examination and trephine biopsy.

HAEMOPTYSIS

Haemoptysis or spitting of blood is usually a symptom of several respiratory and cardiovascular disorders (Table 18). In this the sputum may contain fresh blood or may present as a mixture of blood and sputum. Sometimes heamoptysis may contain small clots while in others there may be profuse haemorrhage.

- **Pulmonary tuberculosis** usually gives rise to undue tiredness, malaise, lassitude, persistent loss of body weight, low-grade fever, usually in the afternoon or evening, and night sweats. Initially there may not be any cough but soon persistent dry cough develops. Sputum is usually scanty at early stage and later, becomes green and purulent in caseous lequefying lesion but yellowish and mucoid in chronic cases. There may be haemoptysis **which** occasionally may also be the first presenting symptom. The haemoptysis varies between slight blood streaks in the sputum and massive haemorrhage. The condition is diagnosed by identification of acid fast bacillus, *Mycobacterium tuberculosis*, from the suptum, tracheal or gastric washings. Pleural and pulmonary biospy are also helpful. Tuberculin test may aid the diagnosis.
- Most **extrapulmonary tuberculosis** develop as complication of pulmonary tuberculosis and, depending upon the site of secondary involvement, may produce haemoptysis. For example, *bronchial tuberculosis* gives rise to inflammation, localised or extensive granulomatous mucosal ulcerations, and haemoptysis.
- The manifestations of **pneumonia** include haedache, chills and fever. There is also haemoptysis, pleuritic pain and cough. The haemoptysis vary and the sputum may be rusty, brick-red or bloody, and gelatinous, copious, mucoid, sticky and difficult to expectorate. Diagnosis of the condition is made on clinical grounds. The responsible causative organism may be identified from sputum and blood.
- **Bronchiectasis** gives rise to chronic cough, usually worse in the morning and often induced by postural changes, with large amount of purulent and sometimes foul or putrid sputum. The patient complains of offensive breath after coughing, and haemoptysis, which vary between blood streaked sputum and massive fatal haemorrhage. There is also recurrent pneumonia in the affected area of the lung. Diagnosis of the condition is made on clinical grounds, and may be confirmed by bronchographic examination.
- Manifestations of **lung abscess** include fever, chills, malaise, sweats, and aches and pains. There is irritating, dry and exhaustive cough, followed by large amount of expectoration of purulent, sometimes fetid and occasionally blood-streaked, sputum. Sometimes there may also be frank haemoptysis. The condition is diagnosed on chest x-ray which, in early stage, shows dense homogeneous opacities with segmental or lobular consolidation.
- In **bronchial carcinoma** symtoms vary considerably, and most cases remain

TABLE 18
Differential features of some cases with Haemoptysis

Disorder	Chest pain	Chills	Fever	Dyspnoea	Cyanosis	Sweating
Pulmonary tuberculosis	yes\no	—	low-grade	present	—	night
Pneumonia	pleuritic	yes	yes	present	present	yes
Bronchiectasis	—	perhaps	yes/no	present	—	night
Bronchitis	yes	yes	slight	present	present	—
Lung abscess	yes\no	yes	yes	yes/no	—	yes
Bronchial carcinoma	yes\no	—	—	present	—	—
Pulmonary infarction	yes	—	yes	present	present	—
Mitral stenosis	rarely	—	—	present	present	—
Cardiac failure	—	—	—	present	present	yes
Silicosis	yes\no	—	—	present	—	—
Aspergillosis	—	yes	yes	—	—	—
Goodpasture's syndrome	—	yes/no	yes/no	present	—	—
Legionnaires' disease	pleuritic	yes	non-remittent	present	—	—

asymptomatic initially. Otherwise, there is persistent cough, and repeated but unexplained slight haemoptysis. Diagnosis of the condition is made from chest x-ray which initially may show abnormal shadow and later, dense, irregular, hilar opacity. The diagnosis is confirmed by suptum cytology.

- **Acute bronchitis** presents with symptoms of upper respiratory tract infection and slight sore throat, followed by irritating, non-productive cough with restrosternal discomfort or pain. Later, there is expectoration, at first scanty, mucoid, viscid, and may be streaked with blood, and then changing to mucopurulent and more copious. Diagnosis is made on clinical grounds.
- **Chronic bronchitis** gives rise to dry irritating cough in the morning with little sputum, usually in the winter, which increases in severity with the advancement of time and finally, paroxysms of cough persist throughout the year. The suptum is usually scanty, tenacious, mucoid, occasionally streaked with blood and later, may be copious and frankly purulent. Diagnosis of the condition is made on clinical grounds.
- **Whooping cough** is characterised by paroxysms of cough ending in a 'whoop' upon inhalation. The strain of cough makes the face puffy between the attacks and may give rise to sub-conjunctival haemorrhage, epistaxis and blood-streaked sputum. Diagnosis of the condition is made on clinical grounds, supported by isolation of *Bordetella pertussis.*
- **Idiopathic pulmonary haemosiderosis** gives rise to haemoptysis, accompanied by recurrent episodes of fever. Development of iron deficiency anaemia is common. Diagnosis of the condition is made on clinical grounds.
- **Silicosis** in its course gives rise to dyspnoea on exertion and cough which is dry initially but later becomes productive, frequently with blood-streaked sputum and haemoptysis. History of exposure to silica dust make the diagnosis easy. Pulmonary function test reveals all king of abnormalities. Radiological exmination of the chest gives the characteristic features.
- In pulmonary involvement **aspergillosis** may give rise to productive cough and dyspnoea. Otherwise, a rapid spread of pulmonary infection may occur with necrotizing pnoumonia or haemoptysis. Chest x-ray shows tumour-like dense opacity of round fungus ball with cresent of thin layer of air in a lung cavity or cyst.
- **Mitral stenosis** begins with exertional dyspnoea which later progresses to nocturnal dyspnoea and orthopnoea. Pulmonary congestion may give rise to cough while pulmonary hypertension may cause haemoptysis. The condition is accompanied by tapping apex beat, pulsation on left of sternum, and lateral shifting of right border of cardiac dullness. First sound appears accentuated, intense, sharp and of snapping type. It characteristically gives rise to low-pitched early diastolic crescendo murmur along the left sternal border which increases in intensity and then ceases suddently, usually accompanied by a thrill. The patient may often give a history of rheumatic fever. Diagnosis is made on clinical grounds.
- In **cardiac failure**, left-sided cardiac failure presents with tachycardia, dyspnoea, and orthopnoea, including paroxysmal nocturnal dyspnoea. The condition gives

rise to cough which is usually non-productive initially but later becomes productive with frothy white, rusty or brown sputum. Occasionally, there may also be frank haemoptysis. Diagnosis of the condition is made on clinical grounds, supported by detection of the underlying causes.

- **Aortic stenosis** may be asymptomatic or may give rise to fatigue, pallor and dyspnoea. Dizziness is common. Angina may occur from poor coronary blood flow. There is pulmonary congestion, and as the stenosis progresses, pulmonary oedema develops. Eventually there is right-sided cardiac failure and repeated haemoptysis from persistent pulmonary hypertension. There is also loud, rough, ejection systolic murmur at aortic area, transmitted to the neck, often accompanied by thrill and diminished or absent second aortic sound, paradoxial splitting of second sound occurs, and there may be fourth sound.
- **Pulmonary infarction** may not give rise to any symptom or else the condition may present with pleuritic pain, dyspnoea, tachycardia, fever, cyanosis, dry and unproductive cough, and haemoptysis. There may be pleural effusion, and both pulse and respirations are rapid. X-ray of the chest shows pulmonary opacity or linear scar, elevation of diaphragm and presence of pleural fluid.
- Cases of **hereditary haemorrhagic telangiectasia** characteristically present with telangiactasia which tend to bleed spontaneously or even from trivial trauma. There may also be epistaxis, haemoptysis and gastrointestinal bleeding. The bleeding gradually leads to anaemia.
- The most characteristic feature of **malignant hypertension** is papilloedema. There may also be haemorrhagic manifestations, such as haemoptysis, haematemesis and haematuria. The diastolic blood pressure is 130 mm of Hg or more.
- **Goodpasture's syndrome** is manifested by severe haemoptysis and dyspnoea. Frank or miscroscopic haematuria and proteinuria are common. So is the iron deficiency anaemia. The condition is diagnosed on clinical grounds. Chest x-ray shows progressive, migratory, asymmetrical, bilateral densities.
- **Legionnaires' disease** may present with anorexia, malaise, profound weakness, pleural pain, recurrent shaking chills and non-remittent fever, which rises like typhoid fever in a stepladder fashion, with relative bradycardia. Diarrhoea begins early in the course of the condition, and is watery. Initially there is dry cough but as the condition progresses, there may be purulent, watery, frequently blood-stained sputum. Proteinuria is common. X-ray of chest shows patchy, often multilocular, consolidation and patchy infiltration.
- **Chronic renal failure** may remain asymptomatic or may present with vague symptoms. Nocturia is however a common feature. There may also be shortness of breath, hiccoughs and pruritus. In addition, there is haemoptysis and haemorrhages. The patient may give a history of previous renal disease, symptoms of lower urinary tract obstruction or of exposure to certain offending agents. Urine shows small amount of protein, white cells, epithelial cells, granular and waxy casts, and low level of creatine, creatinine, uric acid and potassium.
- **Coccidioidomycosis** cases may be asymptomatic or may present with

influenza-like illness or nonspecific upper respiratory tract infection. The codition therefore gives rise to chills, fever, aches, chest pain, sore throat and haemoptysis. Diagnosis of the condition is made from identification of *Coccidioides immitis* from sputum, pleural fluid, gastric aspirates, cerebrospinal fluid, pus from abscesses and from biopsy.

- **Thoracic aortic aneurysm** may give rise to pain, especially in the back, cough, wheezing, or haemoptysis from tracheal or bronchial compression or erosion. Chest x-ray can reveal the aneurysm.
- In **anthrax** when the spores of *Bacillus anthracis* are inhaled, it gives rise to primary pneumonia with mild fever, malaise, haedache, dyspnoea, cyanosis, cough, haemoptysis and severe systemic disturbances. Occupational history of the patient serves a useful guide in the diagnosis. The organism can be identified from blood and suptum.
- **Gas gangrene** is characterised by local cellulitis and anaerobic myositis, Toxaemia is usually profound, and the condition may give rise to tachycardia, haemoptysis, jaundice, lowered blood pressure, stupor, delirium, shock and coma. Diagnosis of the condition is made on clinical grounds.
- **Plague** may sometimes involve the respiratory system (*pneumonic plague*) and may give rise to fulminating symptoms with pneumonitis, leading to copious, bloody, frothy and liquid sputum. The causative organism can be indentified from blood.
- **Melioidosis** may be asymptomatic or may follow fulminatig course with septicaemia, or may follow a chronic indolent course with multiple abscess formation. In acute condition, pulmonary infection may be the commonest form. It then gives rise to cough with bloody and purulent sputum. The condition is diagnosed by identification of *Pseudomonas pseudomallei* from blood, sputum and urine.
- Occasionally a single cyst in **hydatid disease** may develop in the lung, frequently in the base of the lung. The condition is usually symptomfree except when it assumes large size and obstruct the bronchi, causing segmental collapse, or when the cyst ruptures, giving rise to frequent cough, haemoptysis, and the expectorations show hydatid elements.
- Involvement of lung in the tertiary (late) stage of **syphilis** is rare, and yet when it does, the condition may remain asymptomatic or may give rise to dyspnoea, haemoptysis and night sweats, or may present as pneumonia, bronchiectasis or fibrosis of lung. Conventional serological tests for syphilis are always positive in the condition, some even with non-treponemal antigens also.
- During the larval migration through the lungs in both **ascariasis** and **ankylostòmiasis**, there may be fever, cough and slight haemoptysis for a very transient period. Later, both the conditions are diagnosed by identificaion of respective eggs in the stools.

HEMIPLEGIA

Hemiplegia, though encountered only in a few disorders, is a distressing as well as a disabling symptom. It represent paralysis of one side of the body.

This also includes ***hemiparesis,*** another symptom or may well be a synonymous, which represents slight paralysis, affecting one side of the body.

- In **intracranial neoplasms** development of clinical manifestations depend on the site of involvement and the rate of growth. The condition may however give rise to drowsiness, lethargy, disturbed memory, impaired judgement, mood changes, papilloedema and headache. There may also be visual alterations and hallucination, speech disturbances, aphasia or dysphasia, ataxia, monoplegia, hemiplegia, hemianaesthesia, facial palsy, intention tremor, vertigo and tinnitus. Clinical features may at times be suggestive of the condition but most cases are diagnosed through radiography and radionuclide encephalography.
- **Stroke** may present with headache, dizziness, drowsiness, mental confusion, derangement of speech, thought, motion or of vision, or there may be fever, headache, mental changes, nuchal rigidity, convulsions and coma. There may also be disturbances in micturition, staggering gait, ataxia, deafness, vertigo, double vision, loss of consciousness, epileptic fits, hemiparesis, monoparesis and hemiplegia. Diagnosis of the condition is made on clinical grounds.
- **Subarachnoid haemorrhage** begins with severe headache, followed by impairment or loss of consciousness. Soon dizziness, vertigo, convulsions, diplopia, hemiparesis and aphasia develop. Hemiplegia however develops late in the condition usually as a complication. Diagnosis of the condition is suggested on clinical grounds, and is confirmed by computed tomography and cerebral angiography.
- Hemiplegia may develop late in the course of **multiple sclerosis**. Otherwise, in general, the condition gives rise to weakness of one or more limbs. There may be paraesthesia or numbness in one or more extremities, trunk or one side of the face, hemianaesthesia to pain, vertigo, ataxia, swinging motion of the head, body and extremities on walking, and ocular nerve atrophy. The clinical course of repeated exacerbations and remissions, and inconsistent sites in the central nervous system involvement for the neurological symptoms and signs are often diagnostic.
- During the late or tertiary stage **syphilis** may involve central nervous system, causing *neurosyphilis* with four different clinical entities, such as asymptomatic neruosyphills, meningovascular syphilis, general paralysis of insane and tabes dorsalis.

  Of the several involvement ***meningovascular syphilis*** presents with headache, dizziness, lassitude, blurred vision, and neck rigidity, and positive Kernig's sign. There may also be aphasia, papilloedema, epileptiform seizures, inequality of tendon reflexes, and extensor planter reflex, and monoplegia or hemiplegia. Presence of Argyll Robertson pupil is an important feature of the condition.

General paralysis of insane gives rise to mental manifestations, such as irritability, insomnia, headache, difficulty in concentration, failure of memory and changes in behaviour. Mania or melancholia, and euphoria become a feature of the condition. Mental deterioration progresses, and bladder disturbances become frequent. Coarse tremors develop, and speech becomes slow and tremulous. Tremors in hands cause difficulty in writing legibly. There is also epileptiform seizures, and monoplegia or hemiplegia.

In such a late stage of the condition, a history of syphilitic infection may or may not be remembered by the patient. However, cerebrospinal fluid usually shows increased pressure, elevated protein content and lymphocyte, and gives a paretic or leutic colloidal gold curve. Serological tests for syphilis are positive.

- Long standing cases of **hypertension** may give rise to symptoms and signs of left ventricular hypertrophy, angina pectoris or myocardial infarction, and cerebral involvement may present with hemiplegia, aphasia and sudden haemorrhage from rupture of small intracerebral aneurysms.
- In **malaria**, severe form of falciparum infection may produce ***cerebral malaria,*** and may give rise to high fever, confusion, delirium, seizures, stupor, followed by coma persisting for a few hours. There may also be various paresis and hemiplegia.
- When **schistosomiasis** develops due to *Schistosoma japonicum,* the condition gives rise to hemiplegia, Jacksonian epilepsy, blindness and terminal coma. Otherwise, the condition presents with abdominal pain and frequent stools with blood stained mucus. Diagnosis of the condition is made from identification of the eggs from faeces or rectal snip.
- **Viral encephalitis** begins with high fever, malaise, sore throat, headache, nausea and vomiting. There are also lethargy, confusion, delirium, hallucination, delusion, stupor, coma and convulsions. There may be hemiparesis. Cerebrospinal fluid is clear but the pressure and protein content are often elevated, with normal glucose content. Colloidal gold curve is of paretic type in some cases.

HICCOUGH

Hiccough is a benign symptom, and has no clinical importance in terms of diagnosis. It is also a natural manifestation in gastric irritation, following heavy meals or from swallowing air when it develops due to reflex stimulation of phrenic nerve. The symptom is however quite distressing and annoying.

- **Fulminant hepatic failure** gives rise to weakness, nausea, vomiting, fever, sweating, delirium and hypotension. Later, there may be confusion, changes in sleep pattern, slurred speech, hiccough, yawning, disorientation and, finally, convulsion. The patient gives a sweet smell on breathing (fetor hepaticus) and the extended hands show flapping tremors.
- **Hiatus hernia** is almost always asymptomatic. There may however be epigastric or mid-thoracic pain and occasional hiccough. Diagnosis of the condition is made by barium meal x-ray. Endoscopy can also reveal the condition.
- In maintenance phase, **acute renal failure** presents with oliguria or anuria, hiccough and paraesthesia. There may also be mental confusion, apathy, delirium, muscular twitching, fits and coma. There is gallop rhythm and an elevated blood pressure.
- **Chronic nephritic syndrome** when symptomatic may present with fatigue, nausea, vomiting, polyuria, thirst, pruritus and diarrhoea. There may also be hiccough, muscular twitchings, drowsiness, vague muscle and bone pain, dyspnoea, and haematuria. Urine shows small amount of protein, red cells, granular and hyaline casts, and increased level of creatinine. The patient often gives a history of acute nephritic syndrome or of nephrotic syndrome.
- **Epilepsy** is characterised by sudden disturbances in consciousness. In its prodromal phase there may be abdominal pain, hiccough, headache, palpitation, feeling of chocking and depression.
- **Leptospirosis** may present with fever, chills, headache, muscle pains, anorexia, nausea and frequent vomiting. In more severe cases, jaundice develops along with hiccough, Cheyne-Stokes respiration and coma. The causative organism can be isolated and identified in blood and urine during the first 10 days. Identification of the organism is also possible from animal inoculation.

HOARSENESS OF VOICE

Hoarseness is often a disturbing symptom and the patient presents with huskiness of voice. The symptom in general encountered in the disorders which involve the larynx.

- **Laryngitis** is manifested by dryness and soreness of throat, and gives rise to a feeling of tickling and rawness in the throat. Voice becomes hoarse or the voice may be lost. In acute condition, the patient complains of an irritating non-productive cough. In chronic condition, however, the patient feels a constant urge of clearing the throat.
- Persistent hoarseness is however a characteristic feature of **tumour of larynx.** In addition, there may be throat discomfort, dysphagia or mild cough. Laryngeal examination usually reveals a mass or ulceration at the tumour site.
- **Acute coryza** begins with tickling sensation in the nose. Sometimes there may also be slight sore throat, sneezing and perhaps congestion of the eyes. In addition, there is mild hoarsness. Diagnosis of the condition is made on clinical grounds.
- **Acute laryngotracheobronchitis** initially produces common cold-like symptoms, followed by violent spasmodic cough, hoarseness and stridor, commonly seen at night. Diagnosis is made on clinical grounds. X-ray may show subepiglottic narrowing.
- In **extrapulmonary tuberculosis,** *tubercolous laryngitis* usually develops as a complication of pulmonary tuberculosis, and presents with constant hoarseness of voice. There is pallor of the mucous membrane of the pharynx and palate, and irregular-sized ulcers, usually bilateral. Epiglottis may be greatly thickened and ulcerated. Vocal cords are red and thickened.
- In **pulmonary tuberculosis**, the infection may rarely spread and give rise to oral ulcers, painful laryngeal involvement with hoarseness of vioce, or gastrointestinal tuberculosis. The causative organism can be identified from the sputum and tracheal washings. Tuberculin test is also a helpful aid.
- **Syphilis** gives rise to variable symptoms in secondary stage. There may be mild constitutional symptoms of malaise, fever, sore throat, hoarseness of voice, bone and joint pain, and widespread skin rash of various forms.

  In tertiary (late) stage of the condition gumma of larynx may develop and may thus produce hoarseness, aphonia and laryngeal stenosis.

  The condition is diagnosed on serological tests for syphilis.
- **Mediastinal tumour** produces symptoms and signs from compression and distortion of surrounding structures. It may therefore produce hoarsenss from compression paralysis of the thoracic portion of the left recurrent laryngeal nerve. Diagnosis of the condition can be made from barium swallow x-ray and through mediastinoscopy and mediastinotomy.
- **Thoracic aortic aneurysm** produces sympoms and signs due to pressure on the

surrounding structures. Hoarseness develops when it exerts pressure on the left recurrent laryngeal nerve. Aortography can reveal the aneurysm. Ultrasonography or CT scan is also helpful.

- **Adrenal virilism** is characterised by virilising effects. In adult women, it gives rise to decreased menses or amenorrhoea, enlarged clitoris, atrophied breasts and genitalia, loss of female contour, hoarseness or deepened voice, and hirsutism. Urine shows elevated level of 17-ketosteroid, but the level of 17-hydroxycorticosteroids is either normal or low. There is also excessive excretion of pregnanetriol.

- **Hypothyroidism** begins with weakness, lethargy, absence of sweating, dryness and roughness of skin, and dryness and brittleness of hair and nails. The face appears dull and swollen with puffy eyelids, thick lips and enlarged tongue. There may be tingling of the fingers, deafness, gain of body weight, hoarseness of voice, dizziness, pruritus and dyspnoea.

  In ***cretinism,*** the infant presents with cold extremities, thick lips, large tongue protruding from the mouth, coarse facies with broad flat nose, dryness and brittleness of hair, and hoarse cry. There is also retarded mental development and growth.

  Measurement of total serum T_4 and serum TSH are diagnostic but of T_3 is not however always of much help. Urinary concentration of 17-ketosteriods and 17-hydroxycorticosteroids may be very low.

- **Premenstrual tension** most frequently gives rise to nervousness, irritablity, depression, fatigue, lethargy and unreasonable temper. Occasionally, however, paraesthesia of hands and feet, vertigo, hoarseness of voice and syncope may accompany other symtoms.

JAUNDICE

Jaundice represents yellowish staining of the sclerae, skin and mucous membrane that is almost always develop whenever the liver function is impaired. Althogh the depth of its coloration depends on the level of accumulation of bilirubin in the blood, even when jaundice appears in a most lightest form, it becomes evidence from the tint in the sclerae and palatal mucosa. Jaundice therefore not only represents as a symptom but also as a sign. Table 19 illustrates some cases with jaundice.

- **Cholestatic jaundice** presents with yellow coloration of the sclerae, skin and mucous membrane of the mouth, clay-coloured or pale stools and steatorrhoea. Urine may be dark due to renal excretion of conjugated bilirubin. There may be haemorrhagic tendency, ascites, bradycardia and anorexia. Liver is enlarged and tender. Gall bladder may be palpable in some cases.
- Jaundice is the characteristic feature of **acute viral hepatitis**, even though many cases may remain non-icterus. Prior to development of jaundice the patient complains of chills or chilliness, headache, malaise and influenza-like fever. There may be severe anorexia, nausea and vomiting. Urine may be dark and becomes darker progressively, and stools become pale when jaundice deepens. Liver is usually tender and firm, and may be palpable. Splenomegaly may occur, especially in the children. Diagnosis of the condition is made on clinical grounds, supported by liver function test.
- **Chronic active hepatitis** gives rise to fatigue, anorexia and jaundice, which may be mild or moderate, or may be absent. There are also fever, arthralgia, epistaxis, superficial bruising, spider telangiectasia, and heaptosplenomegaly. Diagnosis of the condition is made on histopathological evidence.
- **Indian childhood cirrhosis** initially presents with anorexia or voracious appetite, lassitude, abdominal distension with flatulence, low-grade fever, and constipation or diarrhoea with clay-coloured stools. Liver become enlarged and, along with the advancement of the condition, continuels to become more enlarged with more firm and nodular surface and sharp irregular border, causing abdominal protuberance, with visible superficial veins. In some cases, however, instead of becoming larger, liver may show a shrinkage. Jaundice develops at this stage and beomes more deepen as the condition progresses. Spleen is also enlarged and feels hard. In the later stage, however, the liver shrinks. Dietary habits may be suggestive of the condition. Otherwise, the diagnosis is usually made on clinical grounds, and is confirmed by liver biopsy.
- In **carcinoma of liver, *hepatocellular carcinoma*** gives rise to unexplained deterioration of cirrhotic patients. The condition is then manifested by loss of body weight, cachexia, abdominal pain, jaundice, ascites and oedema, which may be rapidly recurring. Liver is enlarged and tender, and a mass may be palpable at right upper quadrant of abdomen. A bruit or friction rub may be heard over the tumour.

TABLE 19

Cases presenting with Jaundice

Condition	Fever	Abdominal Pain	Stools	Oedema/Ascites	Liver	Gall Bladder	Spleen
Cholestatic jaundice	perhaps with rigors	right upper quadrant	pale stools and steatorrhoea	ascites	enlarged, tender	perhaps palpable	may/may not palpable
Acute viral hepatitis	influenza-like	constant, right upper	diarrhoea	---	enlarged, tender	---	sometimes enlarged
Chronic active hepatitis	yes	---	-----	ascites	enlarged	---	enlarged
Cirrhosis of liver	yes	uneasiness on liver region	diarrhoea/constipation	ascites	enlarged initially later small & hard	----	enlarged
Indian childhood cirrhosis	low-grade	---	diarrhoea/constipation	ascites	enlarged initially later shrinks	----	hard and enlarged
Fulminant hepatic failure	yes	rarely, hypochondrium	diarrhoea	oedema, ascites	palpable earlier later non-palpable	-----	rarely enlarged
Cholangitis	slight	intermittent colicky, right upper	diarrhoea	-----	enlarged, tender	----	----
Chronic cholecystitis	---	bouts in epigastrium, right hypochondrium	constipation	---	enlarged, tender	may/may not be palpable	----
Carcinoma of liver	Yes	abdominal	-----	recurring ascites, oedema	enlarged, tender	-----	-----
Biliary cirrhosis	Yes	upper abdonil	steatorrhoea	ascites	enlarged, hard	----	enlarged
Carcinoma of gall bladder	----	constant in right upper quadrant	constipation	------	enlarged	palpable & tender	----
Portal hypertension	----	abdominal	-----	ascites	enlarged, tender	----	enlarged
Chronic pancreatitis	---	persistant/recurrent, upper abdomen	steatorrhoea	----	enlarged	palpable	----
Carcinoma of pacreas	----	epigastrium	diarrhoea	ascites	firm, enlarged	palpable	enlarged
Amoebic liver abcess	intermittent	constant, liver region	diarrhoea/constipation	----	enlarged, tender	-----	-----
Cardiac failure	----	right hypochondrium	------	oedema, ascites	enlarged, tender	---	---
Haemolytic disease of newborn	----	-----	------	oedema	enlarged	----	enlarged
Thalassaemia	-----	---	------	------	enlarged	-----	enlarged
Schistosomiasis	yes	abdominal	frequent with blood stained mucus	sometimes ascites	enlarged	------	enlarged
Laptospirosis	yes, with hills	—	—	—	enlarged	—	enlarged
Yellow fever	yes, with chills	epigastrium	constipation	—	—	—	—

In ***metastatic carcinoma,*** jaundice develops if there is biliary obstruction. Liver is enlarged and hard, and may also be tender. There may be splenomegaly. Hepatic bruit or friction rub is however not common.

Detection of high concentration of α-fetoprotein is practically diagnostic. CT scan and hepatic angiography are helpful diagnostic aids. Diagnosis is however confirmed by liver biopsy.

- **Cholangitis** presents with intermittent colicky pain in the right upper abdomen. Often there is flatulence, dyspepsia, fullness or oppression in the epigastrium, coming soon after food but worse after fruits or fried food, and is relieved after belching or vomiting. There is also obstructive jaundice. Liver is enlarged and there is tenderness in the right hypochondrium.
- The principal manifestation of **sclerosing cholangitis** is gradual development of progessive cholestatic jaundice. In addition, there is other symptoms of cholangitis. The liver is enlarged, with considerable tenderness on palpation. Diagnosis of the condition may be made by ultrasonography or CT scanning, and can be confirmed by endoscopic retrograde cholangiopancreatography.
- **Cholangiocarcinoma** usually presents with obstructive jaundice. There may also be pain in the upper abdomen and intense generalised itching.
- **Cracinoma of stomach** is usually asymptomatic in the early stage. Later, it may however give rise to progressive dyspepsia, increasing anorexia, nausea, pain or discomfort, and vomiting. Dysphagia is common. There is change in bowel habit. In addition, there are pallor, ascites, jaundice, palpable abdominal mass, visible peristalsis, haematemesis and melaena. Barium meal x-ray may show filling defect but double contour x-ray is more helpful during the early stage.
- **Carcinoma of pancreas** usually gives rise to epigastric pain which becomes exaggerated following foods and from lying supine but is relieved by crouching forward. In late stage, painless obstructive jaundice develops and deepens progressively. Liver becomes firm and enlarged, and the distended gall baldder may be palpable, or there may be ascites. There may also be intractable pruritus secondary to jaundice, leading to heavy excoriations and thickening of skin. The condition is diagnosed by ultrasonography, CT scanning, angiography and retrograde pancreatography.
- **Acute pancreatitis** presents with presistent, intense abdominal pain, nausea, vomiting, fever and prostration. There may also be tachycardia, hypotension, sweating and mild jaundice. The abdomen may be distended. There may be little or no guarding of abdominal muscles and rigidity, and the peristaltic sounds may not be audible. Proteinuria is common. Increased levels of both serum and urine amylase and lipase are valuable diagnostic aid.
- **Chronic Pancreatitis** presents with persistent or recurrent pain in the upper abdomen. In addition, there are anorexia, malaise and vomiting. Mild attack of obstructive jaundice may accompany the pain. Steatorrhoea is common. The condition gives rise to discomfort and distension in upper and middle abdomen, diffuse tenderness in the abdomen and

mild muscle guarding. Barium meal x-ray, ultrasonography and CT scan can demonstrate the pancreatic enlargement.

- **Choledocholithiasis** is usually asymptomatic. Otherwise, it presents with severe pain in the right hypochondrium or epigastrium, nausea, vomiting and jaundice. It is diagnosed on clinical grounds but otherwise by cholangiography, ultrasonography or CT scanning.
- **Gallstones** may be asymptomatic or may present with abdominal distress, pain, nausea, vomiting, belching and bloating. Otherwise, there may be recurrent bililary colic or severe pain in the epigastrium and right hypochondrium, restlessness, pallor, sweating and vomiting. In other circumstances, there may be obstructive jaundice and fever. Plain x-ray can reveal radio-opaque stone. Ultrasonogram can confirm the diagnosis.
- In **carcinoma of gall bladder**, often a history of recurrent biliary colic and chronic cholecystitis are available. The condition gives rise to constant pain in the right upper quadrant. There may also be jaundice. A firm, tender mass of gall bladder may be palpable. In cases of jaundice, a cholecystogram may show filling defect in the gall bladder and the gall bladder appears non-functioning.
- **Gilbert's syndrome** presents with mild jaundice, which appears intermittently with exacerbations. It is a benign congenital condition of unconjugated hyperbilirubinaemia, with no pathological abnormality.
- **Fulminant hepatic failure** presents with sudden severe impairment of liver function and hepatic encephalopathy. The patient presents with a sweet smell in breathing, *fetor hepaticus,* and the extended hands show flapping tremors. There may also be purpura and overt bleeding, and rapidly progressing jaundice. The liver is initially palpable but later becomes impalpable. So is the hepatic dullness. Splenomegaly is rare. Ascites and oedema develop several days after. Diagnosis of the condition is usually made on clinical grounds.
- **Fatty liver** is often asymptomatic. Otherwise, there may be pain in the right upper quadrant, jaundice and perhaps diarrhoea. Liver is enlarged with no tenderness. Percutaneous liver biopsy can establish the diagnosis.
- In **cirrhosis of liver,** there may be mild or no jaundice, which may however be progressive in cases of liver failure. Otherwise, the condition gives rise to weakness, fatigue, loss of body weight, nausea, vomiting, flatulence, diarrhoea or constipation, muscle wasting and spider telangiectasia. Enlargement of spleen is common. Liver is usually enlarged in the early stage with blunt edges but later becomes small and hard, often with nodular surface. The condition gives rise to fetid breath. Tongue appears furred. Blood shows elevated levels of alkaline phosphatase, acid phosphatase, amylase, lactate dehydrogenase, total lipids, cholesterol, bilirubin, asperate aminotransferase (formerly, SGOT) and alanine aminotransferase (formerly, SGPT).
- **Biliary cirrhosis** when presents as *primary biliary cirrhosis* gives rise to pruritus, more severe and marked on the palms and soles, and jaundice. Liver is enlarged. The condition may show association with the rheumatiod arthritis, scleroderma and autoimmune thyroiditis.

Secondary biliary cirrhosis presents with intermittent or chronic jaundice that persists over months or years. Skin is of bronze colour with xanthomatous lesions, particularly around the eyes, elbows, knees, buttocks and on the creases of the hands. Liver is enlarged and tender. Blood shows elevated levels of alkaline phosphatase, bilirubin, aminotransferase, amylase, lactate dehydrogenase, cholesterol and total lipids. Liver biopsy can confirm the diagnosis.

- **Acute cholecystitis** gives rise to slight fever, malaise, epigastric discomfort, severe abdominal pain, restlessness, pallor, nausea, vomiting and sweating. Occasionally, there may also be jaundice. The gall bladder may be palpable. Diagnosis of the condition is made on clinical grounds.
- **Chronic cholecystitis** may present with flatulence, nausea, heartburn, belching, borborygmi, abdominal distress, and bouts of pain in the epigastrium and right hypochondrium, usually worsen by fatty and fried foods. There is also jaundice. Deep pressure causes tenderness in the right hypochondrium. The gall bladder may or may not be visible on cholecystogram.
- In **cardiac failure,** right-sided cardiac failure gives rise to fatigue, general weakness, anorexia, nausea, bloating, and a feeling of fullness in the neck and abdomen. There may be polyuria and nocturia but oliguria during the day. There may also be peripheral cyanosis, peripheral coldness, and dependent oedema and ascites. Pain in the right hypochondrium occurs due to hepatic congestion. Later, jaundice develops. Liver is enlarged and tender. Although the condition gives a disturbed liver function, development of severe jaundice or hepatic failure is rare. Diagnosis of the condition is made on clinical grounds.
- **Portal hypertension** gives rise to abdominal pain and ascites. There may also be jaundice. Liver is enlarged, soft and tender. Spleen is also enlarged. Diagnosis of the condition is made by endoscopy, angiography, hepatic venography, hepatic scintiscanning and ultrasound or CT scan.
- **Amoebiasis** may sometimes lead to the development of *amoebic liver abscess,* the condition then gives rise to pain in the liver region, which is aggravated by body movements. The patient presents with intermittent fever, chills, sweating, nausea, vomiting and, in some cases, diarrhoea or dysentery. Infrequently there may also be mild jaundice. Liver is enlarged and tender. X-ray may show elevation and fixation, or impaired extension of the right leaf of the diaphragm. The abscess can be detected by ultrasonogram and radioisotope scanning. A needle biopsy may show pus.
- In **malaria,** falciparum infection gives rise to an irregular fever. The condition also presents with vomiting, cough, diarrhoea, jaundice, postural hypotension and normocytic anaemia. Diagnosis of the condition is made by detection of characteristic malarial parasities within the erythrocytes.
- In heavy infestations, **fascioliasis** presents with fever, abdominal rigidity, tender heptomegaly and eosinophilia. There may also be cholangitis, obstruction of common bile duct and jaundice. Diagnosis of the condition is made by identification of unembryonated operculated eggs of *Fasciola hepatica* in the stools and in the duodenal aspirates.

- **Clonorchiasis** is however asymptomatic, generally. In heavy infestation the condition may give rise to fever, chills, mild jaundice, tender hepatomegaly and eosinophilia. Blood shows elevated levels of alkaline phosphatase and bilirubin. Diagnosis of the condition is made by identification of small operculated and embryonated ovum of *Clonorchis sinensis* in the faeces or in the duodenal contents.
- When **hydatid disease** involves the liver, the condition is asymptomatic till the cyst ruptures or assumes sufficient large size to produce pressure symptoms. The liver enlarges slowly over the years, and feels smooth, globular, elastic and, sometimes, fluctuating. Jaundice however develops when the cyst obstruct the bile ducts. Intradermal test (Casoni test) with inactivated hydatid fluid is a helpful diagnostic aid.
- **Infective endocarditis** presents with fever, chills, malaise, lassitude, anorexia, night sweats and pallor. Other manifestations of the condition are pain in the abdomen, chest or flanks, myalgia, and arthralgia or swelling and redness of the joints. There may be haemorrhage, petechial haemorrhage, and the spleen may just be enlarged and palpable. Embolism is a common feature of the condition, which may be gross or minute. There may therefore be symptoms and signs of embolism occuring at various sites, high venous pressure, jaundice, pulsating liver, stroke or renal failure. A history of fulminating infection or of rheumatic, congenital or atherosclerotic heart disease is often suggestive for the condition. The causative organism can also be isolated from blood or bone marrow.
- **Relapsing fever** presents with chills, fever, nausea, vomiting, intense headache, muscle and joint pains, and varieties of skin rash. Presence of photophobia is common. Pulse is rapid, face is flushed, and eyes are injected. There may be abdominal pain and tenderness. Liver and spleen are frequently palpable and tender. Jaundice is common. There may be subcutaneous or intestinal haemorrhage. The causative organism, *Borrelia* species, can be isolated and identified from peripheral blood during the febrile period.
- **Leptospirosis** presents with headache, usually frontal, severe muscle pain, anorexia, malaise, chills and rapidly rising fever. Prostration is always severe. Sore throat is common. In a large number of cases liver as well as spleen may be palpable, and jaundice develops in many cases on the fourth to sixth day and may frequently be associated with fever, renal dysfunction and disturbances in consciousness. In more severe cases, jaundice deepens along with hiccough, Cheyne-Stokes respiration and coma. The causative organism can be identified in blood and urine by dark-field microscopy during the first 10 days. Agglutination antibodies appear from the sixth day, reaching a peak at 5 to 8 weeks after the infection.
- **Bronchial carcinoma** is characterised by cough, dyspnoea, and endocrine, biochemical and neruomuscular disorders. During the late stage, symptoms are produced due to metastases and may give rise to headache, bone pain, jaundice, epileptiform seizures or presonality changes, and haematuria, Diagnosis of the condition is usually made on chest x-ray.
- In **haemolytic disease of newborn,** jaundice usually develops 24 hours after birth and may progrsess to further deepening. There may be oedema and enlargement of liver. Spleen may also be enlarged.

- **Thalassaemia** when develops as *thalassaemia major* there may be progressively severe anaemia, leg ulcers, gallstones, jaundice and hepatosplenomegaly. There are also thickening of cranial bones, molar eminences and other changes giving rise to a mongoloid appearance. Blood shows leucocytosis, large number of nucleated erythroblasts, target cells, increased platelets, and both mean corpuscular volume (MCV) and mean corpuscular haemoglobin concentration (MCHC) are below the normal level.
- In **hereditray spherocytosis** there may be no or mild to severe anaemia. Presence of jaundice is constant but is usually mild. Patients complain of a feeling of fullness and discomfort in the left upper quadrant. Spleen is often palpable and firm. In addition, there may be hepatomegaly. A familial history of the condition may be available. Blood shows decreased number of red cells, with increased osmotic fragility, presence of spherocytes, leucocytosis and hyperbilirubinaemia.
- **Glucose 6-phosphate dehydrogenase deficiency** may present with anaemia, haemoglobinuria, and other symptoms and signs of haemolysis. There is also jaundice and reticulocytosis. Blood shows irregularly contracted cells, reticulocytosis and Heinz bodies. The condition is diagnosed by specific erythrocytic enzyme assay.
- Manifestations of **sickle cell anaemia** include fatigue, increased susceptibility to infection, acute abdomen, malaise, jaundice and episodes of severe pain, commonly occuring in the bones and spleen. Scleral icterus is a constant feature. Blood shows abnormal haemoglobin (HbS).
- **Hodgkin's lymphoma** is characterised by progressive, painless and generalised enlargement of lymphoid tissue. It does not give rise to any symptom as such generally but the symptoms are produced due to pressure of lymph node mass on the neighbouring structures. There can therefore be dysphagia, dyspnoea, jaundice, venous obstruction and paraplegia. Diagnosis of the condition is made by lymph node biopsy and is confirmed by the presence of Reed-Strenberg cells.
- Development of **herpes simplex** infection in the newborn (***neonatal herpes***) is extremely rare and yet when it does, it causes generalised vesiculation of skin, fever, jaundice, dyspnoea and haemorrhages. Isolation of the virus is possible for the diagnosis of the condition.
- **Infectious mononucleosis** presents with fever, vomiting, malaise, anorexia, sore throat, severe frontal headache and myalgia. The condition may occasionally give rise to skin rash, jaundice, hepatitis and abnormal liver function test. Demonstration of rising titre by immunofluorescence and other technique are helpful for the diagnosis.
- **Yellow fever** presents with malaise, headache, muscle pain, backache, chills or rigor and fever. Characteristically the pulse is initially rapid and bounding but becomes slow from the second day for the degree of temperature (Faget's sign). Albuminuria appears about the second day and increases. There may be moderate jaundice, along with bilirubinaemia and bilirubinuria. In mild cases, Faget's sign is suggestive of the condition. In severe cases, presence of jaundice, aluminuria and haematuria is diagnostic.

- **Q fever** presents with malaise, chills, fever, retro-orbital headache and myalgia. Fever may persist for as short as 1 day or as long as 3 weeks. Some cses may however give rise to pain at right upper quadrant, jaundice and enlargement of liver while in others, there may be hepatitis and endocarditis. Diagnosis of the condition is made on clinical grounds. Occupational history of close contact with domestic animals, particularly cattle, sheep and goats, is helpful in diagnosis.
- **Syphilis** in its secondary stage gives rise to mild constitutional symptoms and widespread non-itching skin rash of various forms. Generalised, firm, non-tender lymphadenitis is also common. In this stage, extremely infections, condylomata lata, also appears. Occasionally, some cases may present with splenomegaly, hepatomegaly, and jaundice, nephrosis or acute uveitis. Identification of the causative organism by dark-ground microscopy is possible from the cutaneous and mucous membrane lesions. Serological tests for syphilis are positive in most cases.
- **Psittacosis** presents with a wide range of symptoms from mild inapparent infection to a severe pneumonia and sepsis. Mild hepatomegaly is common but development of jaundice is rare and when it occurs, it is considered to be of bad prognostic value. Occupational history of handling birds is a useful guide. The organism, *Chlamydia psittaci,* can be identified from blood and sputum.
- **Amyloidosis** involves multisystem and presents with variable but nonspecific features. However, when it involves the liver it causes elevated level of serum alkaline phosphatase but rarely produces jaundice or portal hypertension with oesophageal varices.
- **Schistosomiasis** due to *Schistosoma mansoni* or *S. japonicum* usually presents with abdominal pain and frequent stools with blood-stained mucus. It also gives rise to granulomatous hepatitis and causes hepatomegaly and splenomegaly, but jaundice and hepatic failure are rare. The condition is diagnosed by identification of characteristic eggs in the stools and from rectal snip.

MICTURITION, FREQUENCY OF

Frequency of micturition may be increased than that is the established pattern of an individual in a number of conditions, while it may also be a natural phenomenon in the states of anxiety, fear and tension. Excessive or increasing intake of fluid can also equally increase the frequency of micturition. Along with the increased frequency there may be urgency, generally due to certain inflammation or tumour, and the person cannot withheld urination and, if delayed, involuntary urination may also occur.

The term ***polyuria*** is also frequently used to express an increased frequency of micturition but usually denotes large volume of urination as that can sometimes be seen normally following heavy intake of fluid.

- **Acute pyelonephritis** gives rise to dysuria, strangury and frequent micturition of small amount of cloudy urine. There is also rigor and fever. The condition presents with pain in one or both loins, radiating to the iliac fossa and suprapubic area. The kidney is usually palpable. Urine analysis shows numerous pus cells, red cells and epithelial cells, fragments of renal tissue, and may sometimes also show the causative microorganism.
- **Chronic pyelonephritis** may remain symptomfree or may present with vague and slight manifestation of frequency in micturition, dysuria, and lumbar pain. There may also be uraemia, symptoms of arterial hypertension and faintness. The patient may give a previous history of urinary tract infection or of recurrent acute pyelonephritis. X-ray shows small-sized contracted kidney with clubbing of the adjacent calyces. Renal function is impaired.
- **Acute renal failure** initially gives rise to oliguria or anuria in its maintenance phase which runs for 1 to 3 weeks and followed by recovery phase with increased frequency of micturition, causing uncontrolled loss of water and sodium. Urine shows red and white cells, protein, epithelial cells, granular and dirty brown casts, and increased level of sodium. A progressively daily rise in serum creatinine is diagnostic for the condition.
- **Chronic renal failure** may however remain asymptomatic or may present with vague symptoms but polyuria and nocturia may be common. In addition, there is hypertension, subnormal body temperature, progressive weakness, lethargy and uraemia. Other manifestations of the condition include bad or metalic taste, thirst, diarrhoea, gastrointestinal irritation, burning sensation and dryness of the mouth. Tongue appears dry and brown coloured. Urine shows small amount of protein, white cells, epithelial cells, granular and waxy casts, and low levels of creatine, creatinine, uric acid and potassium.
- **Chronic nephritic syndrome** usually remains asymptomatic till late stage. Otherwise, there may be nausea, vomiting, polyuria, thirst, pruritus and diarrhoea. Urine shows small amount of protein, red cells, granular and hyaline casts, and increased level of creatinine. The patient may often give a history of acute nephritic syndrome or of nephrotic syndrome.

- **Acute tubulointerstitial nephritis** gives rise to variable symptoms, which may include symptoms of urinary tract infection. Others may present with acute renal failure. Occasionally, when there is evidence of tubular dysfunction, there may be polyuria, volume depletion, metabolic acidosis and hyperkalaemia.
- In **chronic tubulointerstitial nephritis,** when the condition develops due to analgesic nephropathy, the patient may complain of polyuria and thirst. Headache and gastrointestinal symptoms are common. Tips of necrotic papillae may be passed in urine, causing gross haematuria or renal colic. In other instances, symptoms are often minimal, and some may give rise to symptoms of tubular dysfunction as they are evident in acute tubulointerstitial nephritis. History of prolonged or excessive consumption of analgesics may be available.
- When **polycystic kidney disease** develops in early or middle adult life, it may give variable symptoms and in some, there may be haematuria followed by polyuria and proteinuria. Symptoms of uraemia develop gradually. Sometimes the kidneys may be palpable as smooth, nodular mass.
- **Urinary tract calculus** often remains asymptomatic, and only causes colicky pain or varying degree or excruciating pain when it causes obstruction in the calyces, renal pelvis or the ureter. In the vesicle however it produces suprapubic pain. In addition, depending upon the site of involvement, there may be frequency of micturition, haematuria, chills and fever. There may be interruption of urinary flow, dysuria, distended bladder and cystocele. Diagnosis of the condition is made by plain x-ray but otherwise by excretory or retrograde pyelography.
- **Caricoma of urinary bladder** presents with dysuria, burning in micturition, frequency of micturition, and haematuria. A suprapubic mass may be palpable at the late stage of the condition. Cytology of urine and cystogram are often helpful in the diagnosis of the condition.
- In **gonorrhoea**, the presenting manifestation of *gonococcal urethritis* vary widely, to the extent many cases, particularly the females, may remain asymptomatic. However, when it presents with symptoms, burning on micturition and increased frequency of micturition are common.

  Gonococcal vulvovaginitis also presents with dysuria and frequcny of micturition. The patient complains of soreness of the vulva or around the anus, discomfort on defaecation, inflammed and swollen vagina, and staining on the underwear.

  Diagnosis of the condition is made by identification of *Neisseria gonorrhoeae* from the exudates.
- **Trichomoniasis** also frequently remains asymptomatic. Otherwise, there may be vaginal discharge, redness and oedema of the vulva and vagina, dysuria and frequency of micturition in females. In males, however, it only produces slight itching or discomfort inside the penis, and slight moisture at the tip of the penis. Diagnosis of the condition is made by identification of *Trichomanas vaginalis* in the exudate.
- In **nonspecific urethritis** symtoms vary and many cases may well remain asymptomatic. Among others there may be urethral discharge, more marked at early in the morning. There may also be dysuria, frequency and urgency of micturition, and pain in the penis, perineum and lower

abdomen. Diagnosis of the condition is made on clinical grounds.

- **Cystitis** causes frequency of micturition. The patient complains of dysuria, and there may be even haematuria. Pain and tenderness in the hypogastrium may be evident. The causative organism can be identified from urine. Excretory urography can establish other causes of its development.
- **Benign prostatic hyperplasia** presents with progressive urinary frequency, urgency of micturition, nocturia, sensation of incomplete urination, decreased size and force of urinary streams, terminal dribbling, and acute urinary retention. The prostate appears large, rubbery and uniform, and frequently shows loss of median furrow.
- In acute state **prostatitis** may present with perineal pain, low back pain, chills, fever, malaise, urinary frequency and urgency, and dysuria. The prostate feels enlarged, tender and boggy, and a mere palpation of it may result in expression of copious purulent discharge.

  In chronic state, there is however relapsing urinary tract infection, and a proportion of cases may give rise to low back pain, mild dysuria, and urgency and frequency of micturition. The prostate may appear slightly tender, firm and irregularly indurated or boggy.

  Diagnosis of the condition is made on clinical grounds. Prostatic secretion shows clumps of leucocytes and lipid-laden macrophages, pus cells and bacteria.
- In **extrapulmonary tuberculosis,** *tuberculous pyelonephritis* usually develops secondary to renal tuberculosis or to tuberculosis elsewhere in the body, and presents with dull pain in the loin which may also be colicky. There is also increased frequency of micturition and characteristically the urine, though show pyuria, is sterile.
- In **schistosomiasis,** haematobium infection usually begins with painless terminal haematuria and later, there is frequcency in micturition and pain over the iliac fossa. It is diagnosed by identification of the eggs in the urine.
- **Canndidiasis** when involves the genitalia, it produces vulvovaginitis with irritation, intense itching and discharge, dysuria and frequency of micturition. In males, the condition produces balanitis or balanoposthitis. The organism can also cause urinary tract infection, giving rise to dysuria and frequency of micturition.
- **Hypoparathyroidism** characteristically gives rise to tetany, with muscle cramps, dyspnoea, urinary frequency and convulsions. Skin appears dry and there may be pruritus. Blood shows low leval of calcium and high leval of phosphate. Alkaline phosphatase and creatinine clearance are normal.
- **Diverticulitis** presents with severe pain in the left lower quadrant but may occasionally be at suprapubic region or even at right lower quadrant, accompanied by muscle guarding and rigidity. When the inflammation spreads to the bladder, the condition then gives rise to urinary frequency and dysuria. A mass may be palpable on left lower quadrant.
- **Carcinoma of vagina** presents with painless bleeding. In the late stage, pain develops and the vagina becomes swollen. In cases of involvement of the bladder, the condition then gives rise to frequency or urgency of micturition.
- **Dysmenorrhoea** presents with cramping, colicky or constant dull pain in the lower abdomen, starting prior to or with

menstrual flow. Accompanying this there are headache, nausea, vomiting and abdominal distension. In addition, there may be urgency and frequency of micturition, pelvic sorenss and, even, diarrhoea. The condition is diagnosed on clinical grounds.

- In **menopausal syndrome** there is no definite mode of symptomatology, and the symptoms vary extremely widely from one individual to another. In general, there may be a sensation of hot flushes, night sweats, anorexia, nausea, vomiting, diarrhoea, dizziness, headache, palpitation, tachycardia or dyspnoea. The patient may also give rise to urinary tract manifestations, which may include urgency and frequency of micturition, incontinence, dysuria and meatal tenderness. The condition is diagnosed on clinical grounds.
- **Cervicitis** presents with acute inflammation and usually gives rise to profuse, odorous, purulent vaginal discharge. There may also be dysuria, and urgency and frequency of micturition. Diagnosis of the condition is made from identification of the causative organism from the vagtinal exudate. Hysterography is another helpful diagnostic aid but is contraindicated in acute condition.
- In **uterine prolapse** there is usually a sense of varying degree of vaginal fullness and pressure. Depending on the extent of prolapse and the pressure it exerts, there may be urgency and frequency of micturition, outflow voiding, urinary tract infection, constipation and painful defaecation.
- **Myoma of uterus** is often asymptomatic unless it exerts pressure due to its size or position, or becomes twisted on its pedicle. When it however assumes large size, it gives rise to pressure symptoms, such as vaginal discharge, dyspareunia, frequency and urgency of micturition, retention of urine, oedema in the lower extremity, constipation and painful defaecation. If the myoma is not small in size, it can easily be felt through bimanual pelvic examination.
- **Sarcoma of uterus** produces abnormal uterine bleeding and leucorrhoea. The abdomen may be enlarged and the patient complains of pelvic discomfort. There may be frequency of micturition. Vaginal cytology may identify the malignant cells. The diagnosis is however confirmed by biopsy of the tumour.
- The symptoms of **carcinoma of Fallopian tube** depend on the size of the tumour and the pressure it exerts on the neighbouring structures. As an extension of such a pressure there may also be urgency or frequency of micturition and painful defaection.
- In **diabetes mellitus** symptoms vary, and there may be polyuria, nocturia, polydipsia, tiredness, general weakness, wasting of body, and non-healing or delayed-healing of cuts and wounds. Diagnosis of the condition is made by high level of fasting blood glucose level. Random blood sugar level and urine analysis for glucose and ketone bodies can also confirm the diagnosis.
- The chief presenting manifestations of **diabetes insipidus** are polyuria and polydipsia. The patient passes large amount of urine, which in absence of appropriate management may lead to dehydration. The urine shows low specific gravity. Glucose tolerance curve is normal.
- **Hyperparathyroidism** is characterised by hypercalcaemia. When the condition

involves the renal and urinary tract, it may give rise to polyuria, polydipsia, renal calculi and associated symptoms and signs. Blood shows elevated levels of calcium, chloride and uric acid. X-ray may show demineralisation or subperiosteal erosion in the phalanges in the early stage and resorption of terminal phalanges and 'pepper-pot' appearance of the skull.

- In both **acromegaly** and **gigantism** there may be excessive appetite, abnormal gain of body weight, polyuria, extraordinary muscle strength in early stage but later arthritis, overgrowth of vertebral bodies and kyphosis, and muscular weakness. Diagnosis of the condition is often made on clinical grounds.
- **Hyperaldosteronism** presents with episodic weakness, polyuria and polydipsia. Hypertension is common but development of oedema is unusual. Blood shows low levels of renin and potassium. The level of aldosterone in blood and urine are increased.
- **Hypercalcaemia** presents with anorexia, nausea, vomiting, abdominal pain and ileus. There is also polyuria, nocturia and polydipsia. Diagnosis of the condition is made on clinical grounds.
- **Hypokalaemia** is characterised by muscular weakness, apathy, mental confusion and paralysis. There may be polyuria and later, secondary polydipsia may develop. Blood shows normal or lowered level of potassium.
- **Metabolic alkalosis** causes irritation and neuromuscular excitation. In cases of potassium depletion, there may also be muscular weakness, lieus, polyuria and uraemia. Blood shows increased pH and elevated level of bicarbonate. Level of CO_2 is also elevated.
- **Undernutrition** gives rise to weakness and loss of body weight and, in children, retardation of growth. The condition characteristically gives rise to famine oedema, often preceded by a period of nocturnal polyuria. Diagnosis of the condition is made clinically.
- In **cardiac failure,** *right-sided cardiac failure* presents with increasing fatigue, general weakness, anorexia, nausea, vomiting, bloating, and feeling of fullness in the neck and abdomen. There may be polyuria and nocturia but oliguria during the day. Liver is enlarged and tender. Blood pressure is high. Diagnosis of the condition is made on clinical grounds.
- **Supraventricular tachycaridia** gives rise to sudden increase of heart rate to 140 to 220 per minute. The patient may or may not however be aware of the transient attacks lasting for a few second or minutes. Otherwise, there is a feeling of sudden increase in heart rate, and the patient may feel faint or breathless. There may be polyuria during or after the attack.
- **Atrial flutter** with its usual form of 2:1 block behaves like paroxysmal supraventricular tachycardia, and the patient feels sudden, rapid, regular fluttering sensation in the chest. There may be weakness, fainting and polyuria. Atrial rate becomes more rapid, ranging between 240 and 440, usual being 300 per minute. Pulse is rapid but regular with a rate of about 150 beats per minute.
- Most cases of **hypertension** do not usually give to any specific symptom. However, the symptoms which most commonly encountered with in the condition are headache, dizziness, flushed face, trembling, nausea, vomiting, espistaxis, muscular irritability, polyuria and nocturia.

NAUSEA AND VOMITING

Complaints of nausea and vomiting may perhaps a quite frequent feature in a large number of disorders. In most cases the symptoms are however nonspecific and usually serve no purpose in terms of physical diagnosis. The symptoms are also usually frequented in conditions whenever there is uraemia.

Although both these manifestations usually occur concurrently, there are some disorders where the patient may complain of a nauseating feeling but without any vomiting while, in some, there may be vomiting but the symptom of nausea may be absent. Emphasis also needs to be made that too heavy meal, particularly rich food, may at times give rise to either nausea or vomiting or both. So it is with the cases of food poisoning.

On the other hand, in certain circumstances vomiting is at times induced voluntarily so as to get relief of the existing distressing symptom.

- **Tropical sprue** characteristically presents with urgency of defaecation, often after meals. There is steatorrhoea with loose, bulky, frothy, pale, fatty, greasy and foul-smelling stools which float on water surface. The patient may also complain of indigestion, flatulence, nausea, vomiting, pallor, muscle weakness and cramps. The condition is diagnosed on clinical grounds.
- In **Crohn's disease** symptoms vary depending on the site and extent of involvement. The patient presents with intermittent bouts of diarrhoea, anorexia, flatulence, nausea, vomiting, low-grade fever and loss of body weight. Development of hypochromic microcytic anaemia is common. Barium meal and barium enema x-rays demonstrate the typical lesions with alteration in intestinal mucosal pattern.
- There may not be any symptom in **gastritis** but otherwise the condition may give rise to anorexia, nausea, vomiting, heartburn, and epigastric pain, discomfort and tenderness. Endoscopic examination can reveal the condition and the diagnosis can be confirmed by biopsy.
- ***Peptic ulcer*** presents with nausea, vomiting and epigastric distress as burning, aching, hunger-pain, occuring in **gastric ulcer** soon after food but about 2 hours after in **duodenal ulcer**. Barium meal x-ray can demonstrate the ulcer.
- **Carcinoma of stomach** is usually asymptomatic during the early stage or there may be vague symptoms of peptic ulcer with slight nausea, abdominal discomfort and loss of appetite. Later, there may be progressive dyspepsia, increasing anorexia, nausea and vomiting. Dysphagia is common. Barium meal x-ray may show filling defect but double contour x-ray is more helpful during the early stage.
- **Intestinal lymphangiectsia** characteristically produces protein-losing enteropathy. There are mild intermittent diarrhoea, nausea, vomiting, and abdominal pain. Diagnosis of the condition is made from jejunal biopsy.
- **Irritable bowel syndrome** presents with abdominal pain. The patient may feel urgency of defaecation, frequently during

or immediately after foods and passes pellet or ribbon-like stools. The patient also complains of intestinal distension, excessive flatus, borborygmi, nausea, vomiting, sore stomach and a sensation of incomplete emptying of the bowel.

- The severity of symptoms in **gastroenteritis** depend on the nature and cause. In general, it begins with anorexia, nausea, vomiting and borborygmi. There are abdominal discomfort and cramps, and diarrhoea which may be watery or formed, and may contain blood and mucus. Repeated attack of diarrhoea gives rise to malaise, muscular ache and prostration. Very frequent and persistent diarrhoea, perhaps along with vomiting, may lead to dehydration and shock. The condition is diagnosed on clinical grounds.
- **Acute pancreatitis** presents with persistent, intense, abdominal pain. There may be nausea, vomiting, prostration and fever. The condition shows little or no guarding of abdominal muscle and rigidity. The levels of amylase and lipase in both serum and urine are elevated.
- **Chronic pancreatitis** presents with persistent or recurrent pain in the upper abdomen. The patient also complains of anorexia, nausea and vomiting. There is discomfort and distension in the upper and middle abdomen, diffuse tenderness in the abdomen, mild muscle guarding and perhaps paralytic ileus. Mild attack of jaundice may accompany the pain.
- **Fulminant hepatic failure** presents with weakness, nausea, vomiting, fever, sweating, delirium, hypotension and tachycardia. Later, there may be confusion, changes in sleep pattern, slurred speech, hiccough, yawning, disorientation and finally convulsion. There may also be purpura and overt bleeding, and rapidly progressing jaundice. Diagnosis of the condition is made on clinical grounds.
- **Cirrhosis of liver** may be asymptomatic or may present with variable symptoms. There may therefore be weakness, fatigue, loss of body weight, nausea, vomiting, anorexia, flatulence, diarrhoea or constipation, muscle wasting and spider telangiectasias. Enlargement of spleen is common. Blood shows increased levels of alkaline phosphatase, acid phosphatase, amylase, lactic dehydrogenase, total lipids, cholesterol, bilirubin, asperate aminotransferase (formerly, SGOT) and alanine aminotransferase (formerly, SGPT).
- **Acute cholecystitis** gives rise to slight fever, rigors, epigastric discomfort and abdominal pain. There may be pallor, nausea, vomiting and sweating. The patient appears restless.
- **Cholangitis** presents with intermittent colicky pain in the right upper abdomen. Often there is fullness or oppression in the epigastrium, coming soon after foods but worse after fruits and fatty or fried foods, and is relieved after belching or vomiting. There may be chilliness, especially in the evening, with slight rise of body temperature, nausea, vomiting and diarrhoea.
- **Choledocholithiasis** is usually asymptomatic. Otherwise, there may be nausea, vomiting, intermittent jaundice and hepatocellular dysfunction. There may also be tenderness in the right hypochondrium or epigastrium, fever, and a history of biliary colic and jaundice. In addition, there is bilirubinuria.
- **Pneumonia** usually preceded by a history of upper respiratory tract infection and

begins with chills, headache and fever. Varying degree of chest pain and cough are always present. Nausea and vomiting may not be infrequent, particularly in pneumococcal pneumonia.

- **Bacterial meningitis** usually begins suddenly with high fever, chills, malaise, intense headache, pain in the back, abdomen and extremity, photophobia, nausea and vomiting. There may be haemorrhagic rash on any part of the skin, mucous membrane or conjunctiva, usually lasting for 3 to 4 days.
- **Cholera** usually presents with profuse watery diarrhoea but without any abdominal pain or colic. Presence of nausea and violent vomiting may be variable. The patient soon reaches to a profound state of dehydration, and presents with subnormal temperature, rapid and shallow breathing, weak and small pulse, and hypotension. In the endemic area and during the epidemics, diagnosis of the condition is made on chinical grounds. Otherwise, diagnosis is made by identification of the vibrios from the excreta.
- In **salmonella gastroenteritis** there is nausea, vomiting, and usually low-grade fever, often accompanied by chills. This is followed by colicky pain in the abdomen and abrupt onset of persistent diarrhoea. Diagnosis is made on clinical grounds, and is confirmed by isolation of the causative organism from the stools.
- Patients with **acute nephritic syndrome** present with puffiness around the eyes and face. There may also be headache, malaise, mild fever, anorexia, nausea, vomiting and respiratory distress. Other features of the condition includes low urinary output with blood-stained urine.
- **Chronic nephritic syndrome** is usually asymptomatic till its late stage. Otherwise, there may be fatigue, nausea, vomiting, polyuria, thirst, pruritus and diarrhoea. There is also oedema of the feet and ankles, ascites, anaemia and osteomalacia. The patient usually gives a history of acute nephritic syndrome or of nephrotic syndrome.
- **Rapidly progressive nephritic syndrome** develops insidiously and often presents with acute nephritic syndrome-like manifestations, including fever, anorexia, fatigue, weakness, nausea and vomiting. Abdominal pain and arthralgia are common features of the condition. Haematuria is also common but proteinuria is variable.
- In **acute pyelonephritis,** the patients complain of nausea, vomiting, fever, dysuria, strangury, and frequent micturition of small amount of cloudy urine. Lumbar region and hypochondrium are tender on palpation and show muscle guarding. The enlarged kidney is usually palpable.
- **Chronic pyelonephritis** may be asymptomatic or may present with slight frequency of micturition, dysuria and lumbar pain. There may be lassitude, tiredness and symptoms of uraemia (fatigue, nausea, vomiting, dyspepsia), and faintness. Previous history of urinary tract infection or of recurrent acute pyelonephritis may be available.
- In **acute renal failure** symptoms develop rapidly with symptoms of uraemia (fatigue, nausea, vomiting, dyspepsia, pruritus), lethargy and diarrhoea. In addition, there are also symptoms of predisposing factors. A progressive daily rise in serum creatinine level is a diagnostic feature of the condition.
- **Chronic renal failure** may give rise to progressive weakness, lethargy, anorexia, nausea, vomiting, pruritus, headache, paraesthesia and vertigo. The patient gives rise to hypertension, subnormal body

temperature, and deposition of grayish urea crystals usually on the face, neck and cheek. Tongue is dry and looks brown in colour.

- **Urinary tract calculus** produces symptoms when it causes obstruction in the calyces, renal pelvis or ureter, and when it is in the bladder. In addition, it may give rise to nausea, vomiting, dysuria, haematuria, frequency and urgency of micturition, chills and fever.
- **Acute viral heaptatis** gives rise to chills or chilliness, headache, malaise and influenza-like fever, followed usually by the development of jaundice. There may also be severe anorexia, nausea, vomiting, myalagia and diarrhoea. Liver is usually firm and tender and may be palpable. Splenomegaly may also occur, particularly in children.
- The onset of **viral encephalitis** may be abrupt or explosive, with high fever, malaise, sore throat, headache, nausea and vomiting. Tremor, stiff neck, signs of meningeal irritation and cranial nerve palsies are common features of the condition.
- **Smallpox** used to begin with severe headache, malaise, prostration, nausea, vomiting and diarrhoea. The condition is characterised by severe constitutional disturbances and centrifugal pattern of skin rash eruption.
- The manifestations of **rabies** may include malaise, anorexia, nausea, vomiting, sore throat and fever. The condition is characterised by the development of hydrophobia, convulsions and paralysis.
- **Hyperparathyroidism** may be mild and asymptomatic, or may present with weakness, lethargy, loss of appetite, nausea, vomiting, abdominal pain, and constipation. There may also be prostration, calcium deposits in the cornea, hypertension and bone deformities. Blood shows elevated levels of calcium, chloride and uric acid.
- **Pheochromocytoma** gives rise to paroxysmal or sustained hypertension. There may be nausea, vomiting, constipation, increased appetite, loss of body weight and sweating. Headache may be severe. There may be glycosuria or hyperglycemia with normal thyroxine level in the blood.
- In diabetes mellitus, too much insulin intake or unaccustomed exercise or eating of no foods for a prolonged time may produce **hypoglycemia.** The condition then gives rise to headache, malaise, nausea, perhaps vomiting, sweating, tremor, palpitations, faintness, dizziness and mental confusion.
- **Streptococcal sore throat** may give rise to sore throat, fever, nausea, pain on swallowing, and enlarged and tender cervical lymph nodes. When the condition however leads to *scarlet fever,* there is sudden onset of fever with headache, muscle ache and vomiting. The pulse appears rapid. Within 24 to 36 hours after the advent of fever, characteristic skin rashes develop.
- **Pernicious anaemia** gives rise to weakness, debility, loss of body weight, soreness of tongue, palpitation and tachycardia. There may be anorexia, nausea, vomiting, dyspepsia, indigestion and diarrhoea. Blood shows hyperchromic macrocytic anaemia with marked anisocytosis, poikilocytosis and fragmented red cells, leucopenia with relative neutropenia, hypersegmented

neutorophils, diminished number of platelets and low level of vitamin B_{12}.

- **Chronic myeloid leukaemia** may give rise to fatigue, weakness, malaise, loss of body weight, night sweats, anorexia, dyspepsia, nausea and vomiting. Spleen is firm, smooth, painless and greatly enlarged, and gives a friction rub. Liver is usually moderately enlarged, with smooth surface. Blood shows normochromic normocytic anaemia, and full range of granulocytes from myeloblasts to mature neutrophils, and a few nucleated erythrocytes.
- Symptoms of **premenstrual tension** usually appear 7 to 10 days before the onset of menstruation and may give rise to varieties of manifestations. The commonest features thus encountered with are nervousness, irritability, depression, fatigue, lethargy and unreasonable temper. Abdominal bloating is common. There may also be nausea and vomiting. Diagnosis of the condition is made on clinical grounds.
- **Intermenstrual pain** runs a mild course and frequently presents with varying degree of pain in the lower abdomen. There may also be nausea and vomiting but abdominal muscle guarding is however absent.
- In **menopausal syndrome** there is however no definite mode of symptomatology. The patient may complain of anything and everything. Complaining about malaise, fatigue, nausea, vomiting, arththralgia, myalagia, dizziness and headache are, however, quite frequent. There may also be tinnitus, fainting, palpitation, tachycardia and dyspnoea.
- In **tubo-ovarian abscess** most patients usually complain of severe lower abdominal and pelvic pain. There is also nausea and vomiting. Body temperature may swing high, and tachycardia is usual. The abdomen appears tender and shows guarding. Pelvic examination is often extremely difficult to perform because of tenderness.
- **Hyperemesis gravidarum** is a physiological condition that develops during the early pregnancy and is characterised by great exaggeration of nausea and vomiting. Most commonly the symptoms occur during the morning hours for which the condition is popularly known as ***morning sickness.*** The severity of symptoms however vary but most cases are quite mild. On the other hand, the severity of the manifestations may compel the patients to go on starvation, which eventually may result hypoproteinaemia and hypovitaminosis.
- In **hydatiform mole** there may be theatened or incomplete abortion-like uterine bleeding, usually by 6 to 8 weeks of pregnancy. A considerable number of patients also present with nausea and vomiting. The condition is diagnosed clinically, and passage of intact or collapsed vesicles is highly suggestive of the condition.
- **Amoebiasis** may give rise to *amoebic liver abscess* which may be mild and vague in many cases. In others, there may be intermittent fever, chills, sweating, nausea, vomiting, weakness, and diarrhoea or dysentery. The liver is enlarged and tender. Infrequently there may also be mild jaundice.
- Many cases of **giardiasis** may remain asymptomatic. In others, there is acute or chronic diarrhoea. There may also be mild abdominal cramps and discomfort, foul eructation, flatulence, anorexia, nausea,

vomiting, malaise, headache and dizziness. The condition is diagnosed by identification of cysts of *Giardia lamblia* in formed stools or both cyst and vegetative trophozoites in liquid stools.

- **Malaria** presents with chills, rigor, cyanosis, nausea, vomiting, headache and, even, convulsions in children. In vivax infection however vomiting may be troublesome. Diagnosis is made by identification of characteristic malarial parasites within the erythrocytes.
- **Myocardial infarction** presents with pain which may be absent or the severity may vary from a feeling of aching or pressure to severe agnoizing pain in the chest. There may also be nausea, vomiting, abdominal distress, pallor, sweating, excessive fatigue, breathlessness, syncope, fever and shock.
- **Hypertension** generally does not give rise to any specific symptom. Otherwise, the symptoms which are usually encountered with are headache, generally suboccipital, dizziness, flushed face, trembling, nausea, vomiting, epistaxis, muscular weakness, tinnitus, palpitation, nervousness, irritability and polyuria.
- In **pellagra** diarrohea is common. There are also anorexia, nausea, vomiting, excessive salivation, soreness of mouth, dysphagia, and dyspnoea. Tongue is swollen and painful with raw 'beefy' appearance.
- Symptoms and signs in **metabolic acidosis** are obscured and are often predominated by the underlying conditions. Otherwise, it presents with lassitude, nausea and vomiting. In severe form, hyperpnoea develops and may lead to further deep and rapid respiration.
- **Peritonitis** gives rise to malaise, nausea, vomiting and septic fever. Prostration may be severe. There is pain and tenderness in the abdomen which may be localised or generalised, with muscle guarding and rigidity. Later, there may be abdominal distension.
- **Perinephric abscess** presents with fever, chills, and pain in the abdomen in one flank, frequently with dysuria. Nausea, vomiting and haematuria occur occasionally. A palpable mass may be felt in the loin or abdomen.
- **Anxiety neuroses** begin with subjective sense or terror for no apparent reason. The cases may therefore present with sweating, tremor, dizziness and palpitations. A feeling of nausea and vomiting may develop in more acute cases. Sleep disturbances are naturally common.
- **Brain abscess** presents with alteration in the patient's mental and general condition. The patient complains of headache, nausea and vomiting. Slight paresis, apathy and drowsiness are common. Cerebrospinal fluid shows increased pressure, mild elevation of protein content and mild pleocytosis. Causative organism can be isolated from cerebrospinal fluid. If however the abscess is well-capsulated, there will be no abnormality in cerebrospinal fluid.
- Manifestations in **polyarteritis nodosa** vary widely. It may give rise to fever, sweating, abdominal pain, hypertension, peripheral neuropathy, oliguria, uraemia. convulsions and coma. There may be nausea, vomiting, precordial pain, pericarditis and myocardial infarction. Diagnosis of the condition is made by biopsy of medium-sized artery.

- Many cases of **leptospirosis** may remain subclinical but the rest may present with headache, severe muscle pain, anorexia, nausea, frequent vomiting, chills and rapidly rising fever. Prostration is always severe. The causative organism can be isolated and identified in blood by dark-field microscopy during the first 10 days. Agglutination antibodies appear from sixth day, reaching a peak 5 to 8 weeks after the infection.
- **Relapsing fever** presents with fever, chills, nausea, vomiting, intense headache, and muscle and joint pain. There may be varieties of skin rash. Development of jaundice is common. There may also be diarrhoea, hypotension and circulatory or cardiac failure. In acute attacks albuminuria is common but casts and erythrocytes are infrequent. Sometimes there may also be frank haematuria.
- **Tularaemia** begins abruptly with nausea, vomiting, malaise, headache, pain in the limbs, chills, high fever, extreme prostration with profuse sweating. History of exposure to the bites of blood-sucking arthropods, abrupt onset of the symptoms and presence of primary lesion at the site of inoculation are highly diagnostic.
- **Bartonellosis** may present as *oroya fever,* giving rise to fever, weakness, nausea, vomiting, diarrhoea, pallor, muscle and joint pain, and severe headache. The condition is diagnosed by identification of the causative organism in the peripheral blood.
- **Haemorrhagic fever** gives rise to fever, headache, nausea, vomiting, pharyngitis, dyspnoea, cough, and abdominal pain. Shock occurs 2 to 6 days after with sudden collapse or prostration. There is also haemorrhagic manifestations with patechae, purpura or ecchymoses at the site of injections
- **Yellow fever** presents with malaise, frontal headache, backache, myalgia, photophobia, and chills or rigor. Then there is nausea and vomiting. The condition characteristically presents with Faget's sign in which the pulse is relatively slow in comparison to the height of temperature. Diagnosis of the condition can be made by isolation of the virus from blood during the first few days of the illness.
- **Meniere's disease** presents with vertigo, nausea and vomiting. The condition is characterised by progressive hearing loss and tinnitus.
- **Lyme arthritis** begins with red, non-itching, macules or papules on trunk and peripheral part of the extremities. This is followed by signs of prostration, including malaise, fatigue, chills, fever, headache and stiff neck. There may also be nausea, vomiting, myalagia, splenomegaly and lymphadenopathy.
- **Legionnaires' disease** generally presents with severe, may even fatal, bronchopneumonia. There are anorexia, malaise, dry cough and non-remittent fever. The patient also complains of headache, nausea, vomiting, dyspnoea, myalagia and arthralgia. Diagnosis of the condition is made by isolation of the causative organism from the lung tissue. However, demonstration of a four-fold increase in indirect fluorescence antibody titre obtained 3 and 6 weeks after the onset of the condition is diagnostic.
- In the prodromal stage of **enteric fever** the patient may complain of anorexia, malaise, lethargy, severe headache, general aches and pains, and nausea. There may be sore throat and non-productive cough. Epistaxis and vomiting may not be infrequent. Bowel

movement disturbance is usual with constipation or diarrhoea. The condition gives rise to a characteristic temperature pattern.

- **Carcinoma of pancreas** gives rise to epigastric pain, usually dull and boring, that radiates to the neck and becomes exaggerated following foods and from lying supine but relieved by crouching forward. In addition, the presence of anorexia, nausea, abdominal discomfort and sometimes vomiting are common. In late stage, painless obstructive jaundice develops. Liver becomes firm and enlarged, and the distended gall bladder may be palpable or there may be ascites.
- **Salpingo-oophoritis** presents with severe lower abdominal and pelvic pain. There is usually high fever, accompanied by tachycarida. Chills or chilly sensation may occur occasionally. Nausea is often present and may or may not be associated with vomiting.
- There may be no symptom or the cases of **chronic cholecystitis** may present with flatulence, nausea, heartburn, belching, borborygmi, abdominal distress, and bouts of pain in the epigastrium and right hypochondrium, usually worsen by fatty and fried foods. There is also jaundice. Deep pressure on the abdomen causes tenderness in the right hypochondrium. Diagnosis of the condition can be made by oral cholecystography.
- In **addison's disease** there may be weakness, tiredness, malaise, anorexia, nausea, abdominal pain, and constipation alternating with diarrhoea. There may be absence of sweating, diminished tolerance to cold, and dehydration. Characteristically the condition produces hypopigmentation of the skin or vitiligo, which may often appear by itself as initial symptom or may precede other manifestations of the condition, perhaps by years.
- **Iron deficiency anaemia** usually gives rise to no or just vague symtoms. There may therefore be weakness, lassitude, anorexia, nausea, dyspepsia, headache, and aches and pains. There may also be cracking of angles of the mouth, sore tongue, flattened or concavity of the nails with brittleness, oedema of ankles and enlargement of liver. Blood shows hypochromic microcytic anaemia.
- **Atrial fibrillation** may give rise to no complaint or the patient may feel of having an irregularly regular pulse. There may also be palpitation, pallor, nausea, weakness and fatigue.
- Symptoms and signs in **sunburn** depend on the intensity and duration of exposure. In severe cases, however, there may be nausea, chills, fever, tachcardia, shock, and oedema of ankles, legs, face and other parts of the body.
- In **cholestatic jaundice**, there are symptoms and signs of the underlying condition. In addition, there are yellow coloration of sclerae, skin and mucous membrane of the mouth, dark coloured urine, and clay-coloured or pale stools. There may also be malaise, anorexia, vomiting and ascites.
- **Gallstones** may remain asymptomatic. Otherwise, there may be recurrent biliary colic or severe pain in the epigastrium and right hypochondrium, causing restlessness, sweating, pallor and vomiting. Plain abdominal x-ray can reveal radio-opaque stones but otherwise ultrasonography is needed for the diagnosis.
- In **extrapulmonary tuberculosis,** the patients may give rise to malaise, loss of

appetite, vomiting, fever, and persistent severe headache in ***tuberculous meningitis.*** It is however common in children aged 1 to 5 years, and the condition develops from haematogenous spread of tubercle bacilli from a localised focus.

- **Wilm's tumour** is usually asymptomatic. It is only occasionaly and that in the advanced stage that there may be pain, fever, anorexia and vomiting. The condition is suggestive whenever a child presents with intrarenal mass in a functioning kidney.
- **Poliomyelitis** in its non-paralytic form may give rise to influenza-like symptoms with severe headache, pain in the back and neck, deep muscle pain, sore throat, and vomiting or diarrhoea.
- **Infectious mononucleosis** gives rise to sudden onset of fever, often with vomiting, along with malaise, anorexia, sore throat, severe frontal headache and myalagia. Profuse sweating is a common feature. Characteristically the condition involves the lymph nodes which are enlarged, firm, elastic, normally discrete, non-tender or slightly painful, and non-suppurative.
- **Migraine** gives rise to paroxysms of severe and throbbing unilateral headache, preceded by depression, irritability, restlessness, anorexia, sweating, photophobia and prostration. Vomiting is common.
- **Stroke** may present with headache, dizziness, drowsiness, mental confusion, derangement of speech, thought, motion or vision, or there may be fever, headache, vomiting, mental changes, nuchal rigidity, convulsions and coma. Consciousness may or may not be lost.
- **Neruofibromatosis** may have different mode of presentation, while a proportion of patients may remain asymptomatic. In some cases the condition may therefore presents with tinnitus, hearing defects, vomiting and papilloedema. The condition usually gives a positive Babiniski sign. Cerebrospinal fluid may show very high protein content.
- **Erysipelas** often involves the face, arms or legs. Its onset is usually abrupt with malaise, chills, high fever, headache and vomiting. Diagnosis of the condition is made on clinical grounds.
- In **kwashiorkor** the infant looks apathetic and miserable, and presents with retarded growth. There are angular stomatitis, cheiliosis, anorexia, perhaps vomiting, smooth tongue and ulceration around the anus. Anaemia is common.
- **Anorexia nervosa** begins with deliberate and desperate effort of losing body weight. A fear of gaining weight make the patients so compelling that frequently they also induce vomiting.
- In **intestinal obstruction,** clinical features vary on the site and nature of obstruction. When the lesion is high in the intestine and develop due to mechanical cause, it gives rise to severe, crampy, intermittent colicky pain, usually at or about the site of obstruction. There may be projectile and intermittent vomiting of foul-smelling fluid. When the obstruction is low in the lower small intestine or colon, pain is less severe but abdominal distension occurs with fulness in the flanks. Vomiting may be absent or may occur lately.
- **Endometritis** presents with lower abdominal pain. There is also anorexia and

malaise. Body temperature rises to 102°F to 103°F (38·8°C-39·5°C). Vomiting may also occur. Lochia is a common feature which may often be profuse and malodorous but may also be scanty and odourless. Diagnosis of the condition is made on clinical grounds.

- Cases of **hypercalcaemia** present with anorexia, vomiting, constipation, abdominal pain and ileus. There may be polyuria, nocturia and polydipsia.
- **Hypomagnesaemia** presents with multiple metabolic and nutritional deficiencies. It gives rise to anorexia, lethargy, vomiting, weakness and tetany. Development of hypocalcaemia and hypokalaemia are common in the condition. Blood shows reduced level of magnesium.
- Vomiting, malabsorption and symptoms simulaing gastrointestinal carcinoma may be the occasional features of **non-Hodgkin's lymphoma.** Otherwise, the condition is characterised by painless lymphadenopathy and symptoms appear due to the size and site of the enlarged lymph node mass and the pressure they exert on the neighbouring structures.
- Symptoms of **warm type autoimmune haemolytic anaemia** vary but anaemia from haemolysis is a common feature. There may also be prostration, fever and vomiting. Haemoglobinuria and haemosiderinuria occur occasionally. Enlargement of spleen is also a common feature.
- **Whooping cough** is characterised by paroxysms of cough ending in a 'whoop' upon inhalation. The strains of cough make the face puffy between the attacks, and may give rise to sub-conjunctival haemorrhage, epistaxis and blood-streaked sputum. Vomiting is common during the paroxysms.
- **Diphtheria** when involves the pharynx (*pharyngeal diphtheria*), the condition then begins with pallor, headache and vomiting. There may be pharyngeal oedema, sore throat and dysphagia. Soon dirty white or grayish yellow pseudomembrane develops, appearing first on the tonsils as thick gelatinous exudate, and then spreading to the pillars and pharyngeal wall, which may occasionally extend to the larynx and bronchi or to the nose.
- **Rat-bite fever** develops due to streptobacillus infection or spirillum infection. In the former, soon after healing of the primary lesion the condition gives rise to chills, septic fever, vomiting, headache and backache. There may also be morbiliform, petechial skin rash on the hands and feet. In the latter, infection however, there may be chills, relapsing fever, regional lymphadenitis, splenomegaly, and leucocytosis.
- **Cryptococcosis** is characterised by granulomatous lesions in the meninges and in other organs of the body and skin. It also gives rise to severe headache, malaise, fever, vomiting, blurred vision, stiffness of neck, and paralysis or convulsion. Diagnosis is made by identification of the causative fungus from sputum, pus, body fluids or cerebrospinal fluid.
- Increasing sore throat, headache, severe muslce ache, malaise, chills, high fever, anorexia and vomiting are the presenting features of **lassa fever.** Pain in the chest and epigastrium is common. Abdominal pain and vomiting become increasingly severe from the second week of the condition. Blood shows leucopenia with relative neutrophilia, and elevated levels of analine aminotransferase (ALT, formerly SGPT), asparate aminotransferase (AST, formerly SGOT), creatine kinase and lactate dehydrogenase.

OEDEMA AND ASCITES

Oedema indicates accumulation of excess fluid in the cells, tissues and serous cavities. Ascites represents accumulation of serous fluid in the peritoneal cavity. Both these manifestations (Table 20) are sometimes encountred with in a wide variety of disorders, more particularly in cardiac, hepatic and renal disorders. They are also reckoned as important signs and thus, serve a useful purpose in cases of diagnosis.

There are several conditions in which both these two manifestations are seen occuring together. Their independent development is not however infrequent, and there are several disorders which include either oedema or ascites.

- **Fulminant hepatic failure** is characterised by sudden severe impairment of liver function with hepatic encephalopathy. In this condition, ascites and oedema develop several days after. Otherwise, the condition presents with weakness, nausea, vomiting, fever, sweating, delirium and hypotension. Later, there may be confusion, slurred speech, hiccough, disorientation and finally convulsion. The patient gives a sweet smell on breathing and the extending hands show flapping tremors. There may also be purpura and overt bleeding, and rapidly progressing jaundice. Liver is initially palpable but later becomes inpalpable. Diagnosis of the condition is made on clinical grounds.
- **Carcinona of liver**, when develops as ***hepatocellular carcinoma***, gives rise to loss of body weight, cachexia, abdominal pain, jaundice, ascites and oedema. An audible bruit or friction rub may be heard over the tumour. Liver is enlarged and tender, and a mass may be palpable at right upper quadrant.

  Metastatic carcinoma gives rise to loss of body weight, ascites and oedema. Liver is enlarged and hard, and may also be tender. Hepatic bruit or friction rub is not common. Jaundice develops if there is biliary obstruction. There may also be splenomegaly.

  A sudden deterioration of pateint's condition with cirrhosis of liver is often suggestive for hepatocellular carcinoma, while in metastatic carcinoma, there is evidence of carcinoma elsewhere in the body.
- In **cardiac failure** symptoms vary due to involvement of the left or right ventricle. The condition however gives rise to dyspnoea, cyanosis, sweating, and cough. Dependent oedema is common, affecting first the ankles and dorsum of the feet. Soon there is pitting oedema in the lower extremities. The oedema gradually extent to the trunk. There may also be ascites. Diagnosis of the condition is made on clinical grounds.
- **Mitral stenosis** presents with dyspnoea and pulmonary hypertension. There may be high-coloured cheeks and lips, oedema of ankles, ascites, and pleural effusion. The condition gives rise to tapping apex beat, pulsation on left of sternum and lateral shifting of right border of cardiac dullness. First sound is accentuated, intense, sharp and of snapping type. Doubling of first sound is heard in the region of the apex beat. X-ray chest shows straightening of

left cardiac border, doubie contour of right border, dilatation of upper pulmonary veins, bat-wing shadow in hilar region, calcification and, in cases of cardiac failure, enlargement of the heart.

- **Tricuspid stenosis** is often associated with mitral stenosis, and pulmonary congestion may be an important presenting feature. There may also be hepatomegaly, distended jugular venis, dependent oedema and ascites. The condition presents with mid-diastolic thrill and low-pitched blowing presystolic murmur, best heard over the fifth intercostal space at lower right or left sternal border.
- In **tricuspid regurgitation,** there may be pleural effusion, oedema and ascites. There may also be cyanosis. The jugular veins are distended, and the liver is enlarged. The condition gives rise to pansystolic blowing murmur, accentuated by inspiration, and is best heard at fourth and fifth intercostal space at left or right sternal edge.
- **Chronic constrictive pericarditis** presents with fatigue, dyspnoea and cyanosis. There is gross ascites with a disproportionately smaller amount of peripheral oedema in the lower extremities and scrotum. Liver is enlarged and the neck veins are markedly distended.
- **Chronic nephritic syndrome** is usually asymptomatic till its late stage. Otherwise, it presents with nausea, vomiting, polyuria, thirst, pruritus and diarrhoea. Skin and tongue may be dry. Face is pale with puffiness of the eyelids and cheeks. There is also oedema of the feet and ankles, ascites, anaemia and osteomalacia. The patient may often give a history of suffering from acute nephritic syndrome or from nephrotic syndrome.
- **Nephrotic syndrome** presents with weakness, anorexia, malaise, puffy eyelids, abdominal pain, protruberant abdomen, and wasting of muscles. The condition is principally featured by hypoproteinaemic oedema and marked proteinuria. There is localised oedema and ascites. There may be pleural effusion, pericardial fullness, laryngeal oedema, hydrarthrosis and scrotal oedema. Oliguria is also common. Renal biopsy can confirm the diagnosis.
- **Kwashiorkor** is a deficiency disorder of protein-energy malnutrition of childhood. The affected infant presents with retardation of growth. The child fails to gain weight, and shows oedema on the feet. There may also be oedema on the hands and face, perhaps little ascites and pleural effusion. Reduced body weight for age in comparison to normal standard is diagnostic for protein-energy malnutrition.
- **Intestinal lymphangiectasia** presents with mild intermittent diarrhoea, nausea, vomiting and abdominal pain. There is oedema which may be massive and is usually asymmetrical. There may also be ascites and chylorous effusions.
- In **ancylostomaisis,** general symptoms vary and depend upon the degree of infestation. Development of anaemia is however common. In severe infestation the condition may give rise to fever, ascites, oedema of the feet and ankles, headache, palpitation, dizziness and tachycardia. Stools always contain occult blood. Diagnosis of the condition is made by the identification of eggs in the feces.
- With heavy infection **fasciolopsiasis** gives rise to cramping epigastric pain, nausea, anorexia and loose motions. Oedema and ascites however develop when the

TABLE 20

Some cases of Oedema and Ascites.

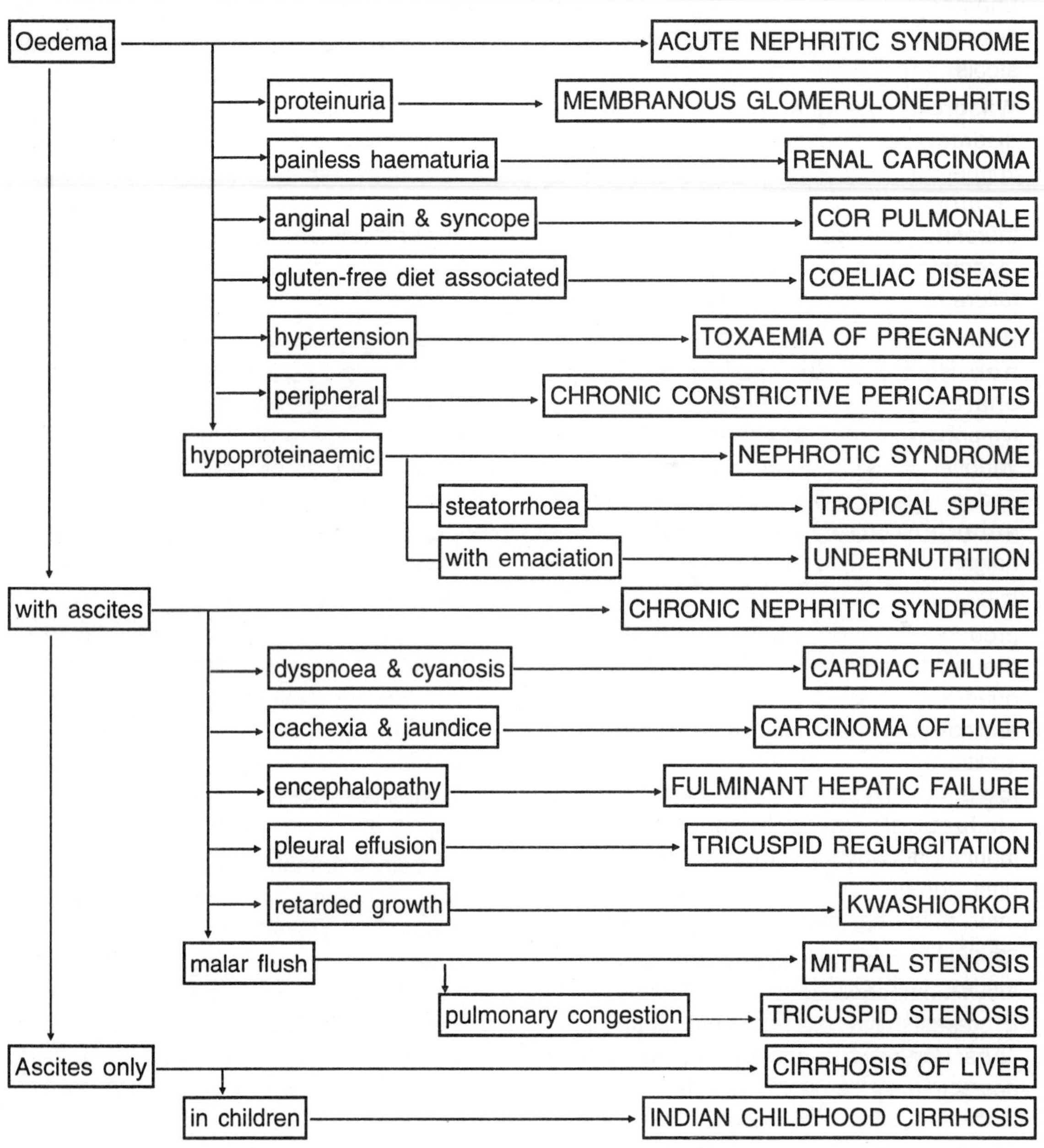

infection is very heavy. Diagnosis of the condition is made by identification of unembryonated operculated ova. Adult fluke may also occasionally be seen in the stools.

- **Wilson's disease** is a rare hereditary disorder resulting due to abnormality in copper metabolism which causes hepatic insufficiency in some. The condition therefore leads to cirrhosis and gives rise to oedema, ascites and progressive liver failure.
- Both **Hodgkin's lymphoma** and **non-Hodgkin's lymphoma** are characterised by generalised lymphdenopathy. They therefore produce varieties of symptoms, including ascites and oedema, from the pressure of the enlarged lymph node mass on the neighbouring structures.
- **Cor pulmonale** may present with chronic productive cough and dyspnoea. Later, there are oedema, pain in right upper quadrant, wheezing, perhaps substernal anginal pain and syncope on exertion. In addition, there are prominent pulsations at lower end of the sternum or at the epigastrium, gallop rhythm, distended jugular veins, pulmonary emphysema and right-sided cardiac failure. Crepitant rales over the lung base and distant breath sounds are heard. Liver is enlarged and tender.
- In **cardiomyopathy** however, *restrictive (obstructive) cardiomyopathy* is characterised by obstruction in ventricular inflow and by endomyocardial fibrosis, and presents with dependent oedema and hepatomegaly. The condition produces dilated neck veins, elevated jugular venous pressure, and left or right sided cardiac failure with normal heart size.
- **Venous thrombosis** may be asymptomatic or there may be tenderness, pain, oedema, local wormth, cyanosis of skin and slight fever. Superficial arterial pulse may be lost. The condition is diagnosed by venography and may be confirmed by impedence plethysmography.
- **Acute nephritic syndrome** has varieties of symptoms but in children, it gives rise to puffiness around the eyes and face. There may be discomfort or pain in the flank or upper abdomen. Also headache, malaise, mild fever, nausea, vomiting, anorexia and respiratory distress may be present. The patient may complain of low urinary output with blood-stained urine. There may be oedema, particularly around the ankles, and pleural effusion in severe cases. There may also be tachycardia, increased pulse rate and raised jugular venous pressure. In adults, the condition however develops insidiously with progressive fatigue and slowly developing oedema of the lower limbs or hypertension.
- **Rapidly progressive nephritic syndrome** develops insidiously and often presents with acute nephritic syndrome-like manifestations. Abdominal pain and arthralgia are common manifestations. Haematuria is also common but proteinuria is variable. Hypertension is an infrequent accompaniment. Oedema develops in many cases.
- **Minimal change nephropathy** begins with massive proteinuria, and the patient presents with generalised oedema, and pale and puffty face. Progressive deterioration of health may be a characteristic feature of the condition. There is however no haematuria or hypertension.
- In **membranous glomerulonephritis** proteinuria is the earliest manifestation but

generalised oedema develops with pale and puffy face when proteinuria is severe. Later, there is progressive deterioration of health. Renal function does not show any impairment, initially.

- **Membranoproliferative glomerulonephritis** is characterised by the manifestations of acute nephritic syndrome or of nephrotic syndrome. Patients present with puffy eyelids. There are haematuria, proteinuria and oedema.
- **Focal segmental glomerulosclerosis** presents with nephrotic syndrome-like manifestations, including generalised oedema wirth accumulation of fluid in the interstitial tissue. Signs of renal function impairment appear as the condition progresses.
- **Renal carcinoma** presents with recurrent painless haematuria but may give rise to renal colic due to blood clot. There may also be pain in the abdomen or flank, long continued fever, symptoms of metastases in the lungs, liver or bones, and oedema of the legs. X-ray may show enlarged kindey. Either excretory urography or retrograde pyelography or both can establish the presence of the tumour.
- In **undernutrition** the person appears emaciated, thin and skinny. In this condition famine oedema develops, often preceded by a period of nocturnal polyuria. There may also be diarrhoea.
- **Beriberi** gives rise to anorexia, malaise, heavyness and weakness of the legs, muscle cramps, little oedema of the legs or face, and fatigue. Diagnosis of the condition is made on clinical grounds.
- **Scurvy** is characterised by haemorrhagic manifestations. In addition there is femoral neuropathy, oliguria, oedema of lower extremities, and impaired vascular reactivity. A suggestive dietary and social history may be available, which may well be diagnostic.
- **Coeliac disease** may be asymptomatic or may present with voluminous, pale, frothy, foul-smelling stools and, in adults, diarrhoea. There is also bone pain, paraesthesia, peripheral neuropathy, oedema, dermatitis herpetiformis and clubbing of finger nails, A trial with gluten free diet brings an immediate dramatic improvement.
- **Tropical sprue** gives rise to urgency of defaecation, often after meals, but in increased frequency in severe cases. There is steatorrhoea with no abdominal pain but abdominal distension and borborygmi are common. Tongue appears sore, fiery, red, furred and painful. There may also be hypoproteinaemic oedema and follicular keratitis. Diagnosis of the condition is made on clinical grounds.
- In **iron deficiency anaemia** the presentation of symptoms depend on the extent of anaemia. Gradually however the condition gives rise to exertional dyspnoea, giddiness and palpitation. There are also cardiac dilatation, systolic murmur, oedema of the ankles, and enlargement of liver. Tongue looks bald and glazed. Blood shows hypochromic microcytic anaemia with anisocytosis and poikilocytosis.
- **Pernicious anaemia** gives rise to weakness, debility, loss of body weight, soreness of tongue, palpitation and tachycardia. Exertional dyspnoea is present but is not so marked. There is also pallor of skin and mucous membrane, oedema of ankles, cardiac dilatation, systolic murmur, spasticity, and hyperreactive reflexes. Tongue is smooth

and atrophic, or red and inflammed. Spleen is enlarged in some cases. Blood shows hyperchromic macrocytic anaemia with aniocytosis, poikilocytosis and fragmented red cells.

- **Sideroblastic anaemia** presents with all symptoms and signs of anaemia. Oedema of ankles however develop in severe cases. Blood shows hypochromic microcytic anaemia and increased level of iron. Bone marrow is hypercellular but may also show dyplastic changes mimicking megaloblastic anaemia.
- In **haemolytic disease of newborn** symptoms vary on the severity. There are however, signs of anaemia, oedema and enlargement of liver. Spleen may also be enlarged. Jaundice usually develops 24 hours after birth and may progress to further deepening. Diagnosis is made on clinical grounds.
- **Chronic lymphatic leukaemia** presents with lymphadenopathy. The condition may therefore present with pressure symptoms due to enlarged lymph nodes and the pressure they exert on the neighbouring structures, causing respiratory difficulties from tracheal compression or oedema of the legs. It presents wih mild but increasing anaemia. Bone marrow shows reduced megakaryocytes and an increase in both small and large lymphocytes.
- **Malaria** is characterised by paroxysms of chills and fever. In severe infection with *Plasmodium malariae* however there may be nephrosis in the children, with generalised oedema, oliguria, proteinuria and hypoproteinaemia.
- The manifestations of **polyarteritis nodosa** vary widely, and may include fever, sweating, abdominal pain, tachycardia, localised oedema, oliguria, convulsions and organic psychosis. Diagnosis of the condition may be confirmed by biopsy of the artery.
- **Mediastinal tumour** produces symptoms due to pressure on the neighbouring structures. When it causes compression on superior vena cava it produces oedema and cyanosis of head and neck. X-ray of chest often reveals the presence of the tumour.
- **Gullain-Barré syndrome** is characterised by flaccid paralysis of the muscle. There may also be hyperhidrosis, oedema and postural hypotension. Diagnosis of the condition is made on clinical grounds.
- In **hypothyroidism** the patient may present with dull and swollen face with puffy eyelids, thick lips and enlarged tongue. The condition gives rise to slow pulse, cardiac enlargement, pericardial effusion, peripheral oedema and clamsy gait.
- The symptoms and signs of **sunburn** depend on the duration and intensity of exposure and may give rise to redness to swelling and perhaps blister formation on the exposed parts of the body. In severe cases, there may also be nausea, chills, fever, tachycardia, shock, and oedema of the ankles, legs, face and upper parts of the body.
- **Premenstrual tension** is characterised by systemic and psychological manifestations which occur prior to menstruation but subside following the onset of menses. In addition, there may be several other symptoms, such as backache, mastalgia, oliguria, oedema and temporary gain of body weight.
- **Myoma of uterus** is usually asymptomatic till its size and site causes pressure symptoms or the myoma becomes twisted

on its pedicle. However, when it produces symptoms there may be vaginal discharge, dyspareunia, frequency and urgency of micturition, retention of urine, oedema in the lower extremity, constipation and painful defaecation. Large myoma can easily be felt through bimanual pelvic examination.

- **Sarcoma of uterus** gives rise to abnormal uterine bleeding and leucorrhoea. There may be frequency of micturition. Oedema develops on the legs. Jaundice may develop occasionally. Cytology of vaginal exudates may identify the malignant cells, but biopsy of the tumour can confirm the diagnosis.
- In **hydatiform mole,** hypertension, generalised oedema and albuminuria develop during the second trimester but due to development of toxaemia of pregnancy.
- In **toxaemia of pregnancy**, the first presenting symptom appears to be sudden excessive gain of body weight in pre-clampsia. Soon this is followed by pitting oedema. Oedema is initially manifested on the feet and ankles. Gradually it becomes apparent in the legs, then to the trunk and upper extremity, and finally to the face. Soon symptoms of hypertension become apparent. In addition, the condition presents with albuminuria.
- In **cholestatic jaundice** there are yellow coloration of the sclerae, skin and mucous membrane of the mouth, clay-coloured or pale stools, and steatorrhoea. There may also be malaise, anorexia, vomiting, ascites, and various neurological manifestations.
- **Chronic active hepatitis** presents with fatigue, anorexia and jaundice. The condition presents with fever, arthralgia, superficial bruising, epistaxis, spider telangiectasia and hepatosplenomegaly. In addition, there may be lymphadenopathy, ascites, haemolytic anaemia, inflammatory skin lesions and urticaria. Diagnosis of the condition is made by liver biopsy.
- **Cirrhosis of liver** may be asymptomatic or may present with variable symptoms. There may therefore be weakness, fatigue, nausea, vomiting, anorexia, flatulence, diarrhoea or constipation, muscle wasting, swelling of parotid gland and spider telangiectasia. There may also be central cyanosis, clubbing of fingers, diffuse erythema on the palms, ascites and peripheral neuropathy.
- **Indian childhood cirrhosis** begins with anorexia or voracious appetite, lassitude, abdominal distension with flatulence, low-grade fever, constipation or diarrhoea with clay-coloured stools, irritability and apathy. Later, there may be jaundice, symptoms of portal hypertension, ascites, anaemia and rapid pulse. Diagnosis of the condition is usually made on clinical grounds.
- The clinical features in **haemochromatosis** depend upon the organ involved. Therefore, there may be cirrhosis of liver with ascites, diabetes mellitus or cardiac failure. Blood shows elevated levels of both iron and ferritin. Diagnosis is confirmed by liver biopsy.
- **Biliary cirrhosis** gives rise to pruritus and jaundice. There may be ascites and portal hypertension. Liver is enlarged, hard and sometimes rough in *primary biliary cirrhosis* but in *secondary biliary cirrhosis*, it is enlarged and tender. Spleen is also enlarged. Liver biopsy can confirm the diagnosis. Ultrasonography and

cholangiography are also useful diagnostic aids.

- **Portal hypertension** gives rise to abdominal pain and ascites. Jaundice may also be present. Liver is enlarged, soft and tender. Spleen is also enlarged. When collateral circulation develops, evidence of gastrointestinal bleeding may be available.
- **Carcionma of stomach** is usually asymptomatic during the early stage. Otherwise, there are vague complaints of abdominal discomfort, loss of appetite, slight nausea and peptic ulcer-like manifestations. Later, there is change in bowel habit, and the patient complains of alternating constipation and diarrhoea. There are also pallor, ascites, jaundice, anaemia, haematemesis, melaena, visible peristalsis, and palpable abdominal mass. Barium meal x-ray may show filling defect. Diagnosis is confirmed by endoscopic examination and biopsy.
- **Carcinoma of pancreas** presents with epigastric pain that radiates to the neck. The pain is exaggerated following food and from lying supine but relieved by crouching forward. In its late stage, obstructive jaundice develops. There may also be ascites.
- **Syphilis** when develops in children as *early congenital syphilis,* it gives rise to rhinitis, mucopurulent or blood-stained nasal discharges, condylomata lata, onychia and paronychia, ascites and splenomegaly.
- **Carcinoma of ovary** is usually asymptomatic in the early stage but otherwise gives rise to vague complaints, usual being nonspecific gastrointestinal symptoms and lower abdominal discomfort. Later, there is pelvic pain. Ascites may also develop. Diagnosis of the condition is made by Papanicolaou test of vaginal smear.
- **Meig's syndrome** presents with abdominal distension or respiratory distress. Development of ascites is common. Diagnosis of the condition is made on clinical grounds but needs surgical exploration for confirmation.

PALPITATION

Palpitation is a subjective symptom of increased pulsation of heart which though often remain benign but may at times cause annoyance. The affected person feels an accelerated heart beat inside the chest, causing no effect. It is frequently seen in the states of fear or anxiety. It may also be a part of general manifestations of several disorders but usually of no clinical significance.

- A subjective sense of terror for no apparent reason is the beginning of **anxiety neuroses**. The patient may present with sweating, tremor, dizziness and palpitations. There may be tachycardia, occasional premature beats, precordial pain and generalised motor weakness. A sense of air hunger may also develop.
- **Ventricular tachycardia** gives rise to palpitation, dizziness and loss of consciousness. There may be hypotension, shock and pulmonary oedema. Ventricular rate varies between 140 and 200 per minute, and carotid sinus massage does not bring any difference. First heart sound may vary in intensity.
- In **supraventricular tachycardia,** the patient may feel a sudden increase in heart beat. In severe attack there is a feeling of tightness in chest, palpitation, chest pain and shortness of breath. There may be polyuria during or after the attack. Fall of peripheral blood pressure is a common feature.
- **Atrial fibrillation** may be asymptomatic or the patient may not be aware of it except in cases of paroxysmal atrial fibrillation, and then the patient may feel of having an irregularly irregular pulse. There may also be palpitation, pallor, nausea, weakness and fatigue. The increasing atrial pressure may eventually lead to cardiac shock or pulmoanry oedema.
- In **atrial flutter** the clinical features are usually indistinguishable with those of paroxysmal supraventricular tachycardia. There are therefore weakness, palpitation, fainting and polyuria. Atrial rate becomes more rapid, ranging between 240 and 400, usual being 300 per minute. Pulse is rapid but regular with a rate of about 150 per minute. Almost all heart sounds are louder than normal, and the first sound varies in intensity from beat to beat.
- **Mitral stenosis** presents with dyspnoea. There is tachycardia and fatigue. Pulmonary cogestion may give rise to cough while pulmonary hypertension may cause haemoptysis. Palpitation and chest pain occur rarely. There is low collapsing pulse but may be irregularly irregular if associated with atrial fibrillation. The condition produces taping apex beat, pulsation on left of sternum and lateral shifting of right border of cardiac dullness. X-ray of the chest shows straightening of left cardiac border, double contour of right border, dilatation of upper pulmonary veins, bat-wing shadow in hilar region, and calcification.
- **Mitral regurgitation** gives rise to fatigue, exertional dyspnoea, followed by paroxysmal nocturnal dyspnoea and orthopnoea, palpitations and symptoms and signs of cardiac failure. The condition

produces strong heaving apical impulse, pansytolic murmur maximum at the apex, often radiating to the axilla and may be associatred with a thrill, displacement of apex beat to the left, prominent third sound or short mid-diastolic murmur, and clicking opening snaps.

- In **cardiomyopathy,** palpitation may be a feature of *hypertrophic cardiomyopathy.* There may also be dyspnoea, anginal pain, syncope and dizziness. The pulse is perhaps jerky but sustained. There are double apical impulse, third heart sound, mid-systolic murmur, mitral regurgitation, and signs of pulmonary hypertension.
- **Hypertension** does not usually give rise to any specific symptom. In general, the symptoms which are commonly encountered with are headache, dizziness, flushed face, trembling, nausea, vomiting, muscular weakness, tinnitus, palpitations, nervousness, irritability and polyuria. Diagnosis of the condition is made on elevation of systolic and/or diastolic blood pressure levels at rest than that is expected to be normal, continued on 3 seprate occasions.
- **Iron deficiency anaemia** usually gives rise to vague symptoms. Gradually the condition gives rise to exertional dyspnoea, giddiness and palpitation. There is pallor of skin and mucous membrane. Blood shows hypochromic microcytic anaemia with aniocytosis and poikilocytosis, reduced haemoglibin, perhpas slightly reduced red cell count, low mean corpuscular haemoglobin and mean corpsucular volume, reduced mean corpuscular haemoglobin concentration, low erythrocyte sodimentation rate, leucocytosis with relative lymphocytosis and thrombocytopenia.
- **Pernicious anaemia** presents with weakness, debility, soreness of tongue, palpitation and tachycardia. Exertional dyspnoea is present which is however not so marked. Blood shows hyperchromic macrocytic anaemia with marked anisocytosis, poikilocytosis and fragmented red cells, raised mean corpuscular volume, leucopenia with relative neutropenia, hypersegmented neutrophils, diminished platelet court, raised erythrocyte sedimentation rate, and low level of vitamin B_{12}.
- **Sideroblastic anaemia** presents with usual symptoms of anaemia. There is also palpitation, dizziness, dimness of vision and paraesthesias in the fingers and toes. Blood shows hypochromic microcytic anaemia and increased level of iron. Bone marrow is hypercellular but may also show dyplastic changes mimicking megaloblastic anaemias.
- **Aplastic anaemia** presents with headache, dimness of vision, bleeding in the skin and mucous membrane, heamaturia, haemorrhagic tendencies, necrotic ulcers in the mouth and throat, coma and stupor or delirium, along with usual symptoms of anaemia. There are pallor, palpitation, tachycardia, systolic murmur and cardiac dilatation. The condition gives rise to normochromic normocytic anaemia. Peripheral blood shows pancytopenia, and reduced number of red cells and platelets.
- In **gastrointestinal bleeding** the severity of clinical manifestations depends on the source and rate of bleeding. In general, there may be weakness, faintness, nausea, sweating, easy fatiguability, palpitation, pallor and irritablity. Massive haemorrhage may eventually cause shock

and renal failure. Diagnosis of the condition is made on clinical grounds.

- **Cushing's syndrome** presents with gain of body weight, central obesity, and accumulation of fat at the lower part of the back of neck with rounding of face, protuberant abdomen and thin extremities. In addition, there are easy bruisability, facial acne, headache and backache. The patient may also complain of dyspnoea, palpitation and hypertension. A history of ACTH treatment may be available. Clinical manifestations of the condition may be suggestive.
- **Pheochromocytoma** presents with paroxysmal or sustained hypertension and extreme pallor or flushing of the face or extremities. Headache may be severe. There may be discomfort in the chest, dyspnoea, palpitations, postural tachycardia and cardiac enlargement. There may be glycosuria or hyperglycaemia with normal thyroxine level in the blood.
- **Hyperthyroidism** may present with increased appetite, loss of body weight, pruritus, increased frequency of bowel movement or diarrhoea, hot and sweaty hands, intolerance to warmth, nervousness, anxiety, fine tremors of the fingers and tongue, mild weakness of proximal muscles and wasting of muscles and bone. There may be tachycardia or arrhythmias, palpitation with or without the symptoms of cardiac failure, increased pulse pressure and perhaps detectable capillary pulsation.
- When **hypoglycaemia** develops as complication of *diabetes mellitus,* the patient then presents with malaise, nausea, tachycardia, palpitations, faintness, dizziness, diplopia and mental donfusion.
- **Ancylostomiasis** characteristically produces anaemia. There may also be fever, ascites, oedema of feet and ankles, headache, palpitation, dizziness, tachycardia, breathlessness and signs of cardiac failure. Diagnosis of the condition is made by the identification of eggs in the faeces. Stool always contain occult blood.
- **Beriberi** is characterised by a triad of peripheral neuropathy, oedema and myocardial weakness. Abdominal discomfort and constipation are common. In addition, there are irritation, poor memory, sleep disturbances, palpitations, and pericardial pain. Diagnosis is made on clinical grounds.
- **Epilepsy** begins with a prodromal phase in which there may be dreamy state or feeling of strangeness, change of mood, sudden myoclonic jerks in the limbs, abdominal pain, hiccoughs, headache, palpitation, feeling of choking, depression and euphoria.
- In **menopausal syndrome** there is no definite mode of symptomatology. The subjective symptoms the condition produce may include many things, most frequent being malaise, fatigue, arthralgia, myalgia, dizziness and headache. There may also be tinnitus, fainting, palpitation, tachycardia and dyspnoea.

PHOTOPHOBIA

Photophobia means fear of light that develops due to abnormal visual intolerance to light. The symptom therefore causes great inconvenience to the affected persons. It is encountered only in a few disorders but has no clinical importance in terms of diagnosis.

- Photophobia is a common manifestation in **measles**. Otherwise, the condition presents with fever, sneezing, coryza, short dry cough, and discharges from the eyes. Conjunctivae appear red and oedematous. Presence of tiny white eruptions surrounded by inflammatory areola (Koplik's spots) on the buccal mucosae and often on the inner conunctival folds and vaginal mucous membrane make the diagnosis easy.
- **Migraine** characteristically presents with severe and throbbing unilateral headache. This may be preceded by depression, irritability, restlessness, anorexia, sweating, photophobia and prostration. The patient complains of a sensation of white or coloured lights. Vomiting is common.
- **Hyperthyroidism** presents with hot and sweaty hands, intolerance to warmth, fine tremors of fingers and tongue, low-grade fever, nervousness, anxiety and mild weakness of proximal muscles. There may also be increased lacrimation, photophobia, pre-orbital oedema, lack of visual accomodation and, even, diplopia.
- **Systemic lupus erythematosus** may involve multisystem and may therefore produce symptoms accordingly. Depending on the system involved the condition can give rise to varieties of symptoms, including transient or migratory arthralgia or more persistent polyarthritis with or without active synovitis, erythematous 'butterfly' rash or dusky red discoloration of skin of the nose and cheeks, pericarditis, endocarditis, myocarditis, generalised lymphadenopathy, pruritus, organic psychosis, hemiplegia, peripheral neuropathy, photophobia and conjunctivitis.
- Large number of cases of **leptospirosis** may remain undiagnosed. In others, there may be headache, severe muscle pain, anorexia, nausea, frequent vomiting, chills and fever. Prostration is always severe. Sometimes there may be cough or chest pain, and conjunctival suffusion with photophobia. Occasionally, the causative organism can be identified in blood by dark-field microscopy during the first 10 days.
- **Relapsing fever** begins with chills, fever, nausea, vomiting, intense headache, and muscle and joint pains. Face is flushed, and eyes are injected. Photophobia is common. There may be varieties of skin rash. Liver and spleen are frequently palpable and tender. Development of jaundice is common. The causative organism can be isolated and identified from peripheral blood during the febrile period.
- The initial lesion in **rickettsial pox** appears as a small, firm, papule at the site of mite bite. About a week after the condition gives rise to intermittent fever, chills, headache, profuse sweating, disseminated aches and pains, and photophobia. Diagnosis of the

condition is made by isolation of the causative rickettsia.

- **Yellow fever** begins with malaise, headache, backache, muscle pains, photophobia, chills or rigor, and fever. Nausea and vomiting develop thereafter. The pulse is initially rapid and bounding but becomes slow from the second day than that is expected from the degree of temperature (Faget's sign).

PRURITUS

Pruritus or itching is a disturbing symptom. It is frequently seen in several dermatological disorders. Its presence in other disorders is however not infrequent.

- **Atopic dermatitis** is charactrised by pruritus. It gives rise to erythematous papular or papulovesicular lesions in the infants. In the older children and adults, the condition shows lichenified lesions.
- Pruritus is a manifestation on **seborrhoeic dermatitis.** The condition usually produces dry, moist or greasy scales with or without erythema. The skin lesions often show remissions and exacerbations.
- **Contract dermatitis** presents with skin rash on the exposed parts of the body. Pruritus is a common feature. There may also be hotness and swelling of the area with exudation and crusting, and excoriation.
- In **exfoliative dermatitis,** the skin is thickened and the patient looks uncomfortable and irritable. There may be itching, chills, rigor, fever or excessive heat loss and, in late stage, loss of hair and nails.
- **Dermatitis herpetiformis** produces vesicles, papules, and urticaria-like lesions on extensor surfaces, usually distributed symmetrically. The lesions are intensely itchy, with burning sensation.
- **Lichen planus** gives rise to flat-topped or umbilicated nodules with whitish puncta or streaks. There may be mild to severe itching.
- **Erythema multiforme** presents with symmetrical erythematous lesions on the skin or mucous membrane with a tendency of recurrences. Sometimes the lesions are urticarial, pustular or haemorrhagic. Erosion of the lesions of mucous membrane of the mouth, genitalia and eyes may occur. There may also be pruritus, burning sensations and fever.
- **Rosacea** is characterised by recurrent episodes of erythema or telangiectasia. It causes itching, burning or stinging.
- **Acne** gives rise to open comedones, closed comedones, papules or pustules. There may be no other symptom or there may be mild soreness, pain or itching, and varieties of emotional disturbances, including embarrassement.
- **Urticaria** may be localised or generalised, and usually presents with intense itching and a burning sensation. This is followed by eruptions of evanscent wheals or hives with rings of erythema and oedema.
- **Psoriasis** presents with characteristic skin lesions. The lesions are well demarcated, usually asymptomatic, and only occasionally may give rise to itching and burning.
- **Miliaria** presents with acute inflammatory eruptions of the skin, accompanied by severe itching, burning and irritation. Repeated scratching may lead to excoriation and infection.
- **Chilblain** produces painful, burning and itchy erythematous lesions with oedema or blistering on the fingers and toes, generally. The affected part is cold, clammy and cyanotic but the colour disappears on pressure.

- **Impetigo** is manifested by localised erythematous areas of itching, stinging and burning on the skin flexures.
- **Sunburn** gives rise to redness, swelling, and perhaps blister formation on the exposed parts of the body. There may be local burning, feeling of warmth, slight itching, pain and tenderness.
- **Scabies** presents with characteristic burrow. Itching is the usual complaint, which is more intense in the night. Scratching may cause secondary infection and pyoderma. Diagnosis of the condition is made by identification of the mite or ova.
- **Pediculosis** gives rise to no complaint except itching and the itching may be very intense even. Scratching may lead to excoriation over the affected areas. Detection of the louse is always possible.
- **Dermatophytosis** presents with patchy or scaling lesions with itching, and gives rise to several clinical entities.

  Tines corporis involves the exposed parts of the body with irregular patches and causes intense itching.

  Tinea capitis involves the scalp with itching or scaling. The lesion may also appear as localised boggy swelling.

  Tinea barbae produces localised boggy swelling on the beard area with itching.

  Tinea cruris involves the groins and presents with severe itching, worse at night and after changes of dresses following continuous use for few hours, and when the part of exposed to general environment.

  Tinea axillaries involves the axillae and, also, undersurface of the breasts in women, and gives rise to tinea cruris-like manifestations.

  Tinea mannum involves the palms and soles with scaling, fissures, papulovesicular or even pustular patches, and itching. There may also be burning, stinging or other sensations.
- **Chickenpox** begins with mild headache, backache, moderate fever, malaise and soon, usually within 24 hours, followed by development of characteristic skin rash and itching. Diagnosis is frequently made on clinical grounds.
- **Vulvitis** gives rise to burning sensation and pruritus on the vulvar region. The vulva appears markedly oedematous and erythematous. Severe itching may often lead to ulceration, vesicle and pustule formation.

  In chronic cases, there is however intractable pruritus and excoriation. Occurence of secondary pyogenic infection is quite common.
- In **vulvovaginitis,** pruritus is the frequent symptom, often associated with varying degree of vaginal discharge. There may also be burning on micturition.
- **Vaginitis** normally presents with vaginal discharge and depending on the organism involved, there may also be pruritus.

  Cases of ***senile vaginitis*** however present with purulent discharge, excoriation and soreness of vulva. There may be pruritus and dyspareunia.
- In **cholestàtic jaundice** there are yellow coloration of the sclerae, skin and mucous membrane of the mouth, clay-coloured or pale stools, and steatorrhoea. There may be discomfort or pain in the right upper quadrant, and pruritus, usually severe and generalised and most marked on the palms and soles. Diagnosis of the condition is made on clinical grounds.

- **Chronic active hepatitis** presents with fatigue, anorexia and jaundice. Other manifestaions of the condition include fever, arthralgia, epistaxis, superficial bruising, spider telangiectasia and haepatosplenomegaly. In addtion, there may be lymphadenopathy, ascites, inflammatory skin lesions and urticaria. Diagnosis of the condition is made by liver biopsy.
- **Billary cirrhosis** presents with pruritus, which is severe and more marked on the palms and soles. There may also be upper abdominal discomfort.
- **Cholangiocarcinoma** usually presents with obstructive jaundice. There may also be pain in the upper abdomen, loss of weight, and intense generalised itching.
- **Carcinoma of pancreas** gives rise to epigastric pain, which becomes exaggerated following foods and from lying supine but relieved by crouching forward. In late stage, painless obstructive jaundice develops and deepens progressively. There may also be intractable pruritus secondary to jaundice, and results to heavy excortiation and thickening of the skin.
- **Enterobiasis** may cause pruritus of perineal region, usually nocturnal. There may also be insomnia, restlessness, irritablity, enuresis and gastrointestinal symptoms. Adult worm can be seen near the anus or can be identified in the stools, and eggs on the perianal region.
- **Loiasis** is charactrised by the development of calabar swelling. Sometimes there may be urticaria, pruritus and allergic dermatitis. Usually *Loa loa* microfilariae can be detected from peripheral blood, and the filaria is strictly diurnal.
- **Rubella** generally begins with malaise and low-grade fever. Characteristically, it presents with enlarged sub-occipital, posterior cervical and postauricular lymph nodes. A fine skin rash appears usually within 24 hours and in adults, the rash may be extremely itchy.
- **Carcinoma of vulva** gives rise to hyperplastic dystrophy of the vulva, but the early lesions appear as chronic dermatitis of the vulva. The condition is usually asymptomatic but otherwise it may present with pruritus. Diagnosis of the condition is made on clinical grounds, supported by histopathological findings of the biopsy material.
- **Anaphylactoid purpura** presents with effusion of blood and plasma into the subcutaneous, submucous and subserous surface. There may be erythematous rash or urticaria and non-thrombocytopenic purpura, particularly evident on the areas of pressure. The skin lesions may be pruritic.
- **Hodgkin's lymphoma** may give rise to progressive weakness, excessive sweating, loss of body weight, puruitus, progressive anaemia, and low-grade fever persisting for several days and alternating with apyrexial periods. The condition is diagnosed by generalised enlargement of lymphoid tissue, and presence of Reed-Strenberg cells in lymph node biopsy.
- **Hypothyroidism** begins with weakness, lethargy, absence of sweating, dryness and roughness of skin, and dryness and brittleness of hair and nails. There is vague muscular and joint pains, decreased sense of taste and smell, and sensitivity to cold. There is also tingling in the fingers, fatigue, deafness, body weight gain, constipation,

hoarseness of voice, dizziness, pruritus and dyspnoea. The face appears dull and swollen with puffy eyelids, thick lips and enlarged tongue.

- In **hyperthyrodism** there may or may not be diffuse or nodular goitre. There may be increased appetite, loss of body weight, pruritus, increased frequency of bowel movement or diarrhoea, hot and sweaty hands, fine tremors of fingers and tongue, nervousness, and intolerance to warmth.
- **Hypoparathyroidism** characteristically gives rise to tetany, with muscle cramps, numbness and stiffness around the mouth, abdominal cramps, wheezing, dyspnoea, stridor and convulsion. The skin is dry and there may be pruritus.
- **Chronic nephritic syndrome** may remain asymptomatic or may present with fatigue, nausea, vomiting, polyuria, thirst, pruritus and diarrhoea. There may also be haematuria, drowsiness, hiccough, muscular twitchings, dyspnoea, loss of vision, fits and coma.
- **Acute renal failure** develops with symptoms of uraemia, such as fatigue, nausea, dyspepsia, vomiting and pruritus. There is gallop rhythm and an elevated blood pressure. Urine shows red and white cells, epithelial cells, granular and dirty brown casts, protein, increased level of sodium in maintenance phase, and low levels of creatine, creatinine and potassium.
- **Chronic renal failure** may be asymptomatic or may give rise to vague symptoms but proteinuria may be common. In others, symptoms develop due to uraemia, with progressive weakness, lethargy, anorexia, nausea, vomiting, pruritus, paraesthesia and vertigo. Tongue appears dry and brown coloured. Urine shows small amount of protein, white cells, epithelial cells, granular and waxy casts, and low level of creatine, creatinine, uric acid and potassium.
- **Polycystic kidney disease** presents with discomfort, pain or colic in the lumbar region, haematuria and slowly progressive hyprtension. Symptoms of uraemia (e.g. fatigue, nausea, vomiting, dyspepsia and pruritus) develop gradually. Urine shows proteinuria, varying degree of haematuria and even pyuria. Ultrasonogram or retrograde pyelogram can make the diagnosis.
- **Toxoplasmosis** may be asymptomatic or may present as mild, acute or chronic condition, with lymphadenopathy of one or more groups of glands. There may be malaise, headache, fever, sore throat, myalgia, arthralgia, stiff neck, maculopapular skin rash, and urticaria.
- Manifestations of **filariasis** vary, and there may be episodes of fever, with or without inflammation of the lymphatics and nodes, that come and go. There may also be chills, headache, malaise and urticaria. Inflammation of spermatic cord, epididymitis and orchitis are common. Diagnosis of the condition is made by identification of the microfilariae in the blood.
- **Onchocerciasis** may remain asymptomatic. Otherwise, there is pruritus and dermatoses which run a chronic course and the skin becomes rough and thickened. There may be one or several subcutaneous fibrous tumours. Diagnosis of the condition is made by identification of the microfilariae in skin snips or excised nodules.

- **Dracunculiasis** is charaterised by blister formation which gives rise to urticaria, nausea, vomiting, diarrhoea, dyspnoea and giddiness. As the blister forms and ruptures, the symptoms subside.
- **Chromomycosis** begins on the foot, leg or on the exposed part of the body where the skin is broken. It gives rise to red or violacious patch with an indurated base, containing small, itching papule, resembling ringworm. New crops of lesions may appear over the path of lymphatic drainage after several weeks or months. History of occupation may be a useful guide in cases of diagnosis.
- **Gout** is characterised by inflammatory arthritis of the peripheral joints, and urate deposits in the subcutaneous and other tissue, bone, cartilage and joints. There may also be fever, chills, rigors, pruritus and tachycardia.
- **Dengue** is characterised by 'saddle-back' pattern of temperature, muscle and joint pain, and lymphadenopathy. A skin rash appears on the third or fourth day of the illness. The rash lasts for several hours to days and may fade leaving desquamation and itching.
- **Pellagra** presents with slightly swollen and well-demarcated areas of erythematous rash which may itch and gives a burning sensation. Dietary habit is a useful guide in the diagnosis of the condition.

SKIN RASH

Skin rash is principally a manifestation of dermatological disorders. Varities of skin rash also occur in several inflammatory conditions as well. In many conditions the development of skin rash may be nonspecific and hence serves no purpose in terms of diagnosis. In other instances, its occurence is distinctive and the pattern by itself appears highly suggestive of a particular condition. In these cases skin rash therefore serves a useful purpose in diagnosis.

- **Chickenpox** begins with mild headache, backache, moderate fever and malaise. Soon, usually within 24 hours, skin rash appears, with itching. The lesion appears as vesicles in the oropharynx initially. Cutaneous rash appears in crops over 1 to 5 days, first appearing on the back or chest, or on the forehead or face, becomes numerous on the trunk and face, and relatively sparse over the extremities where the flexure surfaces are more affected than the extensor surfaces. Skin lesions develop as small, deep pink, slightly raised, ovoid papules, which within a few hours become fragile, thin-walled, translucent, umbilicated, glistening bleb like vesicles, containing clear fluid, surrounded by small red areola, in the most superficial layer of skin. Characteristically all stages of eruptions are seen in any area over any period of time. The vesicles later change to crusts and finally slough out in 7 to 14 days.
- **Smallpox** begins with severe prostration and fever which continues for 1 to 5 days and falls within 24 hours after the appearance of skin rash. The lesions contain macular rash with centrifugal distribution, appearing first on the face and scalp, then on the wrists, hands, neck, back, chest, arms, legs and face. The macules develop into papules in 1 to 4 days, then to vesicles in 1 to 4 days and finally to pustules in 2 to 6 days, Thereafter, crusts form which fall out 2 to 4 weeks after the first sign of skin lesion. Characteristically, all lesions are seen in the same stage of development in any area at any time. Disease does not exist now.
- **Measles** begins with fever, malaise, and short, dry cough. Fever and cough persist until skin rash appears and then subsides within 1 to 2 days. The skin rash appears as pin-head sized papules or dark red macules on the forehead or in front and behind the ears along the hair-line but soon involves the face and the sides of the neck and then spreads to the rest of the body. The rash rapidly increases in number and coalesce to form blotchy maculopapular rash. On the extremities the lesions are more pronounced on the extensor surfaces. The lesion is soft and valvety on touch, and fades on pressure.
- **Streptococcal sore throat** may at times gives rise to ***scarlet fever***. Within 24 to 36 hours after the advent of fever characteristic skin rash develops as small, firm, slightly raised, red papules, superimposed on diffusely erythematous skin surface, with no fluctuations in temperature. The rash blanches on pressure. It appears first at the behind of the ears and rapidly within 24 hours becomes a generalised punctate erythema,

covering the whole body. The distribution of the rash is variable but most intense on the neck, the skin folds and inner aspects of the arms and thighs.

- **Enteric fever** presents with a characteristic pattern of fever. During the second or third week of illness, maculopapular, slightly raised rash (rose spots) usually appears on the upper abdomen or anterior chest but disappears after 2 to 4 days. The rash is however extremely difficult even to recognise in dark-skinned persons.
- **Syphilis,** during its secondary stage, gives rise to widespread skin rash of various forms but often macular or papular. The rashes are non-itching, do not fade on pressure and are symmetrical in distribution, occuring mainly on the chest, abdomen, back and anus. Sometimes the skin lesions may be very faint and sparsely distributed or may appear for the first time or may become intensified due to Jarisch-Herxheimer reaction.
- **Systemic lupus erythematosus** gives rise to erythematous 'butterfly' rash or dusky red coloration of the skin of the neck and cheeks, and discoid and other varieties of skin lesions on the neck, upper chest, back and other parts of the body exposed to sunlight.
- **Discoid lupus erythematosus** presents with localised erythematous plaques with dry, horny, adherent scales, commonly occuring on the exposed parts of the body, particularly on the molar prominences and bridge of the nose and pinnae.
- **Atopic dermatitis** gives rise to bilateral, extremely itchy, erythematous papular or papulovesicular lesions on the cheeks, spreading to other parts, frequently involving the extensor surfaces in the infants. In older childern the lesions may show remissions and relapses, becoming more dry and lichenified, involving flexural areas, particularly the popilteal and antecubital fossae, and fingers, wrists, ankles and toes. In adults the lesions appear as erythematous and lichenified on any part of the body but more so on the flexures.
- **Seborrhoeic dermatitis** is characterised by dry, moist or greasy scales with or without erythema, and pruritus.

  In ***dandruff*** there is fine, thin, powdery, whitish or grayish, dry and slightly greasy scales, on the scalp with mild to moderate itching, or as waxy, grayish or yellowish scales and crusts.

  In ***cradle cap***, occuring in infants during the first month of life, there may be thick or thin, dirty, yellow or brownish-yellow, crusted lesions on the scalp.
- **Contact dermatitis** presents with erythematous macular, papular or papulovesicular eruptions, chiefly involving the exposed parts of the body. The lesions are distributed asymmetrically.
- **Lichen planus** gives rise to pin-head sized, multiple, purplish or violaceous, angular, flat-topped or umbilicated, smooth, glistening, slightly raised papules, with whitish puncta or streaks. The lesions are distributed symmetrically, commonly on the flexure surfaces of the wrists and on the hips, trunk, mouth, glans penis and vaginal mucosa.
- **Erythema multiforme** gives rise to generalised skin eruptions, distributed symmetrically and often arranged in concentric rings. The lesions are slightly raised, erythematous, flat-topped papules

or oedematous macules, wheals, visicles or bullae. The lesions appear on any part of the body but usually on the distal part of the extremities and the face.

- **Urticaria** gives rise to eruptions of evanscent wheals or hives with rings of erythema and oedema. The wheals may coalesce to form larger wheals. Crops of hives come and go. There may usually be intense itching and burning sensation.
- **Dermatitis herpetiformis** presents with tiny vesicles, papules, and urticaria-like eruptions on the face, neck and extensor surfaces of the body. The lesions are distributed symmetrically, with severe itching and burning.
- **Pellagra** presents with slightly swollen and well demarcated areas of erythematous rash, distributed symmetrically on the parts of the body exposed to sunlight, particularly on the neck. The rash may itch and gives a burning sensation.
- **Miliaria** presents with acute inflammatory eruptios, chiefly on the trunk, upper extremities and intertriginous areas, accompanied by severe itching, burning and irritation. Repeated scratching may lead to excoriation and secondary infection.
- **Chronic active hepatitis** may give rise to inflammatory skin lesions and urticaria. The other manifestations of the condition are fatigue, anorexia, jaundice, fever, arthralgia, superficial bruising, spider telangiectasia and hepatosplenomegaly.
- **Respiratory syncytial virus infection** gives rise to cough, dyspnoea, wheezing and bronchiolitis in infants. Rise of body tempreature is common. Occasionally an erythematous rash may appear on the body.
- **Herpes zoster** presents with boring pain with hyperaesthesia and lator, fever, malaise and severe pain in the distribution of the affected nerve root. A few days after, crops of vesicles appear over the skin supplied by the affected nerve.
- In **rubella** a fine, pink, slightly raised, maculopapular rash, initially behind the ears and on the forehead and face, appears usually within 24 hours from the appearance of the first symptom. The rash later extends to the trunk and extremities.
- **Influenza** presents with chills, malaise, anorexia, aches and pains, sore throat, nasal catarrh, substernal burning, dry cough and fever. Occasionally there may also be erythematous or urticarial skin rash.
- **Infectious mononuclcosis** is characterised by enlargement of lymph nodes, fever, petechial eruptions on the palate, and frequent enlargement of spleen. Occasionally the condition may give rise to macular or maculopapular or even petechial skin rash.
- **Typhus,** when develops as ***epidemic typhus,*** presents with severe prostration and sustained high fever. Small, irregular shaped, macular (sometimes papular) rash appears on the fourth to seventh day of illness on the axillae and then over the back and chest and then spreads to the extremities and rest of the body but spares the face, palms and soles. The rash initially fades on pressure but later becomes fixed.

  In ***scrub typhus***, about the end of the first week of fever, generalised macular rash appears on the trunk which may last for few hours or may develop to a maculopapular eruptions, extending over the trunk, face, palms and soles, and may last for a week.

In ***endemic typhus,*** a maculopapular rash appears, maximum on the trunk and fades fairly rapidly, but may also be scanty and transient.

- In **rickettsial pox** initial lesion occurs as a papule at the site of mite bite. About a week after the condition gives rise to intermittent fever. A varicella-like generalised maculopapular skin rash appears during the early stage of fever. The rash spares the palms and soles. Later, the rash changes to vesicles and formation of crusts which is shed within 10 days.
- **Dengue** is characterised by episodes of 'saddle-back' temperature, muscle and joint pain, and lymphadenopathy. A maculopapular, scarlatiniform or petechial rash appears on the thrid or fourth day of illness. The lesion first appears on the dorsum of the hands and feet and then spreads to cover the body but usually spares the face. Both the palms and soles may be oedematous and bright red in colour. The rash lasts for several hours to days.
- **Juvenile chronic arthritis** often accompanied by nonspecific small macular rash, distributed on the limbs and trunk. Along with this there is congestion of the eyes, and arthralgia.
- In **leptospirosis** there may be slightly raised erythematous rash, usually, symmetrical in distribution, appears on the skin of lower legs on about fifth day of the illness.
- **Relapsing fever** begins with chills, fever, nausea, vomiting, intense headache, and muscle and joint pain. There may be varieties of skin rash, varying between erythematous to petechial rash.
- Varieties of skin lesions may be manifested in **African trypanosomiasis.** Otherwise, the condition is characterised by febrile illness and involvement of central nervous system.
- **Rocky mountain spotted fever** presents with fever. After 2 to 6 days of fever small macular rash appears on the skin, initially on the wrists and ankles, and involves the palms and soles, and spreads centripetally for 2 to 3 days to cover the arms, legs, buttocks, trunk, face and neck. The rash later becomes maculopapular, larger and darker, and then petechial which coalesce to form large haemorrhagic area, and finally ulcerates.
- **Rat-bite fever** when develops due to streptobacillus infection, it gives rise to morbiliform petechial skin rash on the hands and feet.

  In spirillum infection however, macular or maculopapular rash sometimes appear but is less marked than that is in streptobacillus infection.
- **Trench fever** is characterised by fever and systemic distrubances. The fever may appear at 5 to 6 days' intervals in some cases and the recrudescence may occur for 1 to 8 times. There may also be transient macular or papular skin rash.
- In **chromomycosis** the initial lesion appears on the foot, leg or other exposed part of the body with broken skin as dull red or violacious, sharply demarcated patch, with an indurated base, containing small, itching papule, resembling ringworm. New crops of lesions may appear over the path of the lymphatic drainage.

SORE THROAT

In upper respiratory tract infection, sore throat is one of the commonest symptoms that is frequently encountered with. In addition, there are several disorders in which the symptom can be complained about. In general, the symptom is however nonspecific and does not serve any purpose in terms of diagnosis.

- **Acute coryza** begins abruptly with tickling sensation in the nose, sometimes accompanied by slight sore throat and a tendency to sneezing and perhaps congestion of the eyes. Later, there is dryness and soreness of throat, with mild hoarseness.
- **Influenza** begins with chills, malaise, anorexia, aches and pains, and prostration. Body temperature rises to 102°F to 104°F (39°C-40°C) but the pulse is relatively slow for the degree of temperature, and bradycardia may develop. There are also sore throat, substernal burning, and dry cough.
- In **laryngitis**, dryness and soreness of throat give rise to a feeling of tickling and rawness in the throat. Voice becomes hoarse or there may even be aphonia. There may also be fever, malaise, throat pain and dysphagia.
- **Pharyngitis** presents with sore throat and pain in swallowing. Throat looks red and inflammaed. The mucous membrane of the pharynx may be covered with membranous or purulent exudate which could be wiped off easily.
- **Tonsillitis** gives rise to sore throat and pain, especially marked on swallowing. Tonsillar pillar and pharynx appear congested. Cervical lymph nodes may be enlarged and tender. The tongue is heavily furred.
- **Acute epiglottitis** presents with sore throat, cough, high fever, dysphagia, dyspnoea, tachypnoea and inspiratory stridor. The glottis and epiglottis may be covered with thick, superficial secretions.
- **Streptococcal sore throat** may present with sore throat, fever, nausea and pain on swallowing. Cervical lymph nodes are enlarged and tender.
- In **diphtheria,** *pharyngeal diphtheria* begins with pallor, headache and vomiting. Usually there is low-grade fever. There may be pharyngeal oedema, sore throat and dysphagia. Soon dirty white or grayish yellow pseudomembrane develops, appearing first on the tonsils as thick gelatinous exudate and then spreading to the pillars and pharyngeal wall. When the pseudomombrane is forcibly removed, it leaves bleeding surface and the membrane is formed again soon.
- In **pneumonia,** mycoplasmal infection gives rise to lassitude, headache, fever, sore throat and cough. Chest pain is common.
- In **extrapulmonary tuberculosis,** *tuberculous pharyngitis* presents with sore throat, pain and dryness of the throat, and pain on swallowing. Mucous membrane of the pharynx shows pallor and widespread 'worm eaten' ulcers. The condition develops as a complication, usually from pulmonary tuberculosis.

  Tuberculous laryngitis presents with constant hoarseness. There is also sore throat. Severe pain on swallowing occurs in the late stage. The condition develops as a complication, usually of pulmonary tuberculosis.

- In the prodromal stage of **enteric fever** patients may complain of anorexia, malaise, lethargy, severe headache, generalised aches and pains, and nausea. There may also be sore throat and unproductive cough. The condition however gives rise to a characteristic pattern of temperature, bradycardia and gastrointestinal disturbances.
- In **acute bronchitis**, initially there are symptoms of upper respiratory tract infection and slight sore thraot, followed by irritating, unproductive cough with retrosternal discomfort or pain. Later, there may be malaise, chilliness, slight fever, sore throat, and muscle pain. The patient complains of a sensation of tightness in the chest, dyspnoea, wheezing and expectoration, at first scanty, mucoid, viscid, and may be streaked with blood.
- **Agranulocytosis** presents with sore throat, fever, chills, extreme weakness and severe prostration. There is progressive necrotic ulceration on the oral mucosa and throat, with little pus formation. Blood shows reduction of absolute number or absence of granular Leucocytes.
- In **acute leukaemia** there may be easy fatitguability, malaise, anorexia, fever and prostration. There is also generalised pain, sore throat, pain and tenderness in the bone and about the joints, and haemorrhagic manifestations. The condition shows enlargement of liver, spleen and lymph nodes.
- In **poliomyelitis,** ***abortive poliomyelitis*** is the commonest form and presents with fever, headache, vomiting, diarrhoea or constipation, and sore throat. The patients recover from the illness in a few days, leaving no trace of the infection but some may progress to non-paralytic poliomyelitis.

  Non-paralytic poliomyelitis presents with influenza-like symptoms with severe headache, pain in the back and neck, deep muscle pain, sore throat, and vomiting or diarrhoea. There may also be lethargy, irritability, stiffness of neck, urinary retention, vertigo, and disturbed vision.
- **Viral encephalitis** begins with high fever, malaise, sore throat, headache, nausea and vomiting. There is also lethargy, confusion, delirium, hallucination, delusion, stupor, coma and convulsions. Tremor, stiff neck, signs of meningeal irritation and cranial nerve palsies are the common findings of the condition.
- **Rabies** may perhaps present with malaise, anorexia, nausea, vomiting, sore throat, fever and mental depression. There is abnormal sensations around the the site of inoculation. The paient may show restlessness, increasing to uncontrollable excitement, and characteristically presents with hydrophobia.
- Secondary stage of **syphilis** usually develops a few weeks after the development of the primary chancre. In this stage there may be mild constitutional symptoms of malaise, fever, headache, sore throat, hoarseness of voice, bone and joint pain, and widespread skin rash of various forms but often macular or papular.
- **Infectious mononucleosis** is characterised by lymphadenopathy and is manifested by fever, often with vomiting. The symptoms also accompany malaise, anorexia, sore throat, severe frontal headache and myalgia. In this condition the lymph nodes of any area may be

affected but those of posterior cervical chain are affected frequently.

- **Dengue** gives rise to malaise, chills, headache, postorbital pain, backache, sore throat and depression. The condition is also manifested by fever, with bradycardia and hypotension. Cervical, epitrochlear and inguinal lymph nodes are anlarged.
- Sore throat is a common feature in **leptospirosis**. The condition however presents with headache, severe muscle pains, anorexia, nausea, frequent vomiting, chills and rapidly rising fever. Prostration is always severe.
- **Toxoplasmosis** may remain asymptomatic or may present as mild, acute or chronic condition, with lymphadenopathy of one or more groups of glands. There may be malaise, headache, fever, sore throat, myalagia, arthralgia, stiff neck, confusion, maculopapular skin rash and urticaria. The causative parasite can be isolated from blood, sputum, cerebrospinal fluid, bone marrow aspirates, and other tissues and body fluids.
- **Haemorrhagic fever** gives rise to fever, headache, nausea, vomiting, pharyngitis with sore throat, cough, and dyspepsia. Shock develops 2 to 6 days after with sudden collapse or prostration, cold clammy extremeties, weak thready pulse and circumoral cyanosis along with haemorrhagic manifestations.
- **Coccidioidomycosis** may give rise to chills, fever, aches, chest pain, sore throat and haemoptysis. History of visiting the endemic area and presentation of obscure illness is often suggestive of the condition.
- In **rickettsial pox**, a small, firm, papule develops at the site of mite bite, followed about a week after by intermittent fever, chills, headache, disseminated aches and pains, photophobia, and profuse sweating. There is also sore throat. Spleen may be enlarged in some cases.
- **Lassa fever** may present with inceasing sore throat, headache, severe muscle aches, malaise, chills, high fever, anorexia and vomiting. Pain in the chest and epigastrium is common. Abdominal pain and vomiting become increasingly severe from the second week of the condition.
- **Rocky mountain spotted fever** presents with malaise, nausea, headache and sore throat. This progresses further till headache becomes severe and accompanies chills, muscle pain, bone and joint pain, abdominal pain, harassing unproductive cough, and fever.
- In **ankylostomiasis** larval migration in the lungs may produce bloody sputum, sore throat, cough, bronchitis and, even, fever but for a very transient period.

SWEATING

Sweating is a symptom that may frequently be complained by the patients or their attendants. Although in many conditions the involvement of the symptom is nonspecific but in other instances, its particular pattern or the way of presentation may be suggestive or cause suspicion for certain conditions.

The symptom may be a localised manifestation or be generalised, and its quantity may vary from scanty to profuse. Again, there are few disorders where the sweating occurs in the night hours only. On the other hand, *there are certain circumstances where there may be no sweating at all.*

- In **gastrointestinal bleeding,** the severity of symptoms depends on the source and rate of bleeding. In general, there may be weaknesss, faintness, nausea, sweating, paplitation, pallor and irritability. There may be haematemesis and melaena.
- **Acute pancreatitis** may present with persistent, intense abdominal pain, nausea, vomiting, prostration and fever. There are also tachycardia, hypotension, sweating, mild jaundice and, in severe cases, shock.
- **Fulminant hepatic failure** characteristically presents with carebral disturbances, altered mood, impaired judgement, poor concentration and lack of sense of awareness, followed by restlessness, aggressive behaviour, mania, drowsiness, and coma. There are also weakness, nausea, vomiting, fever, sweating, delirium and, rarely, pain in the hypochondrium.
- **Acute cholecystitis** presents with slight fever, rigor, epigastric discomfort, and severe abdominal pain, tenderness and rigidity in the right hypochondrium or epigastrium. There may be restlessness, pallor, nausea, vomiting and sweating.
- **Gallstones** may be asymptomatic or may present with abdominal distress, nausea, vomiting, belching, and pain which is usually precipittated by fatty foods. Otherwise, the condition may give rise to recurrent biliary colic or severe pain in the right hypochondrium or epigastrium, causing restlessness, sweating, pallor and vomiting.
- **Lung abscess** begins with chills, fever, malaise, anorexia, sweats, and aches and pains. The patient gives rise to irritating dry and exhaustive cough, followed by large amount of expectoration of purulent, sometimes fetid and occasionally blood-streaked, sputum, and prostration. Diagnosis of the condition is made by chest x-ray.
- **Empyema** may present with high and remittent fever with rigors, sweating, malaise, anorexia and loss of body weight. There are also cough with purulent sputum, pleural pain and, in cases of large deposition of pus, buldging on the intercoastal space of the affected side.
- **Anxiety neuroses** may present with sweating, tremor, dizziness and palpitations. There are tachycardia, occasional premature beats, precordial pain and generalised motor weakness. A sense of air humger may develop. Sleep disturbance is common.

- **Respiratory acidosis** principally presents with the symptoms of encephalopathy. The patient presents with warm extremities, sweating, peripheral vasodilatation, muscle twitchings, flapping tremors, headache, drowsiness, stupor and, in severe cases, coma.
- **Pulmonary embolism** may be fatal. Otherwise, there may be no symptom or there may be dyspnoea, central chest pain, tachycardia, pallor, sweating, cyanosis, syncope, low blood pressure, anxiety, restlessness and shock.
- **Osteomyelitis** usually begins with severe toxaemia in infants but in children, it usually ushered by fever, chills, malaise, and sweating. In acute stage there may be localised pain and tenderness over the bone which is worse on tapping over the bone but in the early stage, the pain may be vague and shifting. X-ray can diagnose the condition but radionuclide scanning is required in early stage.
- **Pleural effusion** begins with little or no pleural pain, pyrexia, especially in the infected cases, sweating, cough and expectoration. There is dyspnoea which may also be the only initial symptom in some cases. Diagnosis of the condition is made by chest x-ray.
- **Cardiac failure** presents with tachycardia, dyspnoea and orthopnoea, including paroxysmal nocturnal dyspnoea, in left-sided cardiac failure. The condition also gives rise to fatigue, weakness, sweating and cough which is initially uproductive but later becomes productive with white or rusty or brownish sputum.
- The cardinal symptom of **myocardial infarction** is pain which may, however, be absent or its intensity may vary widely. In addition, there are nausea, vomiting, abdominal distress, pallor, sweating, excessive fatigue, breathlessness, syncope, fever and shock.
- **Migraine** presents with paroxysms of severe and throbbing unilateral headache. This may be preceded by depression, irritability, restlessness, anorexia, sweating, photophobia and prostration. Vomiting is common.
- **Hypoglycaema** develops perhaps due to intake of excessive insulin or of unaccustomed exercise or of not taking food as a complication in patients with diabetes mellitus, and gives rise to headache, malaise, nausea, perhaps vomiting, sweating, tremor, faintness, dizziness and mental confusion. Skin and tongue appear moist.
- **Amoebiasis** when produces *amoebic liver abscess,* it gives rise to pain in the liver region. Along with it there are intermittent fever, chills, sweating, nausea, vomiting and, in some cases, diarrhoea or dysentry. Liver is enlarged and tender.
- The manifestations of **polyarteritis nodosa** vary widely. It may however give rise to fever, sweating, abdominal pain, peripheral neuropathy, oliguria, uraemia, convulsions and organic psychosis. Development of myalgia and arthralgia is common. There may also be bloody diarrhoea, gastrointestinal haemorrhage, perteinuria and haematuria.
- **Anthrax** characteristically produces necrotic ulcer on the skin or mucous membrane. Sometimes however septicaemia may occur due to haematogenous spread when the scar sloughs. It then gives rise to high fever, prostration, shock, cyanosis, sweating, collapse and even death.

- **Ménière's disease** gives rise to progressive deafness and tinnitus, followed by recurrent paroxysms of vertigo. There may also be nausea, vomiting, sweating, weakness and fainting.
- Mite-borne **typhus** *(scrub typhus)* begins with malaise, chills, headache, backache, and fever. The fever runs a remittent course, with sweating, and falls by lysis usually after twelveth to eighteenth day. In severe cases, there may be apathy and prostration.
- **Trench fever** begins with exhaustion, headache, severe back and leg pains, sweating, coldness of the extremities, fever and dizziness. It is however a rare condition and is only encountered in the armies during the war.
- **Pheochromocytoma** presents with paroxysmal or sustained hypertension and extreme pallor or flushing of the face or extremities. Headache may be severe. There may be nausea, vomiting, constipation, increased appetite, loss of body weight and sweating. Diagnosis of the condition is confirmed by demonstration of increased levels of catecholamines or their metabolites in the urine or plasma.
- In cases of **male hypogonadism** developing after puberty, the condition does not affect the growth but presents with fatigue, flushings, sweating, dizziness, thinning of beards, girdle type of obesity and kyphosis of the spine. External genitalia and prostate gland show atrophy or hyperplasia.
- **Rickets** presents with delayed growth and the infant shows delay in teething, sitting, standing, crawling and walking. It gives rise to irritability, restlessness, distended abdomen and sweating of the forehead and hands. There are also 'bossing' of the skull, 'pigeon chest' and 'bowing' of the legs. History of inadequate intake of vitamin D or of insufficient exposure to sunlight is suggestive.
- In **hyperthyroidism** there may be diffuse or nodular goitre or there may be no goitre. The condition gives rise to increased appetite, loss of body weight, pruritus, increased frequency of bowel movement or diarrhoea, hot and sweaty hands, intolerance to warmth, nervousness, anxiety and low-grade fever. The patient presents with fine tremors of the fingers and tongue. There may also be increased lacrimation, photophobia and preorbital oedema.
- In **miliaria** however there is excessive sweating (hyperhidrosis) initally but later, absence of sweating (anhidrosis). The condition presents with acute inflammatory skin eruption, accompanied by severe itching, burning and irritation.
- **Acromegaly** presents with enlarged bone and soft tissue, widened hands with broad fingers, large feet, jaw, ears, nose, lip, tongue and internal organs. The patients also complain of excessive sweating.
- The manifestations of **Guillain-Barré syndrome** may be variable but most cases give rise to progressive flaccid muscular weakness with muscle tenderness and widespread loss of tendon reflexes. There may also be hyperhidrosis, oedema and postural hypotension.
- In **hodgkin's lymphoma** there may be excessive sweating, loss of body weight, progressive weakness, progressive anaemia, low-grade fever and pruritus. The condition characteristically gives rise to painless enlargement of one group of

superficial lymph nodes. Detection of Reed-Strenberg cells in lymph node biopsy confirm the diagnosis.

- **Chilblain** gives rise to painful, burning and itchy erythematous lesions with oedema or blistering on the fingers and toes from exposure to cold. There may also be macerations and increased sweating. A quick warming up of the affected part worsens the condition.
- **Rabies** may present with malaise, anorexia, nausea, vomiting, sore throat and fever. The patient feels an abnormal sensation around the site of inoculation. There are lacrimation, dilatation of the pupil, increased salivation and perspiration. The condition characteristically gives rise to hydrophobia.
- **Heat exhausition** presents with increasing fatigue, weakness, headache, nausea, loss of appetite, muscle cramps, anxiety and drenching sweating. The skin is cold and clammy. Body temperature falls below normal. Pulse becomes slow and thready. Blood pressure also falls.
- **Q fever** is characterised by fever, headache, and interstitial penumonitis with dry unproductive cough. The condition also gives rise to drenching sweating. It is an occupational hazard to those who come in contact with the domestic animals and handling of animal tissues.
- **Malaria** begins with chills, rigor, pallor, cyanosis, nausea, vomiting and headache. Then there is spiking fever which may last for several hours, followed by profuse sweating, and the temperature drops. The fever comes and goes. As the disease progresses there is splenomegaly. Liver may also be enlarged and tender. Malarial parasites can be seen within the erythrocytes in the blood film.
- **Rheumatic fever** often preceded by a history of group A streptococcal infection, and begins with high temperature or low-grade fever. Accompanying it there are malaise, anorexia, abdominal pain, weakness and loss of body weight. There may be profuse sweating in the adults but may however be absent in children. There is also fleeting or migratory non-suppurative polyarthritis, involving predominently the knees, ankles, shoulders, elbows and wrists.
- **Relapsing fever** begins with fever, chills, nausea, vomiting, intense headache, and muscle and joint pains. Face is flushed, eyes are injected, and development of photophobia is common. There may also be varieties of skin rash. The temperature remains high for 4 to 10 days and then falls by crisis to normal or below, accompanied by profuse sweating.
- **Infectious mononucleosis** gives rise to fever, often with vomiting, and accompanied by malaise, anorexia, sore throat, severe frontal headache and myalgia. Characteristically it involves lymph modes of any area but frequently those of posterior cervical chain, and the lymph nodes are enlarged, firm, elastic, normally discrete, non-tender or slightly painful and non-suppurative. Profuse sweating is a common feature.
- **Kala-azar** presents with fever, generally mild, which is not associated with prostration but may be high in some cases or may even show a daily double rise of temperature in the afternoon and evening. The temperature is usually irregular, remittent or intermittent, or may well be sustained, or there may be wide swings of temperature while there are some cases where there may not be any history of

fever even. Sweating at night is however a constant feature of the condition and is evident even when there is no fever. Spleen is soft and doughy at first and then usually becomes enlarged and very hard. Liver is also enlarged at a later stage but not tender. Lymphadenopathy may be present. Diagnosis of the condition is confirmed by identification of LD bodies in the blood, sternal bone marrow, liver or spleen.

- **Pulmonary tuberculosis** usually presents with undue tiredness, malaise, lassitude, anorexia, dyspepsia, persistent loss of body weight and palpitation. Characteristically the condition presents with low-grade fever, usually in the afternoon or evening, and night sweats.
- In **extrapulmonary tuberculosis,** *miliary tuberculosis* usually develops in children and young adults from massive invasion of blood by tubercle bacilli. It presents with high remittent or intermittent fever in the evening but normal in the morning, chills, malaise and severe night sweats. Unproductive cough and dyspnoea occur occasionally.
- **Dengue** presents with fever, malaise, chills, headache, postorbital pain, headache, pain in the extremities, sore throat and depression. Cervical, epitrochlear and inguinal lymph nodes are enlarged. Spleen appears soft and slightly enlarged. Fever and other symptoms usually persist for 2 to 4 days followed by a remission with profuse sweating. The remission lasts for a few hours to 2 days, but usually 24 hours, and then there occurs second rapid rise of fever.
- **Rickettsial pox** presents with a small papule at the site of mite bite. About a week after there appears chills, fever, headache, profuse sweating and photophobia. During the early stage of fever, the condition also gives rise to varicella-like generalised skin eruptions.
- **Blastomycosis** presents with pneumonia-like manifestations with dry hacking or productive cough, chest pain, chills, fever, dyspnoea and profuse sweating. X-ray of the chest shows patches of bronchopneumonia. The condition is diagnosed by identification of the causative organism.
- **Taluraemia** begins suddenly with nausea, vomiting, malaise, headache, pain in the limbs, chills, high fever and extreme prostration. There is also profuse sweating. Spleen is often enlarged.
- Fatigue, weakness, malaise, loss of body weight, night sweats, anorexia and dyspepsia may be the presenting features of **chronic meyloid leukaemia.** The patient presents with fever, pallor and anaemia. Spleen is firm, smooth, painless and greatly enlarged, with a friction rub over the spleen. Liver is usually moderately enlarged with smooth surface. Lymph nodes are not usually enlarged. Blood shows full range of granulocytes from myeloblasts to mature neutrophils and a few nucleated erythrocytes.
- **Chronic lymphatic leukaemia** begins with lymphadenopathy. The superficial lymph nodes in the cervical, axillary and inguinal regions are enlarged, firm, rubbery, discrete and painless, and distributed symmetrically. There may also be weakness, fatigue, loss of body weight, malaise, exertional dyspnoea, fever and night sweats. It produces anaemia which is mild but generally increasing. Blood shows leucocytosis with absolute lymphocytosis, usually of small variety.

- **Bronchiectasis** gives rise to chronic cough, usually worse at morning and often influenced by postural changes, with large amount of purulent and sometimes fetid or putrid sputum, offensive breath after coughing and haemoptysis. There may be sinusitis, wheezing, dyspnoea, night sweats, fever and shivering on further acute inflammation. Cachexia and clubbing of fingers and toes are common.
- In **AIDS** some cases may present with unexplained persistent lymphadenopathy (AIDS-related complex), perhaps associated with fatigue, malaise, loss of body weight, recurrent fever, night sweats, persistent diarrhoea and candidiasis.
- **Brucellosis** gives rise to fever, which may be septic, sustained, low-grade, intermittent, or chronic and undulant, with chills and emotional irritability. Chronic cases however gives rise to malaise, lethargy, rheumatic pain, night sweats, depression, insomnia and weakness but fever is often absent.
- **Syphilis** does not involve the lung but in tertiary (late) stage only extremely rarely it may involve the lung. The condition may then give rise to dyspnoea, loss of body weight, haemoptysis and night sweats, or may present as pneumonia, bronchiectasis or fibrosis of the lung. Conventional serological tests for syphilis are always positive.
- In **infective endocarditis** fever is a common manifestation which is high with rigor in acute cases but coninuous, low-grade or irregular and occurs for months in subacute cases. There are also chills, malaise, lassitude, anorexia, pallor and night sweats. The causative organism can be isolated from the blood and bone marrow.
- In **sarcoidosis** the patient may present with loss of body weight, fever and night sweats. There may be symmetrical non-destructive inflammatory arthritis associated with erythema nodosum. Cough and dyspnoea may appear in the late stage. There may also be bilateral swelling of parotid glands or iritis.
- **Non-Hodgkin's lymphoma** presents with painless, unexplained enlargement of lymph glands, usually of the cervical or inguinal nodes. The glands are firm, discrete and rubbery but may later become matted. There may also be malaise, tiredness, fever, night sweats, loss of body weight and pressure symptoms from enlarged mass of lymph nodes. Diagnosis of the condition is made from lymph node biopsy.
- In **actinomycosis** when the lesion involves the throax or abdomen, it may present with chills, fever, night sweats, dysphagia, dyspnoea, malaise, cough with sputum formation, pleural pain and abdominal colic.
- **Nocardiosis** usually begins as subclinical pulmonary infection, or may give rise to cough, chest pain, chills, fever, anorexia, night sweats, and loss of body weight. The condition is however characterised by granulomatous ulcer formation.
- In **menopausal syndrome** symptoms vary widely, most common being hot flushes. Among other symptoms most frequently encountered with are anorexia, nausea, vomiting, diarrhoea, constipation, varieties of nonspecific gastrointestinal symptoms, arthralgia, myalgia, dizziness, headache, palpitation, tinnitus, fainting and dyspnoea. In some cases, there may be night sweats, and a sensation of warmth and sweating may cause sleep disturbances.

- *Absence of sweating* is a menifestation of **hypothyroidism**, along with weakness, lethargy, dryness and roughness of the skin, and dryness and brittleness of hair and nails. The face appears dull and swollen with puffy eyelids, thick lips and enlarged tongue. X-ray of bone epiphyses in children and of ossification centre in infants show delayed skeletal maturation.
- *Absence of sweating,* diminished tolerance to cold and dehydration may be the features of **Addison's disease**. In the condition development of hypotension appears to be a most characteristic sign. There is also dizziness, syncope, nervousness and perhaps vertigo. Characteristically the condition produces hyperpigmentation or vitiligo which may often appear by itself as initial symptom or may precede other manifestations of the condition perhaps by years.
- In **heat stroke,** with *absence of sweating,* skin appears hot, dry and flushed. The condition gives rise to headache, vertigo and fatigue, followed by loss of consciousness or convulsions. Body temperature usually swings high to 105·4°F to 106°F (40·7°C-41·1°C) or even may go higher.

TREMORS

Tremor is an alternating rhythmical movement of any part of the body. Although it may be a natural phenomenon in very elderly person or may develop temporarily in a very nervous state, in disease pattern it is an important symptom. The tremors thus present may be fine or coarse. Sometimes it develops when a voluntary movement is made (*intention tremor*) or that may consist of involuntary jerking movements (*flapping tremor*), especially in the hands. Depending on the pattern of the trembling act, tremors are, in fact, classified into several catagories for descriptive purposes, and here all tremors are described without their classification, excepting those of intention tremors and flapping tremors.

- **Parkinsonism** may present with tremor, which starts on the fingers and extends to the proximal part of the arm and later, to the tongue and legs. Stresses and embarrassement aggravate the tremor. The tremors may be present even at rest. Loss of normal arm swinging on walking appears as the early sign of the condition. Characteristically the condition gives rise to slow gait with short and shifting steps, and the patients find difficulty in rising from the chair and in straight walking. Speech becomes monotonous with loss of voice volume.
- **Hereditary ataxias** give rise to ataxia of gait and intention tremor. There may also be dysarthria and nystagmus.
- In **intracranial neoplasms** development of the symptom depends on the site of involvement, the interference of local brain function, and the intracranial pressure. There may therefore be varieties of symptoms including headache, papilloedema, drowsiness, lethargy, disturbed memory, imparied judgement, visual alterations and hallucination, speech disturbances, loss of sense of smell, aphasia or dysphasia, ataxia, monoplegia, hemiplegia, unilateral or bilateral paralysis of cranial nerve, facial palsy, loss of corneal reflex, intention tremor, vertigo, tinnitus, and symptoms and signs of meningitis.
- Manifestations of **multiple sclerosis** are extremely variable, and the condition runs a relapsing and remittent course. There may be paraesthesia or numbness in one or more extremities, trunk or one side of the face, hemianaesthesia to pain, vertigo, apathy, euphoria, scanning speech and difficulties with bladder control. There may also be ataxia, swinging motion of head, body and extremities on walking, intention tremor, diplopia, nystagmus and dimness of vision.
- **Viral encephalitis** presents with high fever, malaise, sore throat, headache, nausea and vomiting. The condition also gives rise to lethargy, confusion, delirium, hallucination, delusion, stupor, coma and convulsions. There may be seizures, personality changes and alteration in consciousness. Tremor, stiff neck, signs of meningeal irritation and cranial nerve palsies are the common findings of the condition.
- In **poliomyelitis**, paralytic variety may follow a mild illness or may develop without any prodromal period, giving rise to upper

respiratory tract symptoms in children but general muscle and bone discomfort in adults. There is irritability. In addition, if the condition follows mild illness, there are tremors and muscle weakness.

- Tremor constitute a feature in **syphilis** in its tertiary (late) stage, producing ***general paralysis of insance (general paresis).*** The condition then gives rise to irritability, headache, insomnia, difficulty in concentration, failure of memory, and changes in behaviour. Coarse tremors develop and affect the lips, facial muscles, tongue, hands and whole body. Speech becomes slow and tremulous. Tremors in the hands cause difficulty in writing legibly. There is epileptiform seizures, and monoplegia or hemiplegia. There may also be optic nerve atrophy and loss of deep reflexes, and sensory changes. Conventional serological tests for syphilis are always positive, some even with non-treponemal antigens. Cerebrospinal fluid usually shows increased pressure, and an increased content of protein and lymphocytes. The colloidal gold curve is either paretic or leutic in type.
- **Anxiety neuroses** begins with a subjective sense of terror for no appearent reason, and development of symptom depends upon the intensity of anxiety. There may therefore be sweating, tremor, dizziness and palpitation. The condition gives rise to tachycardia, occasional premature beats, precordial pain and generalised motor weakness. Sleep disturbacnes are usually common. A feeling of nausea and vomiting may develop in more acute cases.
- **Hyperthyroidism** may give rise to diffuse or nodular goitre or there may be no goitre. The condition may present with increased appetite, increased frequency of bowel movement or diarrchea, pruritus, intolerance to warmth, nervousness, anxiety, low-grade fever, mild weakness of proximal muscles and wasting of muscles and bone. The patients show hot and sweaty hands, and there is fine tremors of the fingers and tongue. There may also be increased lacrimation, photophobia and preorbital odema. Plasma T_4 and T_3 levels and radioactive iodine uptake are high. Plasma T_3 resin uptake may also be elevated. TRH test is also helpful, and the level of TSH is usually low.
- In **diabetes mellitus** when *hypoglycaemia* develops as a complication, the patient then presents with sweating, tremor, palpitation, faintness, dizziness and mental confusion. Skin and tongue appear moist. Respiration is shallow or normal.
- **African trypanosomiasis** gives rise to fever and generalised lymphadenopathy. There may also be tachycardia, skin rash, and enlargement of both liver and spleen. Later, it may present with headache, insomnia, lassitude, changing behaviour, lack of concentration, mental confusion and paresis. The patients show fine tremors of the lips and hands.
- **Respiratory acidosis** gives rise to sweating, muscle twitchings, flapping tremors, headache, drowsiness, stupor and, in severe cases, coma. Extremities appear warm and there is peripheral vasodilatation. There may also be retinal venous distrubances but papilloedema occurs rarely. Blood shows increased concentration of H^+, carbonic acid and $Paco_2$ but the pH is reduced.
- **Hypomagnesaemia** presents with anorexia, lethargy, vomiting, weakness and tetany. The patient presents with choreiform movements with muscle fasciculation and flapping tremors.

Personality changes, confusion, disoriontation and restlessness may be common. Blood shows reduced level of magnesium.

- **Fulminant hepatic failure** is manifested by cerebral disturbances, altered mood, impaired judgement, poor concentration and lack of sense of awareness, followed by restlessness, aggressive behaviour, mania, drowsiness and coma. There are weakness, nausea, vomiting, fever, sweating, delirium, hiccough and finally convulsion. The patient gives rise to a sweet smell on breathing, and the extended hands characteristically show flapping tremors.
- **Pulmonary emphysema** presents with progressive exertional dyspnoea, chronic cough with scanty, mucoid expectorations, wheezing and tightness in the chest. There may be cyanosis, especially on the lips and nail beds, and occasionally there may also be clubbing of fingers. The condition may give rise to anorexia, lethargy, headache, confusion, twitchings and sometimes flapping tremors. The chest looks barrel shaped with diminished movement. Hyperaction of all respiratory muscles are evident during inspiration, including indrawing of costal margins, contraction of sternomastoid and scaleneous muscle, and deepening of suprasternal and supraclavicular fossae.

URINE, SUPPRESSION AND RETENTION OF

Decrease in the quantity of urination is an important symptom, though it is a fact that less intake of fluid or excessive passage of body fluid through perspiration can also cause a decrease in urinary output. There are several terminologies used to describe the nature of suppression. *Oliguria* is one of those terminologies which is used to express scanty urination but *anuria* when there is total suppression of urine. By retention it is however meant that the bladdor contains urine but cannot be voided.

- Oliguria is a common feature of **nephrotic syndrome.** The condition gives rise to weakness, nausea, malaise and pain in the abdomen. The patient shows puffy eyelids, protuberant abdomen and wasting of muscles. The condition is principally featured by hypoproteinaemic oedema and marked proteinuria.
- There is low urinary output wih blood-stained urine in **acute nephritic syndrome.** The young patients usually present themselves with puffiness around the eyes and face. The condition gives rise to headache, malaise, mild fever, anorexia, vomiting and respiratory distress. There is also discomfort or pain in the flank or upper abdomen. In addition, there may be oedema, particularly around the ankles.
- **Rapidly progressive nephritic syndrome** often presents with acute nephritic syndrome. Recurrent haematuria is a common feature of the condition but proteinuria is variable. In late stage of the condition, there may be severe oliguria or even anuria.
- Symptoms of **acute tubulointerstitial nephritis** are variable. Some patients may present with acute renal failure. Only occasionally can it give rise to oliguria in some cases. Otherwise, the condition is characterised by sterile pyuria.
- Development of anuria or oliguria is a characteristic feature of maintenance phase of **acute renal failure.** The condition presents with general weakness, hiccoughs and paraesthesias. There may also be mental confusion, apathy, delirium, muscular twitching, fits and coma. Respiratory embarrassement and cyanosis may develop.
- **Cystitis** characteristically presents with urgency and frequency of micturition but the patient passes small volume of urine, often turbid. Micturition is always associated with burning or pain.
- ***Urethral stricuture*** often develops due to **gonorrhoea** and also from causes which result fibrosis of the urethral mucous membrane. In mild cases, the patients only complain of passing of small quantity of urine and a feeling of incomplete urination. In more established cases, the patient complains of increasing difficulty in passing urine and of having poor urinary stream. Later, stricture may lead to acute retention of urine.
- **Benign prostatic hyperplasia** presents with progressive urinary frequency, urgency of micturition, noctruia, sensation of incomplete urination, decreased size and force of urinary streams, terminal dribbling, and acute urinary retention. Prostate may be enlarged, with rubbery and unifrom in consistency, and frequently shows loss of median furrow. Stasis of urine from incomplete emptying of bladder

may lead to formation of calculus. There is also progressive obstruction to the outflow of urine, and the obstruction may eventually lead to complete retention of urine and development of hydronephrosis.

- **Prostatic carcinoma** is usually asymptomatic till late stage. It then gives rise to urethral obstruction and acute retention of urine. There may also be haematuria and pyuria. Prostate appears firm and stony hard, with obliterated median furrow.
- **Acute circulatory failure** presents with pale, cold and sweaty skin. In addition, there are hypotension and tachycardia. Heart sounds may appear difficult to analyse. Urine output may be low. Later, there is oliguria leading to acute tubular necrosis.
- In **cardiac failure,** *right-sided cardiac failure* presents with polyuria and nocturia but there is oliguria during the day time. Dependent oedema occurs as ankle swelling and pitting oedema in the lower extremities. There may also be ascites.
- **Myocardial infarction** presents with pain in the chest. There is nausea, vomiting, abdominal distress, pallor, sweating, excessive fatigue, breathlessness, syncope, fever and shock. There may be central or peripheral cyanosis, and soft systolic blowing murmur. Blood pressure varies but often there is hypertension. In cases when hypotension develops, the condition gives rise to oliguria.
- The principle manifestations of **cholera** are vomiting and severe diarrhoea. Soon there is a profound state of dehydration with sunken eyes, cold and wrinkled skin, intense thrist, dryness of mouth and eyes, anuria or oliguria, agonizing muscular cramps, shock, coma and death.
- **Tetanus** gives rise to paroxysms of convulsive tonic, and sometimes clonic, contraction of voluntary muscles. There may be dysphagia and irritability. Often there is retention of urine. There is spasm of glottis and respiratory muscles during convulsions, resulting to asphyxia and cyanosis.
- In **poliomyelitis,** the non-paralytic variety presents with influenza-like manifesttions. There may be lethargy, irritablity, stiffness of neck, retention of urine, vertigo and disturbed vision. Muscle spasm is noted at rest or may be elicited by putting each muscle through the maximum range of motion.
- In **syphilis, *tabes dorsalis*** develops during the tertiary stage, and along with its characteristic feature the condition gives rise to paroxysms of painful disorder in the function of various viscera, such as gastric crises, laryngeal crises and peptic ulcers. Retention of urine is frequent.
- Characteristically **malaria** presents with paroxysms of chills and fever, followed by profuse sweating with peripheral vasodilatation. Severe falciparum infection, however, may cause renal damage, while malaria infection is liable to produce nephrosis in children, with generalised oedema, oliguria, proteinuria and hypoproteinaemia.

  Cerebral malaria develops from severe falciparum infection and gives rise to high fever, confusion, delirium, seizures and stupor, followed by coma persisting for a few hours. In addition, there may be renal impairment with low urinary output or persistent oliguria, haemoglobinuria, pulmonary oedema, hypotension and hypoglycaemia.
- **Diphtheria** is characterised by formation of tenacious gray pseudomembrane, which usually attacks the respiratory tract. There may be restlessness, drowsiness and coma. Otherwise, there may be

irregularities with cardiac rhythm, suppression of urine, difficulties with vision or movements of the arms or legs, and progressive enlargement of liver.

- In **diabetes mellitus,** *diabetic ketoacidosis* develops as a complication and is characterised by water and mineral depletion, haemoconcentration and fall of blood pressure with associated renal ischaemia and oliguria.
- **Paraplegia** gives rise to localised pain at the spine, followed by paraesthesia and numbness of the lower limbs. Later, the legs appear heavy, stiff and weak. The arms are relatively or completely spared. There may also be abdominal distension, constipation, faecal impaction, retention of urine and infection.
- Manifestations of **polyarteritis nodosa** vary widely. In general, there may be fever, sweating, abdominal pain, weakness, weight loss, peripheral neuropathy, oliguria, uraemia, convulsions and organic psychosis. Myalgia and arthralgia are common. There are tachycardia, hypertension and localised oedema.
- **Beriberi** may develop in breast-fed infants, usually of 2 to 5 months old, and may give rise to sudden cyanosis with dyspnoea, whining cry and aphonia. There are puffiness of the face, signs of cardiac failure, diminished urinary excretion, restlessness, convulsions and coma.
- **Scurvy** is characterised by haemorrhagic manifestations and abnormal osteoid tissue and dentin of teeth formation. It also gives rise to femoral neuropathy, rheumatoid-like arthritis, oliguria, oedema of lower extremities, and impaired vascular reactivity.
- **Hyponatraemia** presents with tiredness, lethargy, muscular weakness, mental confusion and, in severe cases, convulsions and coma. Skin appears cold, pale and inelastic, Urine output is reduced and soon oliguria supervenes, and finally lead to uraemia.
- **Yellow fever** presents with severe prostration and fever, and characteristically leads to slower pulse rate. In severe cases there may be intense albuminuria and haemorrhagic manifestations. There may also be epigastric distress, constipation, tachycardia, and oliguria or anuria.
- The symptoms of **premenstural tension** vary but most patients complain of nervousness, irritablity, depression, fatigue, lethargy and unreasonable temper. Abdominal bloating is common. Sometimes there may be colicky pain in the abdomen. In addition, there may be several other symptoms, such as headache, mastalgia, oliguria, oedema and temporary gain of body weight.
- **Myoma of uterus** is usually asymptomatic until it assumes appreciably large size or becomes twisted on its pedicle. When the tumour however assumes large size and exerts pressure, pain and bleeding may develop. There may also be other pressure symptoms, such as vaginal discharge, dyspareunia, frequency and urgency of micturition, retention of urine, oedema in the lower extremity, constipation and painful defaecation.

DIFFERENTIAL DIAGNOSIS OF A FEW DISORDERS

Disorder	Abdominal Chest pain	Cough	Cyanosis	Dirarhoea/ Steat-orrhoea	Dyspnoea	Dysuria	Fever	Haema-temesis	Haema-turia	Haemop-tysis	Jaundice	Oedema/ Ascites	Skin rash	Sweating
Actinomycosis	both	yes	—	—	present	—	yes	—	—	—	—	—	—	night
AIDS	chest	yes	—	present	present	—	yes	—	—	—	—	—	—	night
Amoebiasis	abdominal	—	—	present	—	—	yes	—	—	—	yes	—	—	yes
Anaemia, Iron deficiency	chest	—	—	present	present	—	—	—	—	—	—	present	—	—
Anaemia, Pernicious	chest	—	—	present	present	—	yes	—	—	—	—	present	—	—
Angina Pectoris	chest	—	—	—	present	—	—	—	—	—	—	—	—	—
Asthma, Bronchial	chest	yes	present	—	present	—	—	—	—	—	—	—	—	—
Bacillary Dysentery	abdominal	—	—	present	—	—	yes	—	—	—	—	—	—	—
Biliary Cirrhosis	abdominal	—	—	present	—	—	yes	—	—	—	yes	present	—	—
Bronchial Carcinoma	chest	yes	—	—	present	—	—	—	present	present	yes	—	—	—
Bronchiectasis	—	yes	—	—	present	—	yes	—	—	present	—	—	—	night
Bronchitis, Acute	chest	yes	present	—	present	—	yes	—	—	present	—	—	—	—
Cor Pulmonale	both	yes	present	—	present	—	—	—	—	—	—	present	—	—
Crohn's Disease	abdominal	—	—	present	—	—	yes	—	—	—	—	—	—	—
Diphtheria	—	yes	present	—	present	—	yes	—	—	—	—	—	—	—
Diverticulitis	abdominal	—	—	present	—	yes	—	—	—	—	—	—	—	—
Endocarditis, Infective	both	—	—	—	—	—	yes	—	—	—	yes	—	—	night
Enteric Fever	abdominal	yes	—	present	—	—	yes	—	—	—	—	—	yes	—
Hepatic Failure, Fulminant	abdominal	—	—	—	—	—	yes	—	—	—	yes	present	—	yes
Indian Childhood Cirrhosis	—	—	—	present	—	—	yes	present	—	—	yes	present	—	—
Infectious Mononucleosis	yes	yes	—	—	—	—	yes	—	—	—	yes	—	yes	yes
Influenza	chest	yes	present	—	present	—	yes	—	—	—	—	—	yes	night
Kala-azar	abdominal	—	—	present	—	—	yes	—	—	—	—	—	—	night
Leukaemia, Chronic Lymphatic	—	—	—	—	present	—	yes	present	—	—	—	present	—	night
Leukaemia, Chronic Myeloid	abdominal	—	—	present	—	—	yes	—	—	—	—	—	—	night
Liver, Carcinoma of	abdominal	—	—	—	—	—	—	—	—	—	yes	—	—	—

Continued Appendix........Differential Diagnosis of a few disorders

Disorder	Abdominal Chest pain	Cough	Cyanosis	Dirarhoea/ Steat-orrhoea	Dyspnoea	Dysuria	Fever	Haema-temesis	Haema-turia	Haemop-tysis	Jaundice	Oedema/ Ascites	Skin rash	Sweating
Liver, Cirrhosis of	—	—	present	present	—	—	yes	present	—	—	yes	present	—	—
Malaria	—	—	present	present	—	—	yes	—	present	—	yes	present	—	yes
Measles	—	yes	—	—	—	—	yes	—	—	—	—	—	yes	—
Mitral Stenosis	chest	yes	present	—	present	—	—	—	—	present	—	present	—	—
Myocardial Infarction	chest	—	present	—	present	—	yes	—	—	—	—	—	—	yes
Nephritic Syndrome, Acute	abdominal	—	—	—	present	—	yes	—	present	—	—	present	—	—
Nephritis, Acute Tubulointerstitial	abdominal	—	—	—	—	yes	yes	—	present	—	—	—	—	—
Pancreas, Carcinoma of	abdominal	—	—	present		—	—	—	—	—	yes	present	—	—
Pancreatitis, Acute	abdominal	—	—	—	—	—	yes	—	—	—	yes	—	—	yes
Peptic Ulcer	abdominal	—	—	—	—	—	—	present	—	—	—	—	—	—
Pleural Effusion	chest	yes	present	—	present	—	yes	—	—	—	—	—	—	yes
Pneumonia	both	yes	present	present	present	—	yes	—	—	present	—	—	—	—
Prostatitis	—	—	—	—	—	yes	yes	—	present	—	—	—	—	—
Pulmonary Infarction	chest	yes	present	—	present	—	yes	—	—	present	—	—	—	—
Oyelonephritis, Acute	abdominal	—	—	present	—	yes	yes	—	present	—	—	—	—	—
Renal Failure, Chronic	—	—	—	present	present	—	—	—	—	present	—	—	—	—
Syphilis	—	—	—	—	present	—	—	—	—	present	yes	present	yes	yes
Tuberculosis, Pulmonary	chest	yes	—	—	present	—	yes	—	—	present	—	—	—	yes
Ulcerative Colitis	abdominal	—	—	present	—	—	yes	—	—	—	—	—	—	—
Urethritis, Nonspecific	abdominal	—	—	—	—	yes	—	—	present	—	—	—	—	—
Urinary Tract Calculus	abdominal	—	—	—	—	yes	yes	—	present	—	—	—	—	—
Whooping Cough	—	yes	present	—	—	—	yes	—	—	present	—	—	—	—

INDEX OF DISORDERS

INDEX OF SYMPTOMS

INDEX OF SYMPTOMS